Modern API Design with gRPC

Efficient Solutions to Design Modern APIs with gRPC Using Golang for Scalable Distributed Systems

Hitesh Pattanayak

www.orangeava.com

First published: March 2024

Published by: Orange Education Pvt Ltd, AVA™

Address: 9, Daryaganj, Delhi, 110002, India

275 New North Road Islington Suite 1314 London,

N1 7AA, United Kingdom

ISBN: 978-81-97081-83-5

www.orangeava.com

Dedicated To

My Wife and Brother:

Rituja Nayak and Mukesh Pattanayak

My Strength and Support System

About the Author

Hitesh Pattanayak is a Backend Developer with a passion for being involved in building robust and scalable software solutions. Holding a Bachelor's degree in Technology from the GITA Autonomous college, Bhubaneswar, India, Hitesh has honed his skills over the course of an Eight year career.

Specializing in backend development, Hitesh is proficient in a variety of tools and technologies. His expertise spans across languages like Golang, container orchestration systems such as Kubernetes, and communication protocols like gRPC. Notably, he is a Certified Kubernetes Application Developer, demonstrating his commitment to staying at the forefront of cloud-native technologies.

Throughout his career, Hitesh has been part of services and product-based companies. He has worked with organizations like Infracloud Technologies, Sureify, and Thoughtworks, where he has been part of innovative solutions to complex challenges.

Beyond his professional endeavors, Hitesh is an active member of the tech community. He is recognized as an AWS Community Builder and has shared his knowledge and experiences through technical talks at some conferences. His dedication to continuous learning and sharing insights with others underscores his commitment to the advancement of the technology industry.

In his leisure time, Hitesh enjoys indulging in hobbies such as bike riding and cooking, finding balance between his professional pursuits and personal interests.

Connect with Hitesh on LinkedIn at hitesh-pattanayak.

About the Technical Reviewer

Reza Ehsani is a software development professional with a career spanning since 2013, known for his expertise in various programming languages, including PHP, C++, Golang, and Python. His specialization in gRPC and microservices has been a focal point, particularly after his transition to Golang in 2019. Reza's skill set is comprehensive, covering both microservices and monolithic systems design, with a significant focus on gRPC protocols.

As a Senior Back End Developer at Champion Sports since September 2022, Reza has played a crucial role in refining the existing gRPC and microservices architecture, contributing significantly to the iGaming solutions. His earlier experience includes a pivotal role in a major project for Mashhad's public transportation system. In this project, Reza was instrumental in shaping the system's architecture and leading the development efforts, ensuring its scalability and future enhancements. This achievement reflects his ability to manage complex software projects successfully. Holding a Master's degree in E-Commerce/Electronic Commerce and Bachelor's degrees in Information Technology and Computer Software Engineering, Reza's academic background complements his rich professional experience. His career is characterized by a commitment to innovation and excellence in software development, with a particular focus on gRPC and microservices.

Acknowledgements

I would like to express my heartfelt gratitude to my current and previous organizations for affording me the opportunity to participate in projects that revolved around gRPC. Each experience has contributed immensely to my professional growth and understanding of this powerful technology.

A special thank you to Hema Kommoju, who first introduced me to gRPC during my tenure at Sureify. Your guidance and mentorship laid the foundation for my journey with this technology.

I am deeply indebted to Sameer Azazi for his leadership and mentorship during my time at Thoughtworks. Working on the trading and pricing backend system under his guidance not only deepened my understanding of gRPC but also exposed me to invaluable insights, particularly regarding load balancing solutions.

At Infracloud Technologies, I am grateful for the opportunity to continue exploring gRPC within project contexts.

Each project has presented new challenges and learning opportunities, further enriching my grip on this technology. I extend my sincere appreciation to the gRPC community and the invaluable resources available at https://grpc.io/blog . Your contributions have served as a guiding light, enriching the content of this book and ensuring its accuracy.

I would also like to acknowledge the technical reviewers, whose meticulous reviews and insightful feedback played a crucial role in refining the content of this book. Your dedication and expertise have been instrumental in enhancing its quality.

To all those involved in the publication process, your collective efforts have been indispensable. I am grateful for the collaborative spirit that has fueled the creation of "Modern API Design with gRPC."

Lastly, to the readers, thank you for choosing this book as a source of knowledge. It is my sincerest hope that it serves as a valuable companion on your journey to mastering gRPC and navigating the ever-evolving landscape of web development.

Preface

In the dynamic realm of API development, understanding the evolution of APIs over time is crucial. Welcome to "Modern API Design with gRPC" - a journey that delves into the evolution, fundamentals, and advanced concepts of gRPC, a modern and efficient RPC framework.

This book comprises nine chapters, each serving as a complete module, offering a comprehensive guide to mastering gRPC. Whether you're a seasoned developer looking to expand your skills or a newcomer eager to dive into RPC development, this book has something for everyone.

Chapter 1. API Evolution over Time: Evolution with Time sets the stage by tracing the evolution of APIs and their significance in modern software development.

Chapter 2. Fundamentals of gRPC: Introduces you to the core concepts of gRPC, discussing its architecture, protocol buffers, and code generation. It also advocates the usage of gRPC over traditional frameworks in microservices context.

Chapter 3. Getting Started with gRPC: Guides you through the installation process, setting up your first gRPC server and client, and exploring basic gRPC functionalities.

Chapter 4. Communication Patterns in gRPC: Delves into the various communication patterns supported by gRPC, including unary, server streaming, client streaming, and bidirectional streaming.

Chapter 5. Advanced gRPC Concepts: Explores advanced features and techniques in gRPC, such as error handling, metadata propagation, deadline propagation, and cancellation.

Chapter 6. Load Balancing in gRPC: Discusses strategies and techniques for load balancing gRPC services to improve scalability and reliability.

Chapter 7. Secured gRPC: Explores security mechanisms in gRPC, including TLS encryption, mutual TLS authentication, and authentication and authorization mechanisms.

Chapter 8. Production Grade gRPC Applications: Guides you through best practices and considerations for building production-grade gRPC applications, including performance optimization, error handling, and monitoring.

Chapter 9. Case-Studies of Projects Using gRPC: Showcases real-world projects and case studies that leverage gRPC for building scalable and efficient distributed systems.

Filled with practical examples, real-world scenarios, and best practices, this book is a hands-on guide to empower you to harness the full potential of gRPC in your software projects. I hope this journey through gRPC enhances your skills in RPC development and brings you success in your software endeavors.

Get a Free eBook

We hope you are enjoying your recently purchased book! Your feedback is incredibly valuable to us, and to all other readers looking for great books.

If you found this book helpful or enjoyable, we would truly appreciate it, if you could take a moment to leave a short review with a 5 star rating on Amazon. It helps us grow, and lets other readers discover our books.

As a thank you, we would love to send you a free digital copy of this book, and a **30%** discount code on your next cart value on our official websites:

www.orangeava.com

www.orangeava.in (For Indian Subcontinent)

☑ **Here's how:**

Leave a review for the book on Amazon.

Take a screenshot of your review, and send an email to **info@orangeava.com** (it can be just the confirmation screen).

Once, we receive your screenshot, we will send you the digital file, within 24 hours.

Thank you so much for your support – it means a lot to us!

Downloading the code bundles and colored images

Please follow the links or scan the QR codes to download the
Code Bundles and Images of the book:

https://github.com/OrangeAVA/Modern-API-Design-with-gRPC

The code bundles and images of the book are also hosted on
https://rebrand.ly/rdyw3yc

In case there's an update to the code, it will be updated on the existing GitHub repository.

Errata

We take immense pride in our work at **Orange Education Pvt Ltd,** and follow best practices to ensure the accuracy of our content to provide an indulging reading experience to our subscribers. Our readers are our mirrors, and we use their inputs to reflect and improve upon human errors, if any, that may have occurred during the publishing processes involved. To let us maintain the quality and help us reach out to any readers who might be having difficulties due to any unforeseen errors, please write to us at :

errata@orangeava.com

Your support, suggestions, and feedback are highly appreciated.

DID YOU KNOW

Did you know that Orange Education Pvt Ltd offers eBook versions of every book published, with PDF and ePub files available? You can upgrade to the eBook version at **www.orangeava.com** and as a print book customer, you are entitled to a discount on the eBook copy. Get in touch with us at: **info@orangeava.com** for more details.

At **www.orangeava.com**, you can also read a collection of free technical articles, sign up for a range of free newsletters, and receive exclusive discounts and offers on AVA™ Books and eBooks.

PIRACY

If you come across any illegal copies of our works in any form on the internet, we would be grateful if you would provide us with the location address or website name. Please contact us at **info@orangeava.com** with a link to the material.

ARE YOU INTERESTED IN AUTHORING WITH US?

If there is a topic that you have expertise in, and you are interested in either writing or contributing to a book, please write to us at **business@orangeava.com**. We are on a journey to help developers and tech professionals to gain insights on the present technological advancements and innovations happening across the globe and build a community that believes Knowledge is best acquired by sharing and learning with others. Please reach out to us to learn what our audience demands and how you can be part of this educational reform. We also welcome ideas from tech experts and help them build learning and development content for their domains.

REVIEWS

Please leave a review. Once you have read and used this book, why not leave a review on the site that you purchased it from? Potential readers can then see and use your unbiased opinion to make purchase decisions. We at Orange Education would love to know what you think about our products, and our authors can learn from your feedback. Thank you!

For more information about Orange Education, please visit **www.orangeava.com**.

Table of Contents

CHAPTER 1
API Evolution over Time

Introduction

In this chapter, we will delve into the fundamental necessity of APIs and trace their evolutionary journey over time. This exploration is crucial to comprehending the rationale behind our shift to alternative frameworks and messaging formats. We will delve into the prominent frameworks that have emerged over different times and also gaze ahead at the prospective horizons. By the chapter's conclusion, we will have gained a comprehensive grasp of the dynamic evolution that APIs have undergone.

Structure

In this chapter, we will cover the following topics:

- Introduction to API
- Advent of APIs
    - Socket-based network communication
    - Introduction of RPC
    - SOAP
    - REST
- Costs associated with traditional API frameworks
    - Serializing and Deserializing cost

- o Transmitting cost
- o Setting up a connection cost

Introduction to API

An API, or 'Application Programming Interface,' serves as a bridge between software components. I personally perceive the origin of APIs in the pursuit of 'Code Reusability,' akin to the motivation behind crafting functions. What sets APIs apart from functions is their inherent 'Remote-ness,' where APIs are stationed at network-accessible locations. Servers house these functions, with clients establishing connections to utilize them. This interplay requires a shared understanding between clients and servers, a predefined agreement that sidesteps ambiguity.

Several key reasons drove the development of APIs including,

- **Modularity and Reusability**: APIs allow software developers to create modular and reusable components. Instead of reinventing the wheel, developers can leverage existing APIs to access well-defined functionalities, saving time and effort.
- **Abstraction and Encapsulation**: APIs abstract the underlying complexity of software systems. They provide a simplified and standardized interface that shields developers from the internal implementation details of a component, making it easier to use and maintain.
- **Interoperability**: APIs enable different software systems, often developed by different teams or organizations, to work together regardless of their underlying technologies, platforms, or programming languages.
- **Scalability and Specialization**: APIs allow different teams to work on different parts of a system independently. For instance, a frontend team can work on the user interface while a backend team focuses on data processing, as long as they adhere to the defined API contracts.
- **Security and Access Control**: APIs provide a controlled way for applications to access certain functionalities or data. Access can be managed and restricted based on authentication and authorization mechanisms defined in the API.
- **Innovation and Ecosystem Growth**: APIs encourage innovation by enabling third-party developers to build applications or services that extend the capabilities of a platform. This fosters a rich ecosystem and can contribute to the overall success of a technology or product.

- **Updates and Maintenance**: APIs allow software systems to evolve independently. If an internal implementation changes, as long as the API contract remains consistent, other systems using the API won't be affected.
- **Remote Communication**: APIs enable remote communication between different parts of a distributed system. This is particularly important in today's interconnected world, where components might be running on different servers or even in different geographical locations.
- **Standardization**: APIs provide a standardized way of interacting with certain functionalities or services. This standardization ensures consistency and predictability across different applications.
- **Ease of Development**: Developers can build complex applications by leveraging the functionalities provided by APIs without having to create those functionalities from scratch.

In summary, APIs were developed to facilitate seamless communication, integration, and cooperation between different software components, systems, or services. They play a fundamental role in modern software development by enabling interoperability, modularity, and the creation of diverse and interconnected software ecosystems.

Let's explore more on the code reusability aspect of it. Code reusability is one of the key benefits and motivations for writing APIs. APIs provide a way to encapsulate complex functionalities or services into reusable components that can be easily integrated into different applications. This reusability not only saves development time and effort but also promotes consistency and reduces the risk of errors. Developers can leverage existing APIs to avoid reinventing the wheel and focus on building higher-level functionalities. So, yes, code reusability is a significant aspect of the core need to write APIs.

In the absence of APIs, what would the client's course of action entail? It's crucial to grasp the intricacies we would confront if APIs were absent from the equation:

- **Complex Integration**: Integrating different software systems or components would become highly complex and error-prone. Clients would need to develop custom solutions for every interaction, leading to duplicated efforts and increased development time.
- **Lack of Standardization**: Without APIs, there would be no standardized way to interact with external services or functionalities. Clients would need to understand and adapt to the unique protocols and interfaces of each system they want to communicate with.

- **Inefficient Communication**: Communication between systems would be ad-hoc and inefficient. Clients might resort to methods like direct database queries or file exchanges, resulting in slower and less reliable data exchange.
- **Security Implications**: In the absence of APIs, clients may resort to manual data entry or file exchanges, increasing the risk of data breaches due to human error and unstructured data transmission, necessitating enhanced security measures like encryption and access controls.
- **Limited Reusability**: The absence of APIs would hinder code reusability. Developers would need to create functionalities from scratch for every project, leading to a lack of consistency and a higher chance of errors.
- **Higher Development Costs**: Developing custom integrations for each interaction would increase development costs significantly. Clients would need to allocate more resources to handle integration complexities.
- **Reduced Innovation**: Without APIs, third-party developers would struggle to build applications that leverage the capabilities of existing systems. This could stifle innovation and limit the growth of software ecosystems.
- **Vendor Lock-In**: Clients would become heavily dependent on specific vendors or technologies, as switching or migrating to different solutions would require rewriting large portions of code.
- **Maintenance Challenges**: Updates or changes in one system might lead to cascading changes in other systems that interact with it, making maintenance and updates much more challenging.
- **Scalability Issues**: Scaling applications would become more difficult, as custom integrations might not be optimized for performance or adapt well to increased loads.
- **Limited Interoperability**: Different software systems might not be able to communicate effectively, limiting the potential for collaboration and hindering the development of integrated and cohesive software solutions.

In essence, the availability of APIs significantly simplifies and enhances the way software components and systems interact, offering standardization, reusability, efficiency, and the potential for innovation. APIs provide a structured and manageable approach to integration, enabling clients to focus on building higher-level functionalities and creating more robust and flexible software applications.

Advent of APIs

Over time, the evolution of APIs has seen distinct phases of change in both their declaration and definition. In this section, we will delve into a detailed examination of these transformative phases.

Socket-based Network Communication

In earlier days, communicating over a network was a much more low-level and hands-on endeavor. To establish communication with a server, you had to rely on the Sockets library provided by the operating system. This library had no relation to modern concepts like Socket.io or WebSockets; it was a fundamental building block for network communication.

The sockets library offered a relatively simple but raw API with basic functions like **send** and **read** which allowed you to transmit and receive individual bits of character data. However, beyond these functions, you were pretty much on your own.

Working with these raw character bits could be quite cumbersome and error-prone. You had to manually handle the encoding and decoding of data, ensuring data integrity and dealing with potential issues like data fragmentation and reassembly. Essentially, you were responsible for managing the entire communication process from start to finish.

Imagine sending a simple text message. You would need to convert your text into bytes, send those bytes over the network using the 'send' function, then receive the bytes on the other end and convert them back into a readable message. This manual handling of data at the byte level could lead to mistakes and inefficiencies, not to mention the challenges of dealing with different character encodings.

As a result, even though the chat applications served as valuable learning experiences, they also highlighted the need for higher-level abstractions that could simplify and standardize the process of network communication. This need eventually led to the development of more advanced libraries, protocols, and APIs like gRPC, which provide a more structured and efficient way to communicate over networks without the low-level intricacies of managing individual character bits.

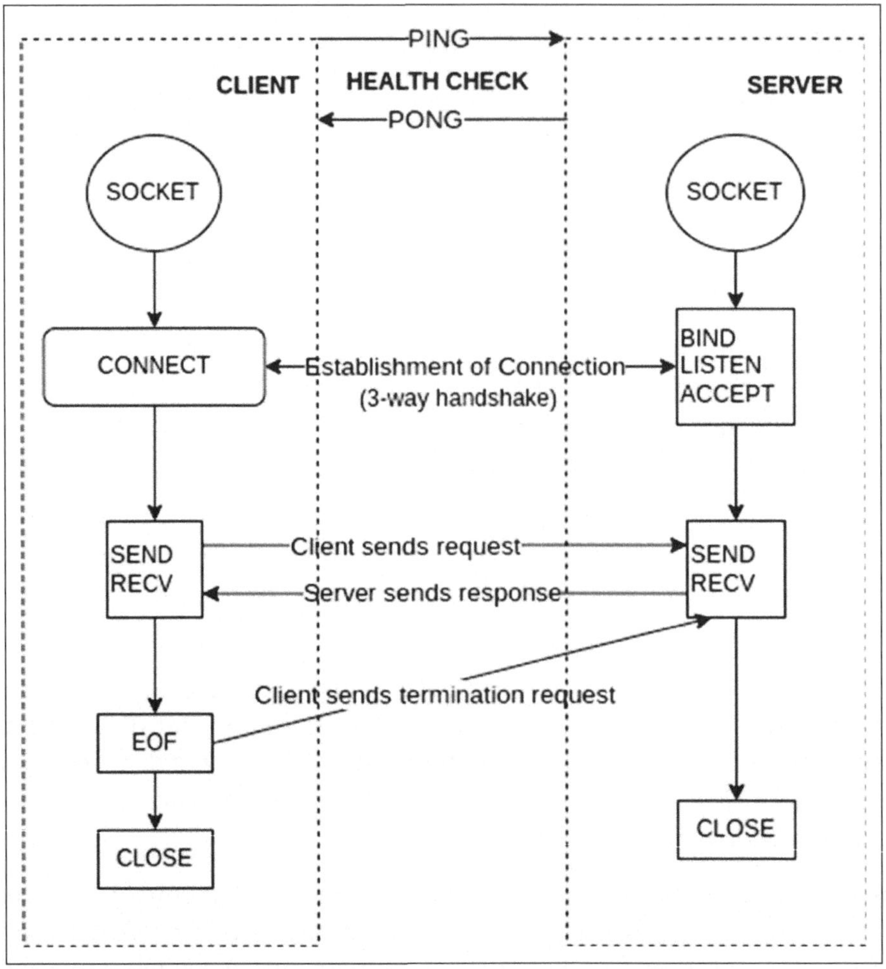

Figure 1.1: *Networking in socket-based communication*

In those earlier days of network communication, simplicity coexisted with complexity. The reliance on the Sockets library for connecting to servers introduced a world of raw data transmission. While it provided fundamental functions for sending and receiving character bits, it left the burden of data management squarely on the shoulders of developers.

Consider the task of sending a text message. It involved the meticulous conversion of text into bytes, followed by the transmission of those bytes using the 'send' function. On the receiving end, these bytes had to be carefully decoded back into a human-readable message. This manual byte-level handling not only introduced room for errors but also created inefficiencies, especially when dealing with various character encodings.

As the demand for network communication grew, so did the need for standardized, simplified, and efficient methods. REST APIs simplified communication by abstracting away the complexities associated with raw data transmission. Developers could now design APIs that offered a more straightforward interface, making it easier to transmit and receive data in a format that aligns with the principles of REST. While REST APIs served as a significant improvement over raw socket-based communication, they still had limitations, especially in scenarios where high-performance and real-time communication were crucial. Developers yearned for even more efficient ways of handling communication over networks, paving the way for the evolution of libraries, protocols, and APIs like gRPC. These yearnings acted as a catalyst for the development of gRPC, a high-performance RPC (Remote Procedure Call) framework developed by Google. Unlike REST, which relies on JSON over HTTP, gRPC uses Protocol Buffers over HTTP/2, providing a more efficient and faster communication protocol.

In this brave new world, developers could now focus on the essence of their communication, freeing themselves from the intricacies of low-level data management. The advent of gRPC and similar technologies marked a significant leap forward in making network communication more accessible, efficient, and reliable than ever before.

Introduction of RPC

The emergence of the Remote Procedure Call (RPC) concept stemmed from the recognition that much of the complexity in networking arises from managing transmitted bits. People began contemplating a scenario where they could transcend network intricacies, seamlessly invoking functions on remote servers in a manner akin to local function calls. This conceptualization paved the way for the advent of RPC.

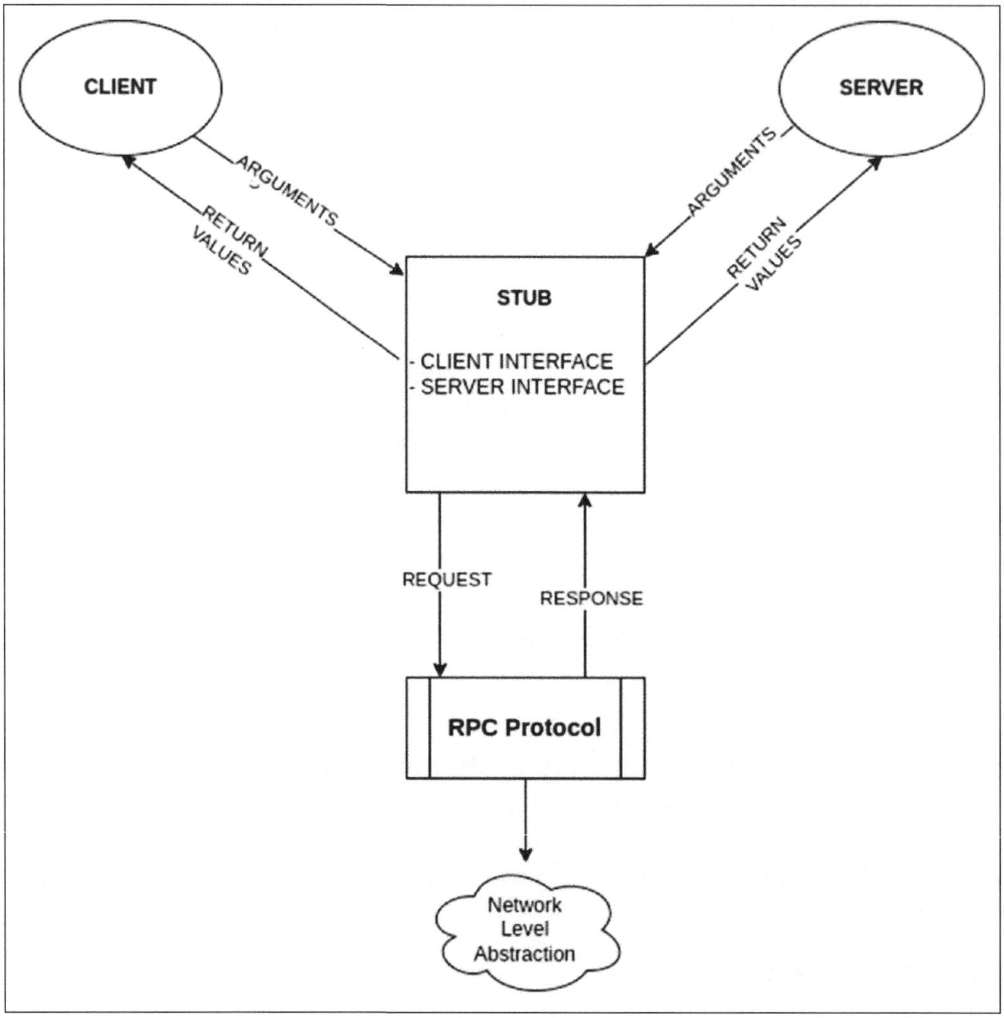

Figure 1.2: *Simplified RPC flow*

To enable such a seamless interaction, the initial step involves defining your API in an Interface Definition Language (IDL) file. Subsequently, you can leverage the IDL compiler tool to generate a code stub. This code stub serves as a fundamental bridge, automating the intricate processes of message serialization and deserialization for both the client and server facets of the communication.

With this code stub in place, the complexity of converting data structures into a format that can be transmitted over the network is significantly alleviated. The stub seamlessly handles the conversion of data into a standardized form suitable for transmission and then transforms the received data back into its original structure.

This automation of serialization and deserialization profoundly simplifies the communication process, liberating developers from the meticulous task of manual data conversion. The generated code stub acts as a mediator that ensures data integrity, format consistency, and reliable communication between client and server. It underscores the essence of abstraction in modern network programming, allowing developers to focus on the core logic and functionality of their applications rather than grappling with the nitty-gritty of data encoding and decoding.

SOAP

Before the era of REST came into full swing, there existed SOAP, a protocol initially introduced by Microsoft. SOAP carries forward many RPC characteristics. Notably, SOAP employs WSDL (Web Service Description Language) as its schema file, encapsulated in XML. This XML-based representation ensures language and platform agnosticism, empowering different programming languages and integrated development environments (IDEs) to seamlessly establish communication channels.

Furthermore, SOAP introduces an additional layer of security. It guarantees privacy and integrity within transactions while enabling message-level encryption. This combination results in a robust framework suitable for transactions of enterprise-grade quality.

However, REST's ascent to prominence was swift, eventually overshadowing SOAP's influence and asserting its dominance in the technological landscape.

Contrary to common belief, SOAP actually emerged subsequent to the concept of RPC. The distinction lies in the fact that during that period, monolithic architecture didn't align well with the principles of RPC. Interestingly, the prevalence of RPC has witnessed a resurgence in contemporary times compared to its earlier adoption.

A typical format of a soap request to get book details would look like this:

```
<?xml version = "1.0">


<SOAP-ENV:Envelope
```

```
   xmlns:SOAP-ENV = "http://www.w3.org/2001/12/soap-envelope"
   SOAP-ENV:encodingStyle = "http://www.w3.org/2001/12/soap-encoding">
   <SOAP-ENV:Body xmlns:m = "http://www.example.com/">
      <m:GetBook>
         <m:ISBN>HVT076236</m:ISBN>
      </m:GetBook>
   </SOAP-ENV:Body>
</SOAP-ENV:Envelope>
```

The corresponding response would be this:

```
<?xml version= "1.0">
<soap:Envelope
xmlns:soap="http://www.w3.org/2003/05/soap-envelope/"
soap:encodingStyle="http://www.w3.org/2003/05/soap-encoding">
<soap:Body>
  <m:GetBookResponse>
    <m:BookName>Modern API Design</m:BookName>
    <m:Publication>AVA Orange</m:Publication>
  </m:GetBookResponse>
</soap:Body>
</soap:Envelope>
```

Understand why SOAP's replacement was considered!

It was because the data size was too big for few details, including response and requests.

REST

Dissimilar from its counterparts, REST distinguishes itself by not prescribing rigid regulations or a standardized toolkit. Rather, it embodies an architectural style, delineating a collection of architectural principles and understandings. An API that aligns with these REST constraints earns the moniker of being RESTful.

The most noteworthy advantage of REST resides in its simplicity and innate comprehensibility. It harnesses standard HTTP methods and adopts a resource-centric approach to API definition. It's akin to transplanting the principles of Object-Oriented Programming (OOP) into the realm of APIs. REST's popularity can be attributed to its accessibility, enabling developers of all backgrounds to craft RESTful APIs with ease.

If we compare SOAP's request-response messages with REST's, we get this:

Request to get a book by ISBN:

```
GET /books/{isbn}
```

and the response would look like:

```
{
  "bookName": "Sample Book",
  "publisherName": "Example Publications"
}
```

Interestingly, it's not uncommon to observe projects predominantly utilizing only the GET and POST HTTP methods. Remarkably, such a streamlined approach does not diminish the potency bestowed by REST's principles.

However, as I highlighted earlier, this lenient standardization also gives rise to certain challenges:

- **Code Maintenance and Reliability**: As a project scales in complexity, the codebase can become convoluted and prone to errors. The flexibility of REST can inadvertently contribute to this challenge.
- **Tight Coupling of Teams**: The interaction between frontend and backend teams can become intricately intertwined due to the unrestricted nature of REST. Any modifications to the API necessitate collaborative efforts from both sides.
- **Multiple API Calls**: RESTful architectures occasionally involve multiple API calls to retrieve necessary information, leading to increased latency and potential performance bottlenecks.
- **Over-fetching and Under-fetching**: The design of REST APIs sometimes results in fetching more data than needed (over-fetching) or not enough data (under-fetching), impacting efficiency and resource utilization.

- **Duplicate Endpoints**: Developers might find themselves compelled to create duplicate API endpoints to cater to diverse client consumers, such as web browsers and mobile applications.

The duality of REST's flexibility, enabling rapid development, and its potential to generate complexities and inefficiencies underscores the importance of careful design considerations to strike a balance between ease of use and system efficiency.

The challenges I previously outlined within the context of REST have found their resolutions in the form of GraphQL, a technology that addresses those limitations head-on. However, it's important to recognize that there are additional underlying intricacies that gRPC, another technology, has effectively tackled. This alignment between gRPC's solutions and the fervent embrace of microservice architecture has proven to be particularly significant.

GraphQL's emergence has been a direct response to REST's issues like over-fetching, under-fetching, and the need for multiple API calls. With GraphQL, the client is empowered to precisely specify the data it requires, facilitating a streamlined and efficient exchange between the client and server. This level of customization effectively eliminates the wastage of resources and improves performance. GraphQL's schema-driven approach enhances discoverability and empowers frontend and backend teams to work more independently, minimizing tight coupling and facilitating iterative development.

On the other hand, gRPC stepped into the scene aligned with the surging adoption of microservice architecture. gRPC's proficiency lies in its efficient and performant communication between distributed services. It employs binary serialization and compact payload, resulting in faster data transfer. gRPC's support for bidirectional streaming enhances real-time interactions. The microservice paradigm, which emphasizes modular and independently deployable components, dovetails well with gRPC's capabilities, enabling seamless communication within these microservices. gRPC's auto-generated code and schema-driven approach expedite development and enhance system maintainability.

In essence, GraphQL and gRPC, while addressing different dimensions of the challenges posed by REST and distributed systems, have significantly contributed to the advancement of modern application architectures. Their impact has been particularly pronounced as technology landscapes evolve towards more modular, efficient, and scalable paradigms, like microservices. This convergence of innovative solutions with changing architectural preferences underscores the dynamic nature of technology's evolution.

In this book, we shall explore the gRPC side of things.

Costs Associated with Traditional API Frameworks

Traditional API frameworks have long been burdened by several inherent costs, each affecting the efficiency and performance of data exchange over networks. Firstly, the expense of transmitting data cannot be overlooked. In the world of traditional APIs, data transfer often incurs high costs, especially when dealing with large payloads. Serialization and deserialization, the processes of encoding and decoding data, come with their own price tag. These operations can consume valuable computational resources and time, leading to delays in response times.

Furthermore, setting up and maintaining network connections adds to the overall cost. Establishing and closing connections can be resource-intensive, and the overhead of creating and managing these connections can hinder scalability and responsiveness. In essence, the traditional approach to APIs has been riddled with these costs, making it imperative for the industry to seek more efficient alternatives.

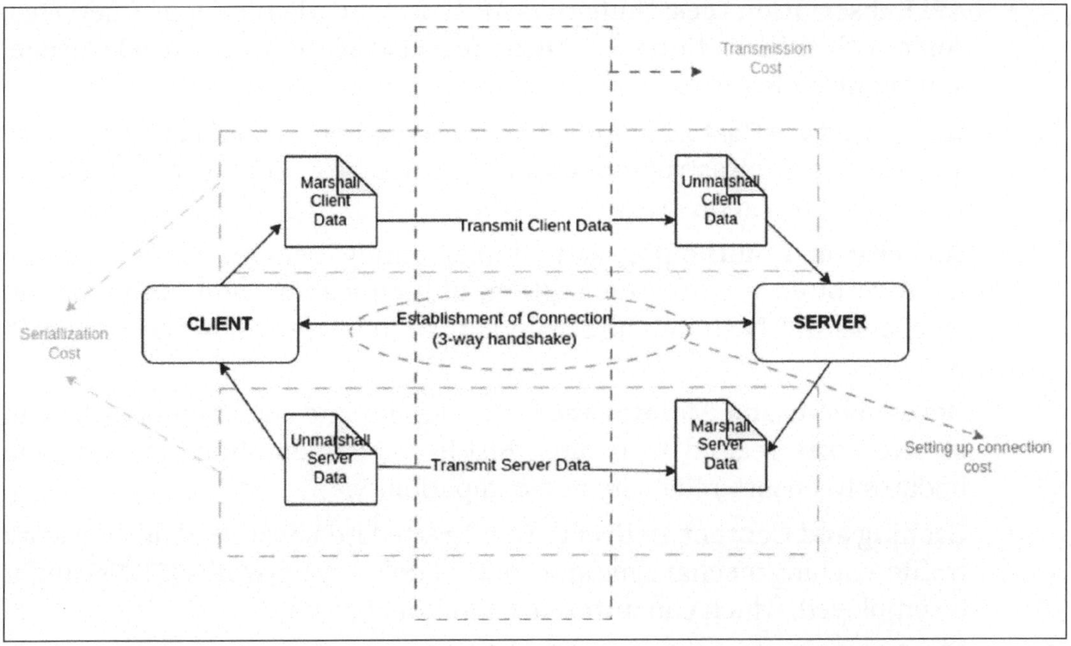

***Figure 1.3:** Illustration of various costs associated with request-response cycle*

Let's detail out the costs associated with accessing APIs over the network.

Accessing APIs over a network can entail various costs, both in terms of financial expenses and performance considerations. Here are some costs associated with accessing APIs over a network:

- **Latency:** Network communication introduces latency, the time delay between sending a request and receiving a response. This delay can **significantly** impact the responsiveness of applications, **especially those relying on** real-time interactions.
- **Network Bandwidth**: API requests and responses consume network bandwidth. Frequent or large API calls can **lead** to increased network traffic, affecting overall performance and potentially **causing** congestion.
- **Data Transfer Costs:** Many cloud providers and API services charge based on the volume of data transferred. APIs with large payloads or high-frequency calls **can result in substantial data transfer costs**.
- **Rate Limiting Charges**: Certain APIs enforce rate limits on the number of requests **within a specified time frame**. Exceeding these limits may **incur additional charges or necessitate** an upgrade to a higher-priced plan.
- **API Subscription Fees**: Numerous APIs, particularly third-party services, come with subscription fees. **These fees, based on access levels, usage, and required features**, contribute to operational costs.
- **Infrastructure Costs**: For APIs that are hosted on a cloud platform, there are associated infrastructure costs for server provisioning, maintenance, and scaling based on usage demands.
- **Security and Authentication**: Implementing secure communication for APIs often requires encryption, authentication, and authorization mechanisms. These measures can add complexity and overhead to API requests.
- **Development and Maintenance**: Developing and maintaining APIs can involve costs related to coding, testing, documentation, and ongoing updates to ensure reliability and compatibility.
- **Caching and Content Delivery**: To mitigate latency and reduce network traffic, caching mechanisms and content delivery networks (CDNs) might be employed, which can introduce additional costs.
- **Monitoring and Analytics**: Effective monitoring and analytics tools are **necessary** to track API usage, performance, and potential issues, incurring costs for required tools and resources.

- **Failover and Redundancy**: Ensuring the high availability of APIs often requires redundant infrastructure, failover mechanisms, and disaster recovery strategies, which can involve additional expenses.
- **Training and Support**: To effectively utilize and troubleshoot APIs, training and support might be needed, which can incur costs for education and access to technical assistance.

It's essential to consider these costs when designing, implementing, and utilizing APIs, as they can impact both the financial aspects and the overall performance of your applications. Balancing cost considerations with the benefits of API usage is crucial for achieving optimal results.

Let's draw our attention particularly on three costs:

Serializing and Deserializing Cost

Serializing and deserializing, also known as serialization and deserialization, refer to the process of converting data structures or objects into a format suitable for transmission or storage and then converting them back into their original form. While these operations are fundamental for data exchange, they come with certain costs that developers should be aware of:

Serialization Costs

- **Computational Overhead**: Serializing data involves converting complex data structures into a format like JSON, XML, or Protocol Buffers. This process requires CPU and memory usage, which can impact the overall performance of the system.
- **Conversion Time**: The serialization process takes time, especially for large or intricate data structures. This can lead to delays when preparing data for transmission.
- **Increased Payload Size**: Serialized data often includes additional metadata and formatting, which can increase the payload size. This can lead to higher network usage and potentially impact response times, particularly in scenarios with limited bandwidth.

Deserialization Costs

- **Processing Overhead**: Deserializing data requires interpreting the serialized format and reconstructing the original data structure. This process also consumes CPU and memory resources.

- **Latency**: Deserialization introduces latency, as the receiving end needs to wait for the entire serialized data to be received and then deserialized before it can be processed.
- **Parsing Complexity**: In more complex data formats, like XML or JSON, parsing and deserialization can become computationally expensive, potentially affecting the system's overall responsiveness.
- **Compatibility Overhead**: Deserializing data may encounter challenges related to versioning and compatibility, especially in evolving systems where data structures may change over time. Ensuring backward and forward compatibility in deserialization processes can introduce additional complcxities. Developers may need to implement strategies such as versioning mechanisms or handling gracefully when encountering different versions of serialized data to prevent errors and maintain system stability.

Mitigating the Costs

- **Efficient Formats**: Choosing efficient serialization formats like Protocol Buffers or MessagePack can reduce both serialization and deserialization costs. These formats are binary and designed for performance.
- **Caching**: Implementing caching mechanisms can help mitigate serialization and deserialization costs. Once data is deserialized, it can be cached to reduce the need for repeated deserialization.
- **Lazy Loading**: For scenarios where not all data needs to be deserialized immediately, lazy loading can be employed. This involves loading data on-demand to reduce upfront deserialization costs.
- **Network Efficiency**: Minimizing the amount of data transmitted can reduce serialization costs. This can be achieved through techniques like data compression or only sending essential data fields.
- **Optimized Code**: Writing efficient serialization and deserialization code, utilizing memory buffers, and reducing unnecessary copying of data can help improve performance.
- **Asynchronous Processing**: In scenarios where immediate data processing is not critical, developers can explore asynchronous processing for deserialization. By decoupling the deserialization process from the main execution thread, the system can continue handling other tasks while deserialization occurs in the background. This approach helps distribute computational load and enhance overall responsiveness, particularly in

situations where the system can operate efficiently without waiting for the completion of deserialization

In conclusion, while serialization and deserialization are essential for data exchange, they do introduce computational overhead, processing time, and potential latency. Developers should be vigilant about backward and forward compatibility during deserialization and address security concerns in serialization. In scenarios emphasizing real-time responsiveness, careful consideration of these costs is crucial. By employing efficient serialization formats, optimizing code, and implementing caching strategies and integrating **Asynchronous Processing**, developers can mitigate these costs and achieve better overall system performance.

Transmitting Cost

Transmitting costs refer to the expenses and considerations associated with sending data over a network, whether it's within a local network, across the internet, or between distributed systems. These costs can have financial implications and affect the performance and efficiency of data transmission. Here are some factors to reflect on regarding transmitting costs:

Bandwidth Usage

- **Data Volume**: The size of the data being transmitted directly impacts bandwidth usage. Larger data payloads consume more bandwidth and may lead to increased costs, particularly in scenarios with limited or metered data plans.
- **Frequency of Transmission**: High-frequency data transmission, such as frequent API calls, can quickly accumulate data usage and incur costs, especially when dealing with cloud-based services that charge based on data transferred.

Financial Costs

- **Data Transfer Fees**: Many cloud service providers charge based on the amount of data transferred. This can include both inbound and outbound data traffic, potentially leading to unexpected costs for high-traffic applications.
- **Service Subscription Costs**: Some APIs and cloud services have subscription tiers based on the level of usage or the features accessed. Higher usage levels might come with increased costs.

- **Content Delivery Networks (CDNs)**: While CDNs can improve data delivery speed, they can also introduce additional costs, particularly for large-scale deployments or extensive data distribution.

Latency and Performance

- **Response Time**: Transmitting data over long distances can introduce latency, affecting the responsiveness of applications. Minimizing latency may require investing in higher-quality network connections or using content delivery networks.
- **Impact on User Experience**: Slow data transmission can lead to poor user experiences, impacting user satisfaction and potentially leading to decreased usage or abandonment of applications.

Optimization and Mitigation

- **Data Compression**: Employing data compression techniques can reduce the amount of data transmitted, decreasing bandwidth usage and associated costs.
- **Caching**: Implementing caching mechanisms can help reduce the need for repeated data transmission by serving cached data to users.
- **Payload Minimization**: Sending only essential data fields and using efficient data formats (for example, binary formats like Protocol Buffers) can minimize payload size and reduce transmitting costs.
- **Network Optimization**: Utilizing efficient networking protocols and technologies can improve data transmission speeds and reduce latency.
- **Rate Limiting**: Implementing rate limiting on API calls can help manage data transmission frequency, ensuring that data transfer costs are controlled.
- **Optimized Code**: Well-optimized code can help reduce the amount of data transmitted by minimizing unnecessary data and optimizing the serialization process.
- **Data Deduplication**: Identifying and eliminating duplicate data before transmission can save bandwidth and reduce the volume of data to be transmitted. This is particularly relevant for applications dealing with redundant or repeated information.
- **Dynamic Scaling**: Utilize dynamic scaling capabilities in cloud environments to automatically adjust resources based on demand. This can help optimize costs during periods of varying data transmission requirements.

- **Quality of Service Measures**: Implement Quality of Service measures to prioritize critical data transmissions over less time-sensitive ones. This ensures that essential data is transmitted promptly, enhancing the overall user experience.

Balancing the need for efficient and responsive data transmission with managing associated costs is crucial for designing high-performance applications. Careful consideration of factors like data volume, frequency of transmission, network infrastructure, and the use of optimization techniques can help mitigate transmitting costs and ensure an optimal user experience while managing expenses.

Setting up a Connection Cost

Setting up a connection cost refers to the expenses and considerations associated with establishing and maintaining network connections between different systems, devices, or components. These costs can impact the performance, scalability, and efficiency of applications that rely on network communication. Here are some factors to reflect on regarding connection setup costs:

Network Establishment

- **Latency**: Establishing a network connection can introduce latency, especially in scenarios where multiple handshakes or negotiation processes are required before communication can begin.
- **Time Delay**: Connection setup takes time, and this delay can impact the responsiveness of applications that require immediate communication.

Resource Utilization

- **Resource Consumption**: Setting up connections consumes computing resources on both the client and server sides. This can impact the overall system performance, particularly in scenarios with a large number of simultaneous connections.
- **Concurrency Management**: Managing concurrent connections requires resources to handle context switching and thread management. This overhead can increase as the number of connections grows.

Financial Costs

- **Infrastructure Costs**: Setting up and maintaining network connections often requires hardware and infrastructure resources, which can lead to associated costs for server provisioning, networking equipment, and maintenance.

- **Cloud Service Costs**: For cloud-based applications, the setup and management of network connections might involve costs based on the amount of data transferred or the level of resources consumed.

Scalability and Efficiency

- **Scaling Challenges**: As the number of connections increases, the complexity of managing and scaling the infrastructure can grow. Balancing connection setup costs with system scalability is crucial.
- **Connection Pools**: Implementing connection pooling strategies can help mitigate connection setup costs by reusing existing connections for multiple transactions.
- **Security Considerations**:
  - **Encryption Overhead**: Implementing encryption for secure connections adds computational overhead during setup, impacting both latency and resource consumption.
  - **Authentication Processes**: Stringent authentication protocols during connection setup contribute to delays, emphasizing the need for a balance between security and performance.
  - **Data Privacy Regulations**: Adhering to data privacy regulations may necessitate additional measures during connection setup, impacting both time and resource requirements.
- **Maintenance and Monitoring**:
  - **Connection Health Monitoring**: Implementing mechanisms to monitor the health of connections helps identify issues early on, reducing downtime and potential performance degradation. But it also includes the cost.
  - **Connection Logging**: Logging connection activities facilitates troubleshooting and auditing, but it comes with the cost of additional storage and processing.

Mitigation and Optimization

- **Connection Reuse**: Reusing established connections whenever possible can help reduce the overhead of setting up new connections for each transaction.
- **Connection Keep-Alive**: Enabling connection keep-alive mechanisms allows connections to remain open for a certain period, reducing the need for frequent reconnections.

- **Connection Pooling**: Utilizing connection pooling techniques allows applications to reuse existing connections from a pool, reducing the overhead of connection setup.
- **Optimized Code**: Efficiently managing connection setup and teardown in code can help reduce unnecessary overhead and improve overall application performance.
- **Load Balancing**: Distributing connections across multiple servers through load balancing can help distribute the connection setup load and improve overall system scalability.
- **Minimized Redundancy**: Avoiding unnecessary or redundant connection setup processes can help reduce resource consumption and latency.
- **Connection Timeout Policies**: Implementing appropriate connection timeout policies helps prevent prolonged waiting times and resource wastage in case of unsuccessful connection attempts.
- **Adaptive Connection Strategies**: Developing adaptive connection strategies that dynamically adjust based on network conditions, load, and application requirements can enhance efficiency.
- **Caching Connection Parameters**: Caching frequently used connection parameters and configurations can reduce the need for renegotiation, improving connection setup speed.
- **Connection Prioritization**: Prioritizing critical connections over less time-sensitive ones can optimize resource allocation and improve the overall user experience.
- **Automated Connection Scaling**: Implementing automated scaling mechanisms that dynamically adjust the infrastructure to handle varying connection loads helps maintain optimal performance.

Balancing the need for efficient and responsive network communication with managing the associated costs of connection setup is crucial for designing robust and high-performance applications. Careful consideration of factors like latency, resource utilization, scalability, and optimization strategies can help mitigate connection setup costs and ensure optimal application performance.

Nonetheless, while it's true that completely eliminating the aforementioned costs might be challenging, it's essential to recognize that in the data-driven era we inhabit, confronting these costs head-on has become imperative. This endeavor is a crucial step towards achieving responses in the sub-millisecond range, a key facet in the quest to build high-performance systems.

Conclusion

As our journey through application development continues, we find ourselves less preoccupied with one central concern: computing power. Thanks to the rise of cloud providers, the intricacies of managing data centers have receded into the background. Within a matter of seconds, resources materialize at our disposal, available on-demand. This paradigm shift also ushers in an era of abundant data, where the generation of big data is a norm, and its transportation occurs through a variety of mediums within singular requests.

However, the expansion in data volume introduces a cascade of activities – serialization, deserialization, and transportation costs – onto the scene. While the management of computing resources might no longer be a pressing issue, latency looms as a significant overhead. The urgency to minimize transportation overhead becomes paramount. Over time, various messaging protocols have emerged, each attempting to address this challenge. While SOAP was robust but burdensome, REST offered a streamlined alternative. Nevertheless, the quest for an even more efficient framework persists. Enter Remote Procedure Calls (RPC), offering a promising solution to this intricate conundrum.

This book embarks on an exploration of the RPC realm, delving into the core concepts of RPC and introducing an implementation known as gRPC. Within these pages, we undertake a comparative journey between REST and RPC, unraveling the nuanced layers that constitute gRPC. From its pivotal role in security to the array of tooling it offers, this book is an illuminating guide that equips readers with a comprehensive understanding of gRPC's multifaceted landscape.

Let's set our sights on the next chapter. Here, we will delve deeper into gRPC's unique approach to API design. Our journey begins at the core of API architecture, exploring the essential components known as 'Message' and 'RPC' within gRPC's framework. These are the building blocks that define gRPC's distinctive structure and functionality.

With a focus on clarity, we will draw comparisons between gRPC and the familiar REST paradigm, ensuring that you can easily grasp the nuances of gRPC by relating it to what you already know. By evaluating the strengths and differences between REST and gRPC, we aim to equip you with the knowledge needed to make informed decisions in your pursuit of modern API design excellence.

Furthermore, we will unravel the message format used by gRPC, which is Protocol Buffers (Protobuf), and highlight the reasons behind this choice. This chapter serves as the foundation upon which we build a comprehensive understanding of gRPC's core concepts, providing you with the tools to excel in modern API design.

Multiple Choice Questions

Let's check our understanding with some multiple choice questions:

1. What is the primary focus of the chapter titled "Introduction to API"?
   a. Exploring the history of APIs
   b. Discussing the advent of APIs
   c. Introducing the concept of API
   d. Analyzing the costs associated with APIs
2. Which section discusses the evolution of APIs and their transformative phases?
   a. Introduction to API
   b. Advent of APIs
   c. SOAP
   d. REST
3. Before the advent of modern communication technologies, what library did developers rely on for network communication?
   a. WebSocket
   b. Socket.io
   c. Sockets library
   d. WebSockets library
4. What does RPC stand for in the context of network communication?
   a. Remote Programming Code
   b. Resource Protocol Communication
   c. Remote Procedure Call
   d. Responsive Protocol Code

5. Which protocol introduced the concept of Web Services Description Language (WSDL) for API contracts?
    a. REST
    b. SOAP
    c. gRPC
    d. WebSocket
6. What is one of the key drawbacks associated with traditional API frameworks?
    a. Efficient data serialization and deserialization
    b. Low costs of transmitting data
    c. Complexity of setting up network connections
    d. Simplified process of managing character bits
7. What cost is discussed in the section titled "Serializing and Deserializing cost"?
    a. Transmitting cost
    b. Setting up a connection cost
    c. Cost associated with efficient data serialization and deserialization
    d. The cost of network infrastructure
8. Which cost is proportional to the size of the data being transferred in traditional API frameworks?
    a. Serializing and Deserializing cost
    b. Transmitting cost
    c. Setting up a connection cost
    d. Network maintenance cost
9. What does the section "Transmitting cost" primarily focus on?
    a. The cost of setting up network connections
    b. The cost associated with data serialization and deserialization
    c. The cost of transmitting data over the network
    d. The cost of API contracts

10. What cost is addressed in the section titled "Setting up a connection cost"?
    a. Serializing and Deserializing cost
    b. Transmitting cost
    c. The cost of establishing and maintaining network connections
    d. The cost of data transfer

Answers

1	c
2	b
3	c
4	c
5	b
6	c
7	a
8	b
9	c
10	c

CHAPTER 2
Fundamentals of gRPC

Introduction

In the preceding chapter, we delved into the historical evolution of APIs, arriving at the pivotal focus of this book: the exploration of gRPC's distinctive approach to API design. It is worth noting that gRPC, in essence, serves as the practical realization of the RPC (Remote Procedure Call) concept. A quick recap reveals that RPC constitutes a significant stride in the journey of API design evolution. Now, as we embark on our journey with gRPC, we will commence with a fundamental principle.

APIs, by their very essence, are the gateways enabling the seamless exchange of data between distinct points. Thus, it becomes paramount for us to embark on a comprehensive exploration of these endpoints. Within the specific terminology of gRPC, these endpoints take on the roles of 'Message' and 'RPC' – the building blocks that underpin the architecture of gRPC. With this lens, we venture into the realm of 'Data' and 'endpoints', unraveling their intricacies.

Within the intricate tapestry of API architecture, gRPC introduces a clear demarcation between these pivotal components. Our journey in this chapter is one of comprehensive understanding, where we delve into the heart of the matter: the concept of 'Message' and 'RPC'. This understanding empowers us to wield the tools that gRPC provides, all the while keeping an eye on the horizon of efficient API design.

As we progress, we bridge the gap between different paradigms by drawing insightful comparisons, particularly between gRPC and the familiar REST. The aim here is lucidity, ensuring that the nuances of gRPC's approach are readily comprehensible through relatable comparisons. Furthermore, by placing REST and gRPC on the scales of assessment, we shall evaluate the strengths and nuances of each, paving the way for an informed choice between the two.

In our realm of familiarity, we acknowledge that the realm of REST employs JSON as the canvas for its data exchange. In a similar vein, the world of gRPC showcases its adherence to a distinct message format, with Protocol Buffers (Protobuf) standing as its chosen means. As we navigate through this chapter, we draw parallels and distinctions, unraveling the reasons behind these choices.

In summation, this chapter serves as the foundation upon which we build our comprehension of the core concepts of gRPC. From 'Data' to 'Endpoints', from 'Message' to 'RPC', our exploration unfolds systematically, gradually illuminating the unique facets of gRPC and elucidating its distinctions from the prevalent alternatives. Through this journey, we gain not only insight but also a platform to make informed decisions in our pursuit of modern API design excellence.

Structure

In this chapter, we will cover the following topics:

- Protocol Buffers
- Message Encoding Using Protocol Buffers
- HTTP/2
- Features that make gRPC standout
  - Clean Contract
  - Size of Data
  - Serialization of Data
  - TCP Connection
  - Code Generation

Protocol Buffers – Foundation of gRPC

Before delving into the intricacies of gRPC, it is crucial to gain a firm grasp of its foundational message format. This foundational understanding will serve as a solid foundation for comprehending the various concepts and mechanisms that make gRPC a powerful and efficient API framework.

Protocol Buffers, often referred to as Protobuf, is a serialization format and language-agnostic interface description language used for efficient and compact data interchange between systems. It was developed by Google and offers a versatile way to structure data, define messages, and generate code for various programming languages.

At its core, Protobuf allows us to define the structure of our data using a simple language in a **.proto** file. Let us illustrate this with an example:

Suppose we want to define a Person message that includes their name, age, and a list of phone numbers.

```
syntax = "proto3";


message Person {

  string name = 1;

  int32 age = 2;

  repeated string phone_numbers = 3;

}
```

In this example:

- We specify that we are using **proto3** syntax.
    - You can use **proto2,** but we recommend that you use **proto3** with gRPC as it lets you use the full range of gRPC-supported languages, as well as avoiding compatibility issues with **proto2** clients talking to **proto3** servers and vice versa.
- We define a Person message with three fields:
    - **name** of type string, tagged with field number 1.
    - **age** of type int32, tagged with field number 2.
    - **phone_numbers** of type repeated string (indicating an array of strings), tagged with field number 3.

After defining the message structure, we can use the Protobuf compiler (**protoc**) to generate code for various programming languages, such as Golang, Python, Java, C++, and more.

This generated code includes methods for serializing and deserializing data, making it easy to work with Protobuf messages in our code.

`protoc` compiler can be installed using the steps mentioned here: https://grpc.io/docs/protoc-installation/

`protoc` is a crucial tool in the Protobuf ecosystem. It takes `` `.proto` `` files as input, which describe the structure of your data, and generates code in various programming languages. This generated code includes classes and methods for easy serialization and deserialization of data, making it a pivotal component for working with Protobuf in different programming environments.

Here is a simple illustration of how Protobuf works:

1. **Defining the Message**:

   You create a `.proto` file where we define our message structure, including the fields and their data types.

2. **Generating Code**:

   Run the Protobuf compiler (`protoc`) on the `.proto` file to generate language-specific code files.

   For example, to generate the code in `` `Golang` `` for the `` `Person` `` message using `` `protoc` `` compiler, we can run the following command:

   ```
   protoc --go_out=. --go_opt=paths=source_relative <path-to-person-proto-file>
   ```

   The complete generated proto code for `` `Person` `` in Golang can be viewed here: https://github.com/OrangeAVA/Modern-API-Design-with-gRPC/blob/main/chapter-2/person/person.pb.go

3. **Using Generated Code**:

   In our application code, we include the generated code. You can then create instances of Protobuf messages, set their values, and use methods provided by the generated code to serialize and deserialize messages.

   Here is how we can use the generated protobuf message to create an instance of the Person in Golang:

   ```
   p := &Person{
       Name:         name,
       Age:          int32(age),
       PhoneNumbers: phNos,
   }
   ```

   The function to create a new `Person` instance using the generated protobuf message can be viewed here: https://github.

com/OrangeAVA/Modern-API-Design-with-gRPC/blob/d22ce567d988376396e5bc9fc5b5681ac4f2f352/chapter-2/person/person.go#L7-L15

4. **Serialization:**

   When we want to send data, we use the generated code to serialize the message into a compact binary format.

   To serialize a generated protobuf message, we can make use of package **"github.com/golang/protobuf/proto"** in the case of Golang, or an equivalent library in other languages.

   Here is an illustration of how to achieve this:

```
import (
"github.com/golang/protobuf/proto"
)
…
serializedPerson, err := proto.Marshal(person)
if err != nil {
retu"" "", err
}
...
```

   Function to serialize a **Person** instance can be viewed here: https://github.com/OrangeAVA/Modern-API-Design-with-gRPC/blob/d22ce567d988376396e5bc9fc5b5681ac4f2f352/chapter-2/person/person.go#L17

5. **Deserialization**:

   On the receiving end, we use the generated code to deserialize the binary data back into a Protobuf message.

   Similarly, to deserialize a protobuf message, we can make use of the same package **github.com/golang/protobuf/proto** in the case of Golang, or an equivalent library in other languages.

   Here is an illustration of how to achieve this:

```
import (
"github.com/golang/protobuf/proto"
)
...
```

```
err := proto.Unmarshal(serializedPerson, &person)
if err != nil {
return nil, err
}

...
```

The function to serialize a **Person** instance can be viewed here: https://github.com/OrangeAVA/Modern-API-Design-with-gRPC/blob/d22ce567d988376396e5bc9fc5b5681ac4f2f352/chapter-2/person/person.go#L28

Protobuf's key benefits include efficiency, compactness, backward and forward compatibility, and support for multiple programming languages. It is particularly useful in scenarios where data serialization and deserialization speed and size matter, such as network communication and storage.

Message Encoding Using Protocol Buffers

Protocol Buffers, often referred to as Protobuf, represent a language-independent data serialization format pioneered by Google. Engineered for the efficient encoding of structured data in a concise binary form, Protobuf employs a schema-like definition approach. This schema is utilized to create a cohesive framework that spans multiple programming languages. Upon definition, the Protobuf compiler takes charge, generating code that handles the seamless serialization and deserialization of data.

Let us take the example of the **BookInfo** message:

```
message BookInfo {
  string isbn = 1;
  string publisher = 2;
}
```

Data:

- ISBN: "1234"
- Publisher: "Ava Orange"

Similar to the way **Person** protobuf message was generated using **protoc** compiler, **BookInfo** message too can be generated by:

```
protoc --go_out=. --go_opt=paths=source_relative <path-to-book-proto-file>
```

Now, let us instantiate and serialize the **BookInfo** message:

```
func NewBook(isbn, publisher string) *BookInfo {
    return &BookInfo{
        Isbn:      isbn,
        Publisher: publisher,
    }
}
```

We can serialize the **BookInfo** message and generate its hexadecimal representation by:

```
func SeriallizeBookInfoInHexaDecimal(isbn, publisher string) (string, error) {
    b := NewBook(isbn, publisher)

    serializedBook, err := proto.Marshal(b)
    if err != nil {
        return "", err
    }

    hexString := hex.EncodeToString(serializedBook)

    return hexString, nil
}
```

Protocol Buffers' encoded byte stream of **BookInfo** message (in hexadecimal representation):

```
0A 04 31 32 33 34 12 0A 41 76 61 20 4F 72 61 6E 67 65
```

Explanation of the byte stream:

`0A` is the tag for the `isbn` field (1), and `04` is the length of the following string in bytes.

`31 32 33 34` is the UTF-8 encoded string "1234".

`12` is the tag for the `publisher` field (2), and `0A` is the length of the following string in bytes.

`41 76 61 20 4F 72 61 6E 67 65` is the UTF-8 encoded string "Ava Orange".

This encoded byte stream represents the provided data according to the Protocol Buffers format.

In this encoded byte stream, the field tags (1 and 2) are used to identify the fields, and the length-prefixing technique is applied to strings to indicate their length before the actual data. This binary format is highly compact and efficient, making it suitable for efficient data serialization and transmission over networks.

It is important to note that the preceding byte stream is a hexadecimal representation for illustrative purposes. In actual programming implementations, the encoded data is represented in binary format. The Protobuf libraries in different programming languages provide functions to serialize and deserialize the data using this binary format.

In Protocol Buffers, tags are used to uniquely identify each field in a message. Tags are essential for serialization and deserialization processes, as they enable efficient encoding and decoding of the data. Tags are also used to maintain compatibility between different versions of the message schema.

The tag is assigned to each field in our message definition. Tags are positive integers and can range from 1 to 2^29 - 1 (536,870,911). However, tags in the range 1 to 15 are more efficient in terms of encoding, as they only require one byte to represent, while tags from 16 to 2,047 take 2 bytes, you also can go higher if you need more.

When we define a field in a message, we assign a tag to it. For example:

```
message BookInfo {

  string isbn = 1;

  string publisher = 2;

}
```

In this example, the field `isbn` is assigned tag 1, and the field `publisher` is assigned tag 2.

Tags play a crucial role in the binary encoding of Protocol Buffers. They are used to identify the field during serialization. The tag is included in the encoded data to specify which field is being encoded or decoded. This allows the decoder to correctly interpret the data even if fields are in a different order or if new fields are added in future versions of the message.

It is important to note that tags should remain consistent across different versions of the message to ensure backward and forward compatibility when dealing with serialized data.

There is a general guideline for assigning tags in Protocol Buffers, especially when we are designing our message schema. While it is not a strict formula, the idea is to ensure that tags are assigned in a way that allows for future changes to our schema without causing conflicts.

Here is a common practice for assigning tags:

- **Reserve Tags**: Reserve a range of tags for each field type you are using. For example, we could reserve tags 1-15 for fields that are unlikely to change and are commonly used. These tags use a single byte in encoding, making them more efficient. Then we can reserve tags 16-30 for fields that might change over time.
- **Avoid Fixed Values**: Avoid assigning fixed values to tags, especially for frequently changing fields, as this might limit our flexibility when evolving our schema.
- **Leave Gaps**: Leave gaps between tag numbers within each range. This allows you to add new fields without having to renumber all the existing tags. This is particularly important for maintaining backward compatibility.
- **Avoid Reusing a Tag Number**: Avoid reusing tag numbers to prevent deserialization issues. Even if a field seems unused, refrain from reusing its tag number. Past live changes might have serialized versions in logs, or old code in other servers could break.
- **Reserve Tag Numbers for Deleted Fields**: Reserve unused field tag numbers (for example, reserved 2, 3) to prevent accidental reuse. No need for types (simplifies dependencies!). Additionally, reserve names like **foo** and **bar** to avoid recycling deleted field names.

- **Avoid Changing the Type of a Field**: Rarely alter a field's type to avoid deserialization issues, similar to reusing a tag number. Refer to the protobuf docs for approved cases (for example, transitioning between int32, uint32, int64, and bool). Changing a field's message type is only acceptable if the new message is a superset of the old one.

Remember that the primary purpose of tags is to uniquely identify fields and provide a means for efficient encoding and decoding. While following a systematic approach to assigning tags is advisable, it is equally important to consider the long-term maintainability and evolution of our message schema.

In the preceding example, the tag **0A** for the isbn field was generated based on the field's assigned number (1) and the field's wire type.

In Protocol Buffers, the tag is composed of three parts:

- **Field Number (3 bits)**: The field number is the identifier we assign to each field in our message definition. It is the part that uniquely identifies the field within the message. Field numbers range from 1 to 2^29 - 1 (536,870,911), but for efficiency, it is recommended to use numbers from 1 to 15 for frequently occurring fields.
- **Wire Type (3 bits)**: The wire type specifies how the data associated with the field should be encoded. For example, strings have a wire type of 2, and variable-length data (like strings) use a length-delimited format.
- **Tag (Varint)**: The tag is a combination of the field number and wire type, encoded as a varint (variable-length integer). The field number occupies the lower three bits, and the wire type occupies the upper three bits.

In the preceding example, for the isbn field:

- Field Number: `1` (assigned in the message definition)
- Wire Type for String: `2`

Combining these two values:

- Field Number (binary): `001`
- Wire Type (binary): `010`

Concatenating the binary representations of field number and wire type, we get: `001010.` Converting this binary value to hexadecimal yields `0A.`

So, the tag **0A** was generated for the **isbn** field, indicating that it's field number `1` and the data associated with it is a string.

Now let us cement our understanding by taking another example:

```
message BookRequest {

  int32 id = 1;

}
```

Data:

- ID: 5
- Wire Type for int (Varint): 0

Let us generate for **'BookInfo'** message by the following command:

```
protoc --go_out=. --go_opt=paths=source_relative <path-to-book-proto-file>
```

We can instantiate the generated **`BookRequest`** protobuf message like this:

```
func NewBookRequest(id int) *BookRequest {

   return &BookRequest{

      Id: int32(id),

   }

}
```

We can serialize the **BookRequest** message and generate its hexadecimal representation by:

```
func SeriallizeBookRequestInHexaDecimal(id int) (string, error) {

   b := NewBookRequest(id)


   serializedBookReq, err := proto.Marshal(b)

   if err != nil {

      return "", err

   }


   hexString := hex.EncodeToString(serializedBookReq)
```

```
    return hexString, nil
}
```

Tag and Wire Type for Field ID:

- Field Number: **`1`**
- Wire Type: **`0`** (Varint)

Combining the Field Number and Wire Type:

- Field Number (binary): **`001`**
- Wire Type (binary): **`000`**

Concatenating the binary representations of the field number and wire type, we get: **`001000.`** Converting this binary value to hexadecimal yields **`08.`**

Now, let us encode the provided data (ID = 5) using the varint encoding:

The binary representation of 5: **`00000101`**

Putting it all together, the Protocol Buffers encoded byte stream for the `` `BookRequest` `` message with the given data is (hexadecimal representation):

```
08 05
```

Explanation of the byte stream:

`08` is the tag for the id field `(1),` and **`05`** is the varint-encoded representation of the integer value **`5.`**

In this example, the encoded byte stream follows the Protobuf structure with the tag indicating the field number and wire type, and the subsequent bytes containing the varint-encoded data. This compact binary format is efficient for serialization and transmission.

In the example provided, the tag **`08`** for the id field was generated based on the field's assigned number `(1)` and the field's wire type.

In this example, the wire type has changed from string to int; the wire type is 0. Please refer to the following table:

Wire type	Category	Field types
0	Varint	int32, int64, uint32, uint64, sint32, sint64, bool, enum
1	64-bit	fixed64, sfixed64, double

Wire type	Category	Field types
2	Length-delimited	string, bytes, embedded messages, packed repeated fields
3	Start group	groups (deprecated)
4	End group	groups (deprecated)
5	32-bit	fixed32, sfixed32, float

Table 2.1: *Protobuf Wire Types and Field Types Mapping*

Combining these two values:

- Field Number (binary): **`001`**
- Wire Type (binary): **`000`**

Concatenating the binary representations of field number and wire type, we get: **`001000`.** Converting this binary value to hexadecimal yields **`08`**.

So, the tag **`08`** was generated for the **`id`** field, indicating that it's field number **1** and the data associated with it is an integer using varint encoding.

Within the context of Protocol Buffers, there are three main message-encoding techniques:

- **Varint Encoding**: Varint (variable-length integer) encoding is used for integer and boolean fields. It is a space-efficient way to encode integers by using a varying number of bytes to represent the value. Smaller values are encoded in fewer bytes, while larger values require more bytes. The most significant bit (MSB) of each byte indicates whether more bytes follow.
- **Fixed-Length Encoding**: Fixed-length encoding is used for fields with fixed-size data, such as 32-bit and 64-bit integers, floats, and doubles. These fields always occupy a specific number of bytes, regardless of the value they hold.
- **Length-Delimited Encoding**: Length-delimited encoding is used for fields that contain a variable amount of data, such as strings, bytes, and nested messages. This technique involves prepending the encoded data with a varint indicating the length of the data. The data itself follows immediately after the length prefix.

The choice of encoding technique depends on the data type of the field and its expected usage. Varint encoding is used to conserve space for smaller integers, fixed-length encoding ensures a consistent size for fixed-size data, and length-delimited encoding accommodates fields with variable-length data.

These encoding techniques contribute to the efficiency of the binary Protocol Buffers format by allowing data to be compactly represented while providing flexibility for different types of data and their variations in size.

Let us use a simplified Book message example to explain each of the three message encoding techniques within Protocol Buffers.

Message Definition:

```
message Book {
  int32 id = 1;
  string title = 2;
  bool available = 3;
}
```

Assuming we are working with the following data:

- **ID**: 123
- **Title:** "The Great Gatsby"
- **Available**: true

As we have been doing earlier, let us generate for 'Book' message by following command:

```
protoc --go_out=. --go_opt=paths=source_relative <path-to-book-proto-file>
```

We can instantiate the generated `Book` protobuf message like this:

```
func NewBookWithTitleAndAvailability(id int, title string, availability bool) *Book {
   return &Book{
      Id:        int32(id),
      Title:     title,
      Available: availability,
   }
}
```

Varint Encoding (ID and Available Fields):

Varint encoding is used for variable-length integers and boolean fields. It is space-efficient, using fewer bytes for smaller values. Let us encode the ID and available fields:

- ID (Field Number: 1):
  - Value: `123`
  - Varint: `1111011`
- Available (Field Number: 3):
  - Value: `true` (encoded as 1)

Encoded Varint Bytes (ID): `7B`

Encoded Varint Bytes (Available): `01`

Fixed-Length Encoding (Title Field):

- **Fixed-Size Numeric Types**: Protocol Buffers support fixed-size numeric types such as fixed32 and fixed64. These types use a fixed number of bytes to represent the value, regardless of the magnitude of the number. For example, a fixed32 field always occupies 4 bytes, and a fixed64 field always occupies 8 bytes.
- **Fixed-Size Byte Arrays:** Protocol Buffers allow the specification of fixed-size byte arrays using the bytes type with a fixed size. Internally, both bytes and string fields are serialized as a sequence of bytes.

For example, the title field is a string, but its size varies. However, in fixed-length encoding, each string occupies a fixed number of bytes based on the maximum possible size.

- Title (Field Number: 2):
  - Value: `"The Great Gatsby"`
  - Fixed Length: 32 bytes (assuming a maximum length of 32 characters)

Encoded Fixed-Length Bytes (Title): 546865204772656174204761473... (32 bytes)

Length-Delimited Encoding (Title Field):

Length-delimited encoding is used for fields with variable-length data. The data is preceded by a varint that indicates the length of the data. Let us encode the title field:

- Title (Field Number: 2):
  - Value: **`"The Great Gatsby"`**
  - Length Prefix (Varint): 00000100 (length is 4 bytes)

Encoded Length-Delimited Bytes (Title): 0A 04 546865204772656174 (12 bytes)

In practice, Protocol Buffers libraries handle the encoding and decoding processes for us, abstracting the low-level details. These encoding techniques contribute to the efficiency of Protocol Buffers by allowing different types of data to be represented compactly while accommodating variable-length and fixed-size fields.

HTTP/2

In gRPC, the concept of a long-duration connection refers to the ability to establish and maintain a persistent connection between a client and a server for an extended period. This is in contrast to traditional request-response communication, where the client sends a request, the server responds, and the connection is closed. Long-duration connections are particularly valuable in scenarios where continuous communication, real-time updates, or efficient resource utilization are essential. Long-duration connections in gRPC provide a powerful mechanism for building efficient, real-time, and resilient communication systems. They enable applications to deliver updates promptly, reduce resource overhead, and offer a seamless and responsive user experience, making them a valuable tool in modern distributed systems.

The ability of gRPC to support long-duration connections is closely tied to its foundation on the HTTP/2 protocol. HTTP/2, the successor to HTTP/1.1, introduced several key features that enable efficient and persistent communication. Here is an expansion on how gRPC inherits this feature from HTTP/2:

1. **Multiplexing**: HTTP/2 introduced the concept of multiplexing, which allows multiple streams (requests and responses) to be sent and received concurrently over a single TCP connection. This is a significant departure from HTTP/1.1, where each request-response cycle requires a separate connection. Multiplexing is a foundational feature of HTTP/2, and gRPC fully leverages it.
2. **Header Compression**: HTTP/2 incorporates header compression using the HPACK algorithm. Headers of HTTP requests and responses are efficiently compressed and decompressed at both ends, reducing

overhead and improving the efficiency of data transfer. This optimization is critical for long-duration connections, where minimizing data transfer overhead is essential.

3. **Flow Control**: Flow control mechanisms in HTTP/2 ensure that data is sent at an optimal pace, preventing congestion and ensuring that neither the client nor the server is overwhelmed. This fine-grained control over data flow is advantageous in scenarios where long-duration connections need to operate efficiently and predictably.
4. **Prioritization**: HTTP/2 allows for the prioritization of streams, enabling more critical data to be delivered first. This is particularly useful when long-duration connections involve multiple streams or channels of communication, ensuring that important updates are prioritized over less critical ones.
5. **Server Push**: HTTP/2 introduced server push, a feature that allows the server to initiate sending data to the client without waiting for a request. While not as common in gRPC as it is in traditional HTTP/2 use cases (for example, web pages), server push can be valuable in scenarios where real-time updates are needed.
6. **Connection Reuse**: HTTP/2 is designed to allow connection reuse, which is essential for long-duration connections. Reusing connections reduces the latency associated with setting up new connections and ensures that clients and servers can maintain ongoing communication efficiently.
7. **Security**: Both HTTP/2 and gRPC prioritize security. They provide mechanisms for securing data transmission using protocols like TLS/SSL, which is crucial for maintaining secure long-duration connections, especially when sensitive data is involved.

To summarize, gRPC inherits the ability to support long-duration connections from its foundation on HTTP/2. This modern protocol offers a range of features that optimize data transfer, prioritize communication, and ensure efficient use of resources. By building on HTTP/2, gRPC is well-suited for applications that require persistent, real-time, and efficient communication between clients and servers.

Let us illustrate the differences between HTTP/2 and HTTP/1.1 using a simplified example of loading a web page that consists of multiple resources (HTML, CSS, JavaScript, and images).

Scenario: Loading a Web Page

HTTP/2:

- When a client (for example, a web browser) requests a web page over an HTTP/2 connection, a single TCP connection is established with the server.
- The client sends a request for the HTML file, and simultaneously, it can send requests for CSS, JavaScript, and image files, all within the same connection.
- The server can respond to these requests in parallel, sending each resource as soon as it is ready.
- Header compression is used to reduce the size of headers, making the transfer of request and response headers more efficient.
- Server push is employed, allowing the server to send critical resources (for example, CSS) to the client without waiting for the client to request them.

HTTP/1.1:

- In the case of HTTP/1.1, each resource request requires a separate TCP connection (or reuse of an existing connection), as the protocol does not support multiplexing.
- The client sends a request for the HTML file, and the server responds with the HTML content. Only after receiving the HTML response can the client send requests for CSS, JavaScript, and images.
- Each resource request is handled sequentially, resulting in potential "head-of-line blocking" as subsequent requests wait for previous responses to arrive.
- Headers are not compressed, leading to larger header sizes that contribute to increased overhead.
- Server push is not natively supported, so the server must rely on techniques like inlining resources in HTML or other workarounds to optimize performance.

Comparison:

- In the HTTP/2 scenario, resources are loaded in parallel over a single connection, reducing latency and improving page load times.
- HTTP/2's header compression and binary framing reduce the size of headers and make more efficient use of network resources.

- Server push in HTTP/2 allows the server to proactively send resources, further improving load times.
- In the HTTP/1.1 scenario, resources are loaded sequentially, potentially leading to slower page load times, especially when there are many resources to load.
- This example highlights how HTTP/2's features, such as multiplexing, header compression, and server push, lead to more efficient and faster web page loading compared to the older HTTP/1.1 protocol, where resources are loaded one after the other, often with more overhead.

Let us consider an example where a client sends an HTTP request to a server to retrieve a book using the gRPC message **`BookRequest`**:

```
message BookRequest {

  int32 id = 1;

}
```

We will assume the **`id`** field has a value of **`42`**.

Now, let us compare how the headers for this request would look in HTTP/2 and HTTP/1.1:

HTTP/2 Request Headers:

In HTTP/2, headers are efficiently compressed using the HPACK algorithm, which reduces overhead and optimizes data transfer. Here is how the request headers might look in:

HTTP/2 in pseudo-headers format:

```
:method: POST

:scheme: https

:authority: example.com

:path: /book-service.GetBook

content-type: application/grpc

content-encoding: gzip

user-agent: grpc-go/2.0

te: trailers
```

```
grpc-accept-encoding: gzip

grpc-timeout: 10000m
```

In this example:

- **`:method: POST`**: Indicates that the request is a POST request.
- **`:scheme: https`**: Specifies the scheme used (HTTPS).
- **`:authority: example.com`**: Specifies the server's authority, which typically corresponds to the server's domain or address.
- **`:path: /book-service.GetBook`**: Specifies the path to the gRPC service method.
- **`content-type: application/grpc`**: Indicates the content type as gRPC.
- **`content-encoding: gzip`**: Specifies content encoding (optional).
- **`user-agent: grpc-go/2.0`**: Identifies the user agent as a gRPC client.
- **`te: trailers`**: Specifies that trailers (additional metadata) will be included in the response.
- **`grpc-accept-encoding: gzip`**: Indicates that the client can accept gzip encoding for the response.
- **`grpc-timeout: 10000m`**: Specifies a timeout for the request (optional).

HTTP/1.1 Request Headers:

In HTTP/1.1, headers are sent in plain text and are less efficient compared to HTTP/2. Here is how the request headers might look in HTTP/1.1:

```
POST /book-service.GetBook HTTP/1.1

Host: example.com

User-Agent: grpc-go/2.0

Content-Type: application/grpc

Content-Length: 6

grpc-timeout: 10000m
```

HTTP/1.1 protocol does not inherently support gRPC semantics, so the mapping of gRPC concepts onto HTTP/1.1 is somewhat forced.

In this example:

- **`POST /book-service.GetBook HTTP/1.1`**: Indicates a POST request with the path to the gRPC service method.

- **`Host: example.com`**: Specifies the server's domain.
- **`User-Agent: grpc-go/2.0`**: Identifies the user agent as a gRPC client.
- **`Content-Type: application/grpc`**: Indicates the content type as gRPC.
- **`Content-Length: 6`**: Specifies the length of the request body.
- **`grpc-timeout: 10000m`**: Specifies a timeout for the request (optional).

Comparison:

- In HTTP/2, headers are more compact due to compression, which reduces overhead and optimizes network efficiency.
- HTTP/2 uses binary framing and multiplexing, allowing multiple requests to be sent concurrently over a single connection, whereas HTTP/1.1 uses textual headers and requires multiple connections for parallel requests.
- The HTTP/2 request includes several built-in headers that facilitate gRPC communication, such as **`'content-type'`, `'content-encoding'`**, and **`'grpc-accept-encoding'`**, which are not present in the HTTP/1.1 request.
- HTTP/2 headers also include special headers like **`':method'`, `':scheme'`, `':authority'`**, and **`':path'`** for efficient routing and processing of requests.
- In HTTP/2, headers are more efficient when dealing with gRPC's binary data, making it well-suited for gRPC-based communication.

Overall, HTTP/2 offers several advantages over HTTP/1.1 in terms of efficiency, multiplexing, and built-in support for gRPC-specific headers, making it a preferred choice for gRPC-based applications.

Features that make gRPC Standout

gRPC stands out due to several key features. Firstly, it offers clean and well-defined contracts between clients and servers, ensuring consistent communication. Secondly, it efficiently handles data size, reducing unnecessary network overhead. Thirdly, it supports bidirectional streaming, allowing both clients and servers to send streams of messages.

Lastly, gRPC's code generation simplifies development by automatically producing client and server code, streamlining the implementation process. These features collectively make gRPC a powerful and efficient framework for modern API design. Let us understand these features in detail.

Clean Contract

The difference in contract management between REST, SOAP, and gRPC is a crucial aspect of understanding why gRPC is gaining popularity. Let us expand on this concept:

- **REST and Swagger**: In the world of RESTful APIs, documentation plays a pivotal role in defining the contract between clients and servers. Tools like Swagger provide a way to document and expose these contracts. However, the contract in REST is not as strict as in other protocols. While Swagger helps document endpoints and data structures, it does not enforce strict adherence to the contract. Developers using REST APIs rely on the documentation but can't be certain that the server's implementation will always match the documentation. Changes on the server-side might not be immediately reflected in the documentation, leading to potential inconsistencies and bugs in client code.
- **SOAP and WSDL**: In the era of SOAP, contracts were exposed via WSDL (Web Service Description Language) files. WSDL defined not only the operations but also the data types and message structures. This provided a more rigid and explicit contract between clients and servers. Clients could generate code directly from WSDL files, ensuring tight adherence to the contract. However, SOAP's strictness came with increased complexity, including verbose XML payloads and extensive tooling for handling SOAP messages.
- **gRPC and Protobuf**: gRPC takes a different approach to contract management. The contract is shared between the client and server in the form of Protocol Buffer (protobuf) files (.proto files). These .proto files define not only the service methods but also the message types used in those methods. This provides a clear and strict contract that both the client and server agree upon. Code can be generated from .proto files, allowing developers to make remote procedure calls (RPCs) as if they were making local function calls. This ensures that both parties are always in sync with the contract. The complexity of managing connections, security, serialization, and deserialization is abstracted away, allowing developers to focus solely on the data and the business logic.

Advantages of gRPC's Contract Approach:

- **Predictability**: With gRPC, developers can be certain about the contract between client and server. Any changes to the contract are explicit and require updates to the .proto files.

- **Code Generation**: Code can be generated from the .proto files, reducing the likelihood of contract mismatches between client and server.
- **Efficiency**: gRPC's binary serialization (protobuf) is efficient in terms of both size and speed, making it a suitable choice for modern, high-performance applications.
- **Abstraction**: gRPC abstracts away many networking and infrastructure concerns, allowing developers to focus on application logic and data.

In summary, gRPC's contract approach combines the strictness of SOAP/WSDL with the simplicity and efficiency of REST, providing a clear and predictable contract between client and server while abstracting away many of the complexities involved in remote communication. This approach has made gRPC an attractive choice for building modern, performant APIs and microservices.

As we progress through this book, we will dive deeper into this concept. For now, let us take a quick look at *Figure* 1.2, which provides a glimpse of how gRPC enforces a strict contract at compile time. This is achieved by sharing generated stubs with both the server and client.

Size of Data

As you may recall from our earlier discussion in the first chapter, we delved into the expenses linked to the interaction between the client and server in terms of the request-response cycle. One key factor affecting these costs is the size of the data being transmitted. Given that gRPC employs protobuf as its messaging format, let us now conduct a comparative analysis with REST and gRPC to better grasp the implications of these choices.

Let us have three proto messages in a file **'info.proto'**

```
syntax = "proto3";


package main;


message BenchSmall {

  string action = 1;

  bytes key = 2;

}
```

```
message BenchMedium {
  string name = 1;
  int64 age = 2;
  float height = 3;
  double weight = 4;
  bool alive = 5;
  bytes desc = 6;
}

message BenchLarge {
  string name = 1;
  int64 age = 2;
  float height = 3;
  double weight = 4;
  bool alive = 5;
  bytes desc = 6;
  string nickname = 7;
  int64 num = 8;
  float flt = 9;
  double dbl = 10;
  bool tru = 11;
  bytes data = 12;
}
```

This is a Protocol Buffers (protobuf) file written in version 3 (**`syntax = "proto3";`**). It defines three message types: BenchSmall, BenchMedium, and BenchLarge. Let us break down what each message represents:

1. **`BenchSmall`**:
    a. `BenchSmall` is a message type that has two fields:

        i. action (field number 1) of type string.
        ii. key (field number 2) of type bytes.

2. **BenchMedium**:
    a. **BenchMedium** is a message type with several fields:
        i. name (field number 1) of type string.
        ii. age (field number 2) of type int64.
        iii. height (field number 3) of type float.
        iv. weight (field number 4) of type double.
        v. alive (field number 5) of type bool.
        vi. desc (field number 6) of type bytes.
3. **BenchLarge:**
    a. **BenchLarge** is similar to **BenchMedium** but with additional fields:
        i. nickname (field number 7) of type string.
        ii. num (field number 8) of type int64.
        iii. flt (field number 9) of type float.
        iv. dbl (field number 10) of type double.
        v. tru (field number 11) of type bool.
        vi. data (field number 12) of type bytes.

These message types define structured data formats that can be used to serialize and deserialize data in a binary format. Protocol Buffers provide a way to define a contract for data interchange between different systems or components. The field numbers are used to uniquely identify each field within a message.

You can use the Protocol Buffers compiler (protoc) to generate code in various programming languages based on this .proto file. This generated code allows you to work with these structured messages in your code, making it easier to serialize and deserialize data and ensure consistency in communication between systems.

We can generate the code in Golang for the preceding proto using the following command:

```
protoc --go_out=. --go_opt=paths=source_relative <path-to-info-proto>
```

Now, let us create three variables for the protos:

```
var (
```

```
  ProtocSmall = BenchSmall{
    Action: "benchmark",
    Key: []byte("data to be sent"),
  }

  ProtocMedium = BenchMedium{
    Name: "Tester",
    Age: 20,
    Height: 5.8,
    Weight: 180.7,
    Alive: true,
    Desc: []byte(`If you've ever heard of ProtoBuf you may be thinking
that the results of this benchmarking experiment will be obvious,
JSON < ProtoBuf.`),
  }

  ProtocLarge = BenchLarge{
    Name: "Tester",
    Age: 20,
    Height: 5.8,
    Weight: 180.7,
    Alive: true,
    Desc: []byte("Lets benchmark some json and protobuf"),
    Nickname: "Another name",
    Num: 2314,
    Flt: 123451231.1234,
   Data: []byte(`If you've ever heard of ProtoBuf you may be thinking that
```

```
the results of this benchmarking experiment will be obvious, JSON <
ProtoBuf.

My interest was in how much they actually differ in practice.

How do they compare on a couple of different metrics, specifically
serialization

and de-serialization speeds, and the memory footprint of encoding the
data.

I was also curious about how the different serialization methods would

behave under small, medium, and large chunks of data.`),

  }

)
```

Let us have the same messages in JSON as well.

```
var (

JsonSmall = `{"action":"benchmark","key":"ZGF0YSB0byBiZSBzZW50"}`


JsonMedium = `{"name":"Tester","age":20,"height":5.8,"-
weight":180.7,"alive":true,"desc":"SWYgeW914oCZdmUgZXZlciBoZWFyZCB-
vZiBQcm90b0J1ZiB5b3UgbWF5IGJlIHRoaW5raW5nIAoJCXRoYXQgdGhlIHJlc3VsdHMg-
b2YgdGhpcyBiZW5jaG1hcmtpbmcgZXhwZXJpbWVudCB3aWxsIGJlIG9idmlvdXMsCgkJSl-
NPTiA8IFByb3RvQnVmLg=="}`


JsonLarge = `{"name":"Tester","age":20,"height":5.8,"-
weight":180.7,"alive":true,"desc":"TGV0cyBiZW5jaG1hcmsgc29tZSBq-
c29uIGFuZCBwcm90b2J1Zg==","nickname":"Another name","num":2314,"-
flt":123451230,"data":"SWYgeW914oCZdmUgZXZlciBoZWFyZCBvZiBQcm90b0J1ZiB-
5b3UgbWF5IGJlIHRoaW5raW5nIHRoYXQKCQl0aGUgcmVzdWx0cyBvZiB0aGlzIGJlbmNob-
WFya2luZyBleHBlcmltZW50IHdpbGwgYmUgb2J2aW91cywgSlNPTiA8IFByb3RvQnVmL-
goJCU15IGludGVyZXN0IHdhcyBpbiBob3cgbXVjaCB0aGV5IGFjdHVhbGx5IGRpZmZl-
ciBpbiBwcmFjdGljZS4KCQlIb3cgZG8gdGhleSBjb21wYXJlIG9uIGEgY291cGxlIG9mI-
GRpZmZlcmVudCBtZXRyaWNzLCBzcGVjaWZpY2FsbHkgc2VyaWFsaXphdGlvbgoJCW-
FuZCBkZS1zZXJpYWxpemF0aW9uIHNwZWVkcywgYW5kIHRoZSBtZW1vcnkgZm9vdHByaW-
50IG9mIGVuY29kaW5nIHRoZSBkYXRhLgoJCUkgd2FzIGFsc28gY3VyaW91cyBhYm91dC-
Bob3cgdGhlIGRpZmZlcmVudCBzZXJpYWxpemF0aW9uIG1ldGhvZHMgd291bGQKCQliZWhhd-
```

mUgdW5kZXIgc21hbGwsIG1lZGl1bSwgYW5kIGxhcmdlIGNodW5rcyBvZiBkYXRhLg==”}`

)

Both proto and json have the same data. For this comparison purpose, we shall only consider the large-size data of both formats.

In order to determine the size of the format, we shall employ the following steps:

1. Serialize JSON data and write to a file
2. Find the size of the file
3. Serialize proto data and write to a file
4. Find the size of the file
5. Compare the sizes

This is illustrated in the following code:

```
package main

import (
  “encoding/json”
  “fmt”
  “os”

  “github.com/golang/protobuf/proto”
)

const (
  jsonOutputPath = “out/data.json”
  protoOutputPath = “out/data.pb”
)

func main() {
  err := os.MkdirAll(“out”, os.ModePerm)
  check(err)
```

```
  jsonData := JsonLarge
  pbData := ProtocLarge

  // seriallize json
  b, err := json.Marshal(&jsonData)
  check(err)

  err = os.WriteFile(jsonOutputPath, b, 0644)
  check(err)
  fileSize(jsonOutputPath)

  // seriallize proto
  d, err := proto.Marshal(&pbData)
  check(err)

  err = os.WriteFile(protoOutputPath, d, 0644)
  check(err)
  fileSize(protoOutputPath)

  err = os.RemoveAll("out")
  check(err)
}

func check(e error) {
  if e != nil {
    panic(e)
  }
}
```

```
func fileSize(path string) {
  info, err := os.Stat(path)
  if err != nil {
    fmt.Println("unable to fetch file stats", err)
  }
  x := info.Size()
  fmt.Printf("size of file at %s is %d bytes\n", path, x)
}
```

To determine the sizes, we can run the preceding code in a terminal:

```
go run <dir-path>/main.go
```

The result will look like this:

```
size of file at out/data.json is 882 bytes
size of file at out/data.pb is 581 bytes
```

We can see the difference in size. Notably, with bigger data, the difference is more prominent.

Serialization of Data

In our previous discussion in the first chapter, we also touched upon the costs associated with serialization and deserialization. It is worth noting that, thanks to Protocol Buffers (protobuf), gRPC outperforms REST in this particular regard. Serialization and deserialization speed is significantly better in the case of Protocol Buffers (protobuf) compared to JSON, especially as data sizes increase. Here is an expanded explanation of why this is the case:

- **Efficient Binary Encoding**: Protocol Buffers use a compact binary encoding format that is highly optimized for both size and speed. This binary encoding is much more efficient than the plain text encoding used in JSON. In JSON, data is represented in human-readable text, which includes field names, data types, and other metadata. This results in larger payloads and slower serialization/deserialization times.

- **Reduced Overhead**: JSON includes a significant amount of overhead in the form of field names and delimiters (for example, quotation marks, colons, commas). This overhead adds up as data sizes increase. Protocol Buffers, on the other hand, use a numeric tag system to identify fields, which is more space-efficient and faster to process.
- **Schema-Driven Approach**: Protocol Buffers rely on a predefined schema (defined in .proto files) that specifies the structure of the data. This schema-driven approach allows for highly optimized serialization and deserialization code to be generated. JSON, being schema-less, requires more runtime reflection and processing to determine the structure of data, resulting in slower performance.
- **Type Information**: Protocol Buffers encode type information for each field directly in the binary format. This eliminates the need for runtime type inference during deserialization, speeding up the process. JSON relies on data types to be inferred from the content itself, which can introduce additional overhead and complexity.
- **Reduced Data Size**: Due to its efficient binary encoding, Protocol Buffers produce smaller serialized payloads compared to JSON for the same data. Smaller payloads mean less data to transmit over the network, resulting in faster data transfer times.
- **Optimized Code Generation**: Code generators (for example, protoc for various programming languages) can produce highly optimized serialization and deserialization code based on the schema definition. This code is tailored for each specific message type. JSON parsers, while efficient, don't benefit from this level of schema-specific optimization, which can slow down processing.
- **Streaming Support**: Protocol Buffers provide native support for streaming, allowing for the efficient serialization and deserialization of data streams. This is especially valuable for high-throughput and real-time applications. JSON can be used for streaming, but it may involve more complex handling of delimiters and parsing.

In summary, Protocol Buffers' binary encoding, schema-driven approach, reduced overhead, and optimized code generation makes it significantly faster for serialization.

If we look at the benchmark results, we could notice the difference between both message formats. For this purpose, we shall utilize all three different sizes of both message formats used previously.

We can use the following code to generate the benchmark results:

```
package benchmarking_test

import (
  "encoding/json"
  "fmt"
  "testing"

  info "github.com/OrangeAVA/Modern-API-Design-with-gRPC/chapter-2/
  serialization"
  "github.com/golang/protobuf/proto"
)

func BenchmarkJSONMarshal(b *testing.B) {
  s := info.JsonSmall
  m := info.JsonMedium
  l := info.JsonLarge

  b.ResetTimer()

  b.Run("SmallData", func(b *testing.B) {
    for n := 0; n < b.N; n++ {
      d, _ := json.Marshal(&s)
      _ = d
    }
    b.ReportAllocs()
  })
  b.Run("MediumData", func(b *testing.B) {
    for n := 0; n < b.N; n++ {
```

```
      d, _ := json.Marshal(&m)
      _ = d
    }
    b.ReportAllocs()
  })
  b.Run("LargeData", func(b *testing.B) {
    for n := 0; n < b.N; n++ {
      d, _ := json.Marshal(&l)
      _ = d
    }
    b.ReportAllocs()
  })
  fmt.Printf("\n")
}

func BenchmarkJSONUnmarshal(b *testing.B) {
  s := info.JsonSmall
  m := info.JsonMedium
  l := info.JsonLarge

  sd, _ := json.Marshal(&s)
  md, _ := json.Marshal(&m)
  ld, _ := json.Marshal(&l)

  var sf []byte
  var mf []byte
  var lf []byte
```

```
  b.ResetTimer()

  b.Run("SmallData", func(b *testing.B) {
    for n := 0; n < b.N; n++ {
      _ = json.Unmarshal(sd, &sf)
    }
    b.ReportAllocs()
  })
  b.Run("MediumData", func(b *testing.B) {
    for n := 0; n < b.N; n++ {
      _ = json.Unmarshal(md, &mf)
    }
    b.ReportAllocs()
  })
  b.Run("LargeData", func(b *testing.B) {
    for n := 0; n < b.N; n++ {
        _ = json.Unmarshal(ld, &lf)
    }
  b.ReportAllocs()
  })
  fmt.Printf("\n")
}

func BenchmarkProtocMarshal(b *testing.B) {
  s := info.ProtocSmall
  m := info.ProtocMedium
  l := info.ProtocLarge
```

```
  b.ResetTimer()

  b.Run("SmallData", func(b *testing.B) {
    for n := 0; n < b.N; n++ {
      d, _ := proto.Marshal(&s)
      _ = d
    }
    b.ReportAllocs()
  })
  b.Run("MediumData", func(b *testing.B) {
     for n := 0; n < b.N; n++ {
       d, _ := proto.Marshal(&m)
       _ = d
     }
     b.ReportAllocs()
  })
  b.Run("LargeData", func(b *testing.B) {
    for n := 0; n < b.N; n++ {
      d, _ := proto.Marshal(&l)
      _ = d
    }
    b.ReportAllocs()
  })
  fmt.Printf("\n")
}

func BenchmarkProtocUnMarshal(b *testing.B) {
```

```
s := info.ProtocSmall
m := info.ProtocMedium
l := info.ProtocLarge

sd, _ := proto.Marshal(&s)
md, _ := proto.Marshal(&m)
ld, _ := proto.Marshal(&l)

var sf info.BenchSmall
var mf info.BenchMedium
var lf info.BenchLarge

b.ResetTimer()

b.Run("SmallData", func(b *testing.B) {
  for n := 0; n < b.N; n++ {
    _ = proto.Unmarshal(sd, &sf)
  }
  b.ReportAllocs()
})
b.Run("MediumData", func(b *testing.B) {
  for n := 0; n < b.N; n++ {
    _ = proto.Unmarshal(md, &mf)
  }
  b.ReportAllocs()
})
b.Run("LargeData", func(b *testing.B) {
  for n := 0; n < b.N; n++ {
```

```
      _ = proto.Unmarshal(ld, &lf)
    }
    b.ReportAllocs()
  })
  fmt.Printf("\n")
}
```

Then, we can run the benchmark test by:

```
go test -bench=. ./... > benchmark.txt
```

This is what the results look like:

```
...
BenchmarkJSONMarshal/SmallData-12          2384252          498.7
ns/op       64 B/op       1 allocs/op
BenchmarkJSONMarshal/MediumData-12          945313         1281 ns/
op       288 B/op       1 allocs/op
BenchmarkJSONMarshal/LargeData-12           425020         3012 ns/
op       896 B/op       1 allocs/op

BenchmarkJSONUnmarshal/SmallData-12         998362         1127 ns/
op       272 B/op       3 allocs/op
BenchmarkJSONUnmarshal/MediumData-12        333024         3336 ns/
op       672 B/op       3 allocs/op
BenchmarkJSONUnmarshal/LargeData-12         119995         9191 ns/
op      1680 B/op       3 allocs/op

BenchmarkProtocMarshal/SmallData-12        4277210          245.8
ns/op       32 B/op       1 allocs/op
BenchmarkProtocMarshal/MediumData-12       2819110          425.6
ns/op      176 B/op       1 allocs/op
BenchmarkProtocMarshal/LargeData-12        1339984          900.7
ns/op      640 B/op       1 allocs/op
```

```
BenchmarkProtocUnMarshal/SmallData-12          5212929              225.3
ns/op         32 B/op        2 allocs/op
BenchmarkProtocUnMarshal/MediumData-12         2532816              474.2
ns/op        152 B/op        2 allocs/op
BenchmarkProtocUnMarshal/LargeData-12          1241935              973.5
ns/op        584 B/op        4 allocs/op
...
```

The benchmark test results compare the performance of JSON serialization and deserialization against Protocol Buffers (protobuf) serialization and deserialization across different data sizes (small, medium, and large). Let us break down what each part of the results means:

Benchmark Name Explanation:

- **`BenchmarkJSONMarshal/SmallData-12`**: This benchmark tests the JSON serialization performance for SmallData.
- **`BenchmarkJSONMarshal/MediumData-12`**: This benchmark tests the JSON serialization performance for MediumData.
- **`BenchmarkJSONMarshal/LargeData-12`**: This benchmark tests the JSON serialization performance for LargeData.

Similarly, there are benchmarks for JSON deserialization and protobuf serialization and deserialization.

Results Explanation (Taking JSON Serialization as an Example):

- **`BenchmarkJSONMarshal/SmallData-12`**: This benchmark indicates that for SmallData, the JSON serialization operation took an average of 498.7 nanoseconds per operation (ns/op). It also tells us that it allocated 64 bytes (B/op) of memory and performed 1 allocation (allocs/op) during each serialization operation.
- **`BenchmarkJSONMarshal/MediumData-12:`** Similarly, for MediumData, the JSON serialization operation took an average of 1281 nanoseconds per operation. It allocated 288 bytes of memory and performed 1 allocation during each serialization.
- **`BenchmarkJSONMarshal/LargeData-12`**: For LargeData, the JSON serialization operation took an average of 3012 nanoseconds per operation. It allocated 896 bytes of memory and performed 1 allocation during each serialization.

Interpretation of Results:

- Lower ns/op values indicate faster performance, meaning that less time is spent on each operation.
- Lower memory allocations (B/op) and fewer allocations (allocs/op) are also desirable because they indicate efficient memory usage.
- Comparing the JSON serialization results with the protobuf serialization results, you can observe that protobuf consistently outperforms JSON in terms of speed and memory efficiency for all data sizes.
- Protobuf serialization is significantly faster (ns/op values are lower) and uses less memory (B/op and allocs/op values are lower) compared to JSON serialization.

Similar interpretations can be made for JSON deserialization and protobuf serialization/deserialization for different data sizes. In each case, protobuf demonstrates superior performance, making it a more efficient choice for data serialization and deserialization tasks, especially when handling larger data.

TCP Connection

gRPC, built on top of HTTP/2, offers the capability to maintain long-duration TCP connections between clients and servers. This is a significant departure from traditional REST and SOAP-based communication methods. Here is an explanation of this concept:

- **Long-Duration Connections**: gRPC allows clients and servers to establish long-duration connections. Unlike traditional REST or SOAP, where each request-response typically opens and closes a connection, gRPC maintains a single connection that can be reused for multiple requests and responses over an extended period. This persistent connection is highly efficient because it avoids the overhead of establishing and tearing down connections for each interaction.
- **Bi-Directional Streaming**: One of the most notable features of gRPC is bi-directional streaming. Both the client and server can send multiple messages to each other over a single connection. This is particularly useful for scenarios where real-time communication, updates, or event-driven interactions are required. An example could be a chat application where users can send and receive messages in real-time without constantly opening and closing connections.
- **Efficiency and Multiplexing**: gRPC multiplexes multiple requests and responses over a single TCP connection. This means that multiple remote

procedure calls (RPC) can be in-flight simultaneously without blocking each other. This improves the overall efficiency and responsiveness of the communication.

- **Reduced Latency**: With long-duration connections, gRPC significantly reduces the latency associated with connection setup and teardown. This is crucial for applications that require low-latency responses, such as online gaming, financial services, or IoT devices.

Comparison with Traditional REST/SOAP-based TCP Connections:

REST/SOAP:

- Traditional REST and SOAP-based approaches typically rely on short-lived connections. Each HTTP request opens a new connection, performs the operation, and then closes the connection. This can lead to a high overhead of connection setup and teardown.
- In REST, clients often use HTTP/1.1, which is a text-based protocol, making it less efficient than binary protocols like gRPC.
- REST and SOAP are primarily request-response models, making it challenging to implement efficient bidirectional streaming, which gRPC excels at.

gRPC:

- gRPC maintains long-duration TCP connections, which are more efficient for scenarios requiring frequent or real-time communication.
- It uses HTTP/2, a binary protocol that reduces overhead and improves efficiency.
- gRPC excels in bidirectional streaming, allowing both clients and servers to send multiple messages without blocking, making it suitable for real-time applications.
- Example: Consider a ride-sharing app where the server continuously sends real-time updates about a user's ride, including the driver's location and estimated arrival time. With gRPC's bidirectional streaming, this information can be efficiently communicated over a single connection.

In summary, gRPC's long-duration TCP connections and support for bidirectional streaming make it a compelling choice for modern applications that require real-time or low-latency communication, as it offers improved efficiency and reduced latency compared to traditional REST or SOAP-based approaches.

Code Generation

Let us delve deeper into the concept of code generation in gRPC and how it simplifies the development process when compared to traditional REST APIs:

Code Generation in gRPC: A First-Class Citizen

In gRPC, code generation is seamlessly integrated into the development workflow, making it a first-class citizen in the ecosystem. This is primarily achieved through its built-in protoc (Protocol Buffers Compiler) tool, which generates language-specific client and server code from .proto service definitions. Here is why this is advantageous:

- **Simplified Development**: With gRPC, developers can focus primarily on the essential aspects of their applications: data and logic. This is because gRPC abstracts many of the lower-level complexities associated with network communication. Instead of writing boilerplate code for marshaling and unmarshaling data, setting up connections, and handling the intricacies of different programming languages, developers can concentrate on defining the data structures they want to send and receive the core business logic of their services.
- **Consistency Across Languages**: gRPC's code generation ensures that client and server code is available in a variety of programming languages, including but not limited to Go, Java, Python, and more. This consistency simplifies the development process for teams working with multiple languages, as they can use the same .proto definitions to generate code in their language of choice.
- **Strong Typing**: gRPC leverages Protocol Buffers as its interface definition language (IDL), which allows for precise data modeling. This strong typing means that data structures are well-defined and strongly typed across languages, reducing the likelihood of runtime errors due to data format mismatches. It also enables better tooling and code editor support, leading to improved development efficiency.

Comparison with REST API Development:

In contrast, traditional REST API development typically lacks native code generation capabilities. Developers often rely on third-party tools like Swagger/OpenAPI to auto-generate client code for API calls in various programming languages. Here is how this compares:

- **Additional Tooling**: In the REST ecosystem, using third-party tools for code generation adds complexity to the development process. Developers must integrate these tools into their workflow, potentially leading to compatibility issues and the need for additional configuration.
- **Less Abstraction**: Unlike gRPC, where much of the communication logic is abstracted away, developers working with REST APIs often need to write more boilerplate code. This includes handling HTTP requests, parsing JSON or XML data, and managing error handling and request/response formatting.
- **Data Format Challenges**: In REST, data format mismatches can occur more frequently due to thc absence of a strongly typed IDL. This can result in runtime errors and debugging challenges.
- **Language-Specific Challenges**: Generating client code for various programming languages in the REST world can lead to inconsistencies and language-specific idiosyncrasies, potentially causing discrepancies in behavior across clients.

In summary, gRPC's native code generation capabilities, facilitated by its integration with Protocol Buffers and the protoc tool, streamline the development process. This approach allows developers to focus on the core aspects of their applications while benefiting from strong typing, language consistency, and reduced boilerplate code. This is in contrast to REST APIs, where additional tooling and manual coding may be required to achieve similar results, often at the cost of increased complexity.

Conclusion

In this chapter, we have embarked on an exploration of gRPC, a powerful and modern API framework known for its efficiency and versatility. We introduced fundamental concepts and technologies that underlie gRPC's functionality, including Protocol Buffers (Protobuf) as the backbone of efficient data serialization and encoding. We delved into the inner workings of message encoding using Protobuf, offering insights into data interchange in gRPC.

We also dissected HTTP/2, the transport layer powering gRPC, and discussed how it significantly enhances the speed and efficiency of data transfer compared to its predecessor, HTTP/1.1. Our exploration extended to highlighting the distinctive features that make gRPC stand out, including clean contracts, optimized data size handling, efficient data serialization, and the advantages of long-duration TCP connections. Additionally, we've touched upon gRPC's code generation capabilities, which simplify development by automatically generating client and server code from service definitions, freeing developers to focus on data and logic rather than low-level networking intricacies.

In the upcoming chapter, we will delve even deeper into the world of gRPC, exploring its use cases, implementation details, and practical applications in building efficient and scalable APIs.

Multiple Choice Questions

1. What is the primary purpose of Protocol Buffers (Protobuf) in gRPC?
   a. To define HTTP/2 headers.
   b. To enable efficient data serialization and encoding.
   c. To implement long-duration TCP connections.
   d. To generate client and server code.
2. What does HTTP/2 bring to gRPC in terms of data transfer?
   a. Slower data transfer compared to HTTP/1.1.
   b. Reduced efficiency in handling large data.
   c. Improved speed and efficiency compared to HTTP/1.1.
   d. Incompatibility with modern networking protocols.
3. Which of the following is NOT a distinctive feature that sets gRPC apart?
   a. Clean contracts.
   b. Efficient data size handling.
   c. Complex data serialization.
   d. Long-duration TCP connections.
4. What is the primary advantage of gRPC's code generation capabilities?
   a. It simplifies the debugging of networking issues.
   b. It allows developers to focus on low-level networking details.
   c. It automatically generates client and server code.
   d. It reduces the need for Protocol Buffers.
5. In gRPC, what is the focus of developers when working with data and logic?
   a. Managing HTTP/2 headers.
   b. Defining low-level networking protocols.

   c. Data serialization and encoding.
   d. Data and logic, abstracting away networking complexities.

6. What role does Protocol Buffers (Protobuf) play in gRPC's data serialization?
   a. It is primarily responsible for generating HTTP/2 headers.
   b. It efficiently encodes structured data for communication.
   c. It defines clean contracts between clients and servers.
   d. It handles long-duration TCP connections.

7. How does HTTP/2 improve data transfer in gRPC compared to HTTP/1.1?
   a. It introduces more complexity and slower performance.
   b. It reduces efficiency and increases latency.
   c. It significantly enhances speed and efficiency.
   d. It focuses on security at the expense of speed.

8. What is the benefit of gRPC's clean contracts in API development?
   a. They increase the size of data, improving network performance.
   b. They simplify data serialization and encoding.
   c. They ensure a consistent understanding of the API between clients and servers.
   d. They reduce the need for code generation.

9. Which of the following aspects does gRPC prioritize in data handling for optimized network usage?
   a. Overloading the network with unnecessary data.
   b. Minimizing data transfer to an extreme degree.
   c. Efficiently handling data size.
   d. Ignoring data size concerns altogether.

10. How does gRPC's code generation feature impact the development process?
   a. It increases the need for low-level networking expertise.
   b. It generates HTTP/2 headers automatically.
   c. It simplifies development by generating client and server code.
   d. It eliminates the need for Protocol Buffers.

Answers

1	b
2	c
3	c
4	c
5	d
6	b
7	c
8	c
9	c
10	c

CHAPTER 3
Getting Started with gRPC

Introduction

In the previous chapter, we delved into the core concepts that form the foundation of gRPC. We commenced our exploration by understanding the significance of Protocol Buffers (Protobuf) in the world of gRPC. Protobuf serves as the chosen means for efficient data serialization and encoding, which is pivotal for streamlined communication. We then transitioned into the realm of HTTP/2, the underlying protocol that gRPC leverages for data transfer. This transition marked a significant step forward in terms of efficiency and speed compared to the earlier HTTP/1.1. Understanding the capabilities of HTTP/2 was crucial in comprehending the enhanced performance that gRPC offers. With a firm grasp of the protocol layer, we moved on to explore what sets gRPC apart. We identified key features, such as the establishment of clean contracts between clients and servers. These contracts ensure a shared understanding of the API's structure, reducing ambiguities and enhancing communication efficiency. Our journey continued as we examined the pivotal role played by data in API design. We dived into the complexities of data size, serialization, and deserialization costs, highlighting the efficiency gains offered by gRPC in handling these aspects. The chapter reached its climax as we explored the intricate realm of TCP connections in gRPC. We understood how long-duration connections between clients and servers are a fundamental characteristic of gRPC, significantly enhancing performance and reducing latency. Finally, we delved into the world of code generation, a feature that is native to gRPC. This capability simplifies the development process by automatically generating client and server code, reducing the need for manual coding and minimizing potential sources of error. In summary, *Chapter 2, Fundamentals of gRPC*, equipped us with a deep understanding of the core elements that empower gRPC's efficiency, from the role of Protocol Buffers to the advantages of HTTP/2, clean contracts, and streamlined data handling. This knowledge forms the bedrock upon which we will build as we proceed further into the realm of gRPC implementation.

In this chapter, our focus shifts to the practical application of gRPC for developing and consuming APIs, or as they are termed within the gRPC context, Remote Procedure Calls (RPCs). We will embark on a journey of setting up a gRPC server, a foundational component that exposes these RPCs to clients. This process involves not only establishing the server but also meticulously defining the contracts that govern the requests and responses, ensuring a clear and structured communication framework.

Additionally, we will be building a gRPC client, which plays a vital role in the consumption of these RPCs. Through a series of hands-on exercises and real-world examples, we will guide through the intricacies of crafting gRPC clients, empowering to harness the full potential of this modern API design paradigm.

However, to facilitate a comprehensive understanding and to draw insightful comparisons, we will not limit our exploration to gRPC alone. In parallel, we will also delve into the world of REST APIs, a more widely recognized and established approach. By concurrently examining these two approaches, we aim to provide a holistic perspective, aiding in the retention of key concepts and making the transition to gRPC smoother. The comparative analysis will illuminate the distinctive strengths and nuances of gRPC, enabling you to make informed decisions and choose the right tool for the right job in your own development projects. So, let us dive into this exciting journey of API development and consumption with gRPC as our guiding star while keeping REST as a valuable point of reference.

Structure

In this chapter, we will cover the following topics:

- Folder structure
- Books CRUD operations
    - Implement REST APIs to perform CRUD operations

        - Implement REST-based books server
        - Implement REST-based books client
        - Testability: using curl and REST client
    - Implement gRPC RPCs to perform CRUD operations
        - Define proto file
        - Generate code using protoc compiler
        - Implement gRPC-based books server
        - Implement gRPC-based books client
        - Testability: using grpcurl and gRPC client
- Contrasting aspects of both implementations

Folder Structure

In this chapter, we embark on the journey of setting up a foundational codebase, one that comprises not only a gRPC-based books server and a gRPC books client but also includes counterparts in the realm of REST: a REST-based books server and a REST books client. This holistic approach allows us to explore and compare the two prominent API paradigms within the same context. We aim to provide a comprehensive understanding of these technologies.

As we commence this endeavor, we recognize the importance of meticulous organization and structure within our project. Given the diverse nature of our applications, spanning different frameworks like gRPC and REST, it becomes paramount to maintain a well-defined folder structure. This structure ensures that each component remains neatly segregated, facilitating streamlined development and clarity as we progressively enhance our codebase in subsequent chapters. The journey begins with establishing this essential groundwork, which will serve as the foundation for our explorations into feature-rich API development.

To commence, let us delve into the folder structure.

Directory: */cmd*

This directory serves as the hub for entry points of primary applications within this codebase. It includes distinct main applications, such as a gRPC-based books client and a gRPC-based books server. Each application is housed within its own subdirectory, and the name of the subdirectory precisely matches the name of the corresponding executable (for example, **`/cmd/grpc-books-client`**).

It is vital to maintain a clear separation of concerns within the **`/cmd`** directory. Typically, the main functions contained here are minimal, serving as entry points that import and execute code from other directories, specifically **`/internal`** and **`/pkg.`** Code located in **`/pkg`** is designed to be reusable across various projects, fostering modularity and enhancing code sharing. Conversely, code placed in the **`/internal`** directory is explicitly intended for internal use within this codebase, limiting its accessibility to external projects.

By adhering to this structured approach, we can ensure clarity of purpose for each component and make it evident whether a given piece of code is intended for broader use or restricted to the confines of this specific project.

Directory: *`/internal`*

The /internal directory is dedicated to housing confidential application and library code, designed exclusively for internal consumption within this codebase. It is the ideal place to store code that should not be imported or utilized by external applications or libraries. It is important to note that this layout pattern is not merely a convention but is also enforced by the Go compiler itself, ensuring the privacy and security of this code.

Within the **`/internal`** directory, we have the flexibility to organize our code further. While it is not mandatory, creating a bit of additional structure within our internal packages can be beneficial, particularly for larger projects. This separation provides clear visual cues, distinguishing between shared and non-shared internal code. For instance, we can structure our application-specific code under **`/internal/apps`** (for example, **`/internal/apps/book-server`**) and place code shared by these applications in the **`/internal/pkg`** directory (for example, **`/internal/pkg/proto`**). This approach enhances code organization and comprehension, especially as our project scales.

Directory: */configs*

The /configs directory serves as a repository for configuration file templates or default configurations. This is where we can store templates or initial configuration settings that our application or services may require. These configurations are often essential for the proper functioning of applications or software.

Directory: */scripts*

The /scripts directory is designated for housing scripts that perform a variety of operations such as building, installing, or can be used to store database migration scripts. By keeping these scripts organized in a dedicated directory, we can maintain a clean and straightforward root-level Makefile, making it easier to manage and execute these operations as needed.

Directory: */deployments*

In the /deployments directory, you will find configurations and templates for deploying our application or services across various infrastructure and orchestration platforms. This can include configurations for IaaS (Infrastructure as a Service), PaaS (Platform as a Service), system deployments, and container orchestration setups like Docker Compose, Kubernetes with Helm charts, or Terraform templates. Depending on our project's conventions, we might also encounter this directory named simply as **`/deploy`** in some repositories.

Directory: */test*

The /test directory plays a pivotal role in housing additional external test applications and test data. We have the flexibility to structure this directory in a way that best suits our project's needs. For more extensive projects, creating a subdirectory like **`/test/data`** or **`/test/testdata`** can be particularly helpful. Note that Go, the language used in this codebase, will automatically ignore the contents of directories with names starting with ".", "_", or "test", ensuring that our test data remains distinct and isolated for testing purposes. This directory is a valuable resource for conducting thorough testing and quality assurance of our code.

The initial folder structure can be viewed here: https://github.com/OrangeAVA/Modern-API-Design-with-gRPC/tree/chapter-3-folder-structure

CRUD Operations on 'Books'

Now that we have a solid understanding of the folder structure, let's embark on the implementation phase. Our primary goal here is to create APIs that can perform CRUD (Create, Read, Update, Delete) operations on book resources within our application. This means we should be able to seamlessly add, update, fetch, and delete books to or from a data store or repository. To ensure flexibility and versatility, we will initially implement REST-based APIs and subsequently extend our capabilities to include gRPC-based RPCs.

Breaking down our requirements for REST APIs, we can outline the following key steps:

1. **Definition of Book Models**: We will start by defining the data models for books, outlining their attributes and structure.
2. **Book Repository**: To manage book objects effectively, we will create a dedicated book repository responsible for storage and retrieval.
3. **Book Service**: To interact with the book repository, we will develop a book service layer, facilitating seamless communication between our application and the data store.
4. **Routes and URLs**: Defining the routes and URLs is crucial for mapping API endpoints to specific functionalities within our application.
5. **Handlers**: We will establish handlers to process incoming requests and execute the corresponding actions, ensuring a smooth flow of data.

Additionally, we need to consider some non-functional requirements to enhance the overall performance and maintainability of our application. These include:

- **Dockerization**: Containerizing our applications for easy deployment and scalability.
- **Migration Scripts**: Developing scripts to handle the initial data population in the database.
- **Makefile Commands**: Compiling various commands into a Makefile for streamlined project management.
- **Configuration Management**: Implementing robust configuration management to handle different environments.
- **Testing Scripts**: Developing scripts to rigorously test the functionality of our APIs.

While the functional requirements address the core functionality of our application, these non-functional requirements are equally vital in ensuring the success of our project. They enhance maintainability, scalability, and overall efficiency, making our application robust and adaptable.

Implementing REST APIs to perform CRUD Operations

Let us begin by defining the models. Since we will be working with `Book` resources, it is crucial to establish their structure.

Path: ~/books-app/internal/pkg/model/book-db.go

```
package model
```

```
type Tabler interface {
  TableName() string
}

type DBBook struct {
  Isbn int `json:"isbn"`
  Name string `json:"name"`
  Publisher string `json:"publisher"`
}

func (DBBook) TableName() string {
  return "books"
}
```

Path: ~/books-app/internal/pkg/model/book.go

```
package model

type Book struct {
  Isbn int `json:"isbn"`
  Name string `json:"name"`
  Publisher string `json:"publisher"`
}
```

We have defined two structs, **`Book`** and **`DBBook`**, in our code. Let us break down their purposes and how they relate to each other:

- **`Book struct`**: This struct represents a book model that is used across different parts of our application (**tiers**). It includes the following fields:
  - **`ISBN`**: An integer field representing the **ISBN** of the book.
  - **`Name`**: A string field representing the name or title of the book.
  - **`Publisher`**: A string field representing the publisher of the book.

- **`Tabler Interface`**: This interface, named **`Tabler`**, defines a contract that other structs can implement. However, it is not directly related to the **`Book`** or **`DBBook`** structs.
- **`DBBook Struct`**: This struct is specifically designed for interaction with a database. It includes the same fields as the **`Book`** struct. Additionally, it defines a method **`TableName()`** that returns the table name associated with this struct, which is set to **`"books"`**.

The purpose of having two similar structs (**`Book`** and **`DBBook`**) might be to separate concerns within our application. The **`Book`** struct could be used for general application logic and API responses, while the **`DBBook`** struct is tailored for database interactions, possibly for an ORM (Object-Relational Mapping) framework. This separation helps maintain clean architecture and avoid mixing database-specific details with our core application logic.

Now that we are here, let us examine how we have implemented a mapper package. A mapper serves as a centralized component for handling the conversion logic between a **`Book`** and a **`DBBook`**, streamlining the process and reducing redundancy wherever it is needed.

Path: ~/books-app/internal/apps/rest-books-server/mapper.go

```
package restbooksserver


import (
  "github.com/orangeava/Modern-API-Design-with-gRPC/books-app/internal/
  pkg/model"
)



func DBBook(book *model.Book) *model.DBBook {
  dbBook := &model.DBBook{
    Isbn: book.Isbn,
    Name: book.Name,
    Publisher: book.Publisher,
  }
```

```
  return dbBook
}

func Book(dbBooks *model.DBBook) *model.Book {
  book := &model.Book{
    Isbn: dbBooks.Isbn,
    Name: dbBooks.Name,
    Publisher: dbBooks.Publisher,
  }

  return book
}
```

The preceding code defines two functions within the **restbooksserver** package.

The **DBBook** function takes a **model.Book** object as input, creates a new **model.DBBook** object, and populates it with the same values from the input **Book**. It then returns the resulting **DBBook** object.

Conversely, the Book function performs the reverse operation. It takes a **model.DBBook** object, creates a new **model.Book** object, and copies the values from the input **DBBook** to the output **Book**. It then returns the resulting **Book** object.

These functions serve as mapping utilities for converting between the two data models, **Book** and **DBBook**, making it easier to work with these objects across different parts of the application. This helps centralize the conversion logic, reduces redundancy, and improves code maintainability.

Next, we will need a repository to handle the storage of our book resources. Let us explore how we can go about implementing this essential component.

Path: ~/books-app/internal/pkg/repo/book.go

```
package repo

import (
  "github.com/orangeava/Modern-API-Design-with-gRPC/books-app/internal/
  pkg/model"
```

```
  "gorm.io/gorm"
)

type BookRepository struct {
  db *gorm.DB
}

func GetNewBookRepository(db *gorm.DB) *BookRepository {
  return &BookRepository{db: db}
}

func (br *BookRepository) AddBook(book *model.DBBook) {
  br.db.Create(book)
}

func (br *BookRepository) UpdateBook(book *model.DBBook) {
  br.db.Model(&book).Where("isbn = ?", book.Isbn).Update("name",
  "publisher")
}

func (br *BookRepository) GetBook(isbn int) *model.DBBook {
  var book model.DBBook
  br.db.First(&book, isbn)
  return &book
}

func (br *BookRepository) GetAllBooks() ([]*model.DBBook, error) {
  books := make([]*model.DBBook, 0)
  err := br.db.Find(&books).Error
```

```
  if err != nil {
    return nil, err
  }
  return books, nil
}

func (br *BookRepository) RemoveBook(isbn int) {
  br.db.Delete(&model.DBBook{}, isbn)
}
```

Here is a detailed breakdown of the book repository code:

1. The code belongs to the **`repo`** package. It imports necessary packages, including a model for the book model definition and GORM for interacting with a relational database using the **`GORM`** library.
2. **`BookRepository`** is a struct that represents a repository for managing book resources. It contains a field db of type **`*gorm.DB`**, which is used for interacting with the database.
3. **`NewBookRepository`** is a constructor function that creates and returns a new BookRepository instance, initialized with a GORM database connection.
4. **`AddBook`** is a method of the **`BookRepository.`** It takes a **`*model.DBBook`** as input, which represents a book. The **`Create`** method of the GORM database is used to insert the book data into the database.
5. **`UpdateBook`** is a method for updating book information. It takes a **`*model.DBBook`** as input. It uses the GORM Model and update methods to find a book by **ISBN** and update its **`name`** and **`publisher`** fields in the database.
6. **`GetBook`** retrieves a book by its **ISBN** (unique identifier). It takes an **ISBN** (an integer) as input. It uses the GORM first method to find the first book with the specified **ISBN** and returns it.
7. **`GetAllBooks`** retrieves all books from the database. It returns a slice of **`*model.DBBook`** representing all books. If there is an error during retrieval, it returns the error.
8. **`RemoveBook`** deletes a book from the database by ISBN. It uses the **`GORM Delete`** method to delete the book with the specified ISBN.

Overall, the preceding code defines a **BookRepository** struct that provides methods for adding, updating, retrieving, listing, and removing books from a database. It uses the **GORM** library to interact with the underlying database, and it is designed to work with the **model.DBBook** data structure representing books.

Path: ~/books-app/internal/pkg/service/book.go

```
package service

import (
  "fmt"

  "github.com/orangeava/Modern-API-Design-with-gRPC/books-app/internal/
  pkg/model"
  "github.com/orangeava/Modern-API-Design-with-gRPC/books-app/internal/
  pkg/repo"
  "github.com/pkg/errors"
)

type BooksService struct {
  booksRepo *repo.BookRepository
}

func GetNewBooksService(booksRepo *repo.BookRepository) BooksService {
  return BooksService{booksRepo: booksRepo}
}

func (bs *BooksService) AddBook(book *model.DBBook) {
  bs.booksRepo.AddBook(book)
}

func (bs *BooksService) GetBook(isbn int) (*model.DBBook, error) {
```

```
  book := bs.booksRepo.GetBook(isbn)
  if book != nil {
    return book, nil
  }
  return nil, errors.New(fmt.Sprintf("book with isbn %d was not found",
  isbn))
}

func (bs *BooksService) GetAllBooks() ([]*model.DBBook, error) {
  books, err := bs.booksRepo.GetAllBooks()
  if err != nil {
    return nil, err
  }

  if len(books) == 0 {
    return nil, errors.New("No books present")
  }
  return books, nil
}

func (bs *BooksService) RemoveBook(isbn int) {
  bs.booksRepo.RemoveBook(isbn)
}

func (bs *BooksService) UpdateBook(book *model.DBBook) {
  bs.booksRepo.UpdateBook(book)
}
```

Here is a detailed breakdown of the book service code:

1. The code belongs to the **`service`** package. It imports necessary packages, including model for the book model, repo for the book repository, and errors for error handling.
2. **`BooksService`** is a struct that represents a service for managing book resources. It contains a field **`booksRepo`** of type **`*repo.BookRepository`**, which is used to interact with the book repository.
3. **`GetNewBooksService`** is a constructor function that creates and returns a new **`BooksService`** instance, initialized with a book repository.
4. **`AddBook`** is a method of the **`BooksService.`** It takes a **`*model.DBBook`** as input, which represents a book to be added. It delegates the task of adding the book to the **`booksRepo`** (book repository).
5. **`GetBook`** is a method for retrieving a book by its **ISBN** (unique identifier). It takes an **ISBN** (an integer) as input. It uses the **`booksRepo`** to get the book. If the book is found, it returns it along with no error. If the book is not found, it returns an error indicating that the book with the given ISBN was not found.
6. **`GetAllBooks`** is a method for retrieving all books from the repository. It uses the **`booksRepo`** to get all the books. If there is an error during retrieval, it returns the error. If there are no books present, it returns an error indicating that no books are present. Otherwise, it returns the list of books.
7. **`RemoveBook`** is a method for deleting a book by its **ISBN**. It delegates the task of book removal to the **`booksRepo`**.
8. **`UpdateBook`** is a method for updating book information. It delegates the task of book update to the **`booksRepo`**.

The preceding code defines a **`BooksService`** struct that encapsulates the logic for adding, retrieving, listing, removing, and updating book resources. The service relies on a book repository (**`booksRepo`**) to perform these operations on the database. Additionally, it uses the **`fmt`** and **`errors`** packages for error handling and formatting error messages.

With our repository and service functionalities in place, the next step is to create handlers and routes. This will allow us to make the service accessible and handle requests for CRUD operations.

Path: ~/books-app/internal/app/rest-books-server/handlers.go

```
package restbooksserver
```

```
import (
  "encoding/json"
  "net/http"
  "strconv"

  "github.com/orangeava/Modern-API-Design-with-gRPC/books-app/internal/
  pkg/model"
  "github.com/orangeava/Modern-API-Design-with-gRPC/books-app/internal/
  pkg/service"
  "github.com/gorilla/mux"
)

const SuccessResponseFieldKey = "status"
const ErrorResponseFieldKey = "error"

type BooksHandler struct {
  bookService service.BooksService
}

func GetNewBooksHandler(bookService service.BooksService) *BooksHandler
{
  return &BooksHandler{bookService: bookService}
}

func (bh *BooksHandler) GetBookList(w http.ResponseWriter, r *http.
Request) {
  books, err := bh.bookService.GetAllBooks()
  if err != nil {
    respondWithError(w, http.StatusNotFound, err.Error())
```

```
    return
  }
  respondWithJSON(w, http.StatusOK, books)
}

func (bh *BooksHandler) GetOrRemoveBookHandler(w http.ResponseWriter, r
*http.Request) {
  muxVar := mux.Vars(r)
  isbnStr := muxVar["isbn"]
  isbn, err := strconv.Atoi(isbnStr)
  if err != nil || isbn == 0{
    respondWithError(w, http.StatusInternalServerError, err.Error())
    return
  }

  if r.Method == "GET" {
    book, err := bh.bookService.GetBook(isbn)
    if err != nil {
      respondWithError(w, http.StatusNotFound, err.Error())
      return
    }
    respondWithJSON(w, http.StatusOK, Book(book))
}else if r.Method == "DELETE" {
    bh.bookService.RemoveBook(isbn)
    respondWithJSON(w, http.StatusOK, map[string]string{"message": "book
    removed"})
    }
}
```

```
func (bh *BooksHandler) UpsertBookHandler(w http.ResponseWriter, r *http.
Request) {
  var book *model.Book
  decoder := json.NewDecoder(r.Body)

  if err := decoder.Decode(&book); err != nil {
    respondWithError(w, http.StatusBadRequest, err.Error())
    return
  }

  if r.Method == "POST" {
    bh.bookService.AddBook(DBBook(book))
  } else if r.Method == "PUT" {
    bh.bookService.UpdateBook(DBBook(book))
  } else {
    respondWithError(w, http.StatusMethodNotAllowed, "invalid request
    method")
    return
  }

  respondWithJSON(w, http.StatusOK, map[string]string{"message": "book
  upserted"})
}

func respondWithError(w http.ResponseWriter, code int, message string) {
  respondWithJSON(w, code, map[string]string{SuccessResponseFieldKey:
  message})
}
```

```
func respondWithJSON(w http.ResponseWriter, code int, payload interface{})
{
  response, _ := json.Marshal(payload)

  w.Header().Set("Content-Type", "application/json")
  w.WriteHeader(code)
  w.Write(response)
}
```

Here is a breakdown of the handler code:

1. **`Imports`**: The code imports necessary packages for handling HTTP requests (**`net/http`**), routing (**`gorilla/mux`**), JSON encoding/decoding (**`encoding/json`**), and internal packages for models and services.
2. **`BooksHandler`**: This struct contains a bookService instance, allowing it to interact with the book-related services.
3. **`GetNewBooksHandler:`** A constructor function that creates a new BooksHandler instance with the provided bookService.
4. **BooksHandler Methods:**
    a. **`GetBookList`**: Handles GET requests to retrieve all books. It calls the **`GetAllBooks`** method from the **`bookService`** and responds with the book data in JSON format.
    b. **`GetOrRemoveBookHandler`**: Handles GET and DELETE requests for specific books based on ISBN. It extracts the ISBN from the request, calls **`GetBook`** or **`RemoveBook`** methods from the **`bookService`**, and responds accordingly.
    c. **`UpsertBookHandler`**: Handles POST and PUT requests to add or update a book. It decodes the JSON payload from the request body, calls **`AddBook`** or **`UpdateBook`** methods from the **`bookService`**, and responds with a success message.
5. **Helper Functions**:
    a. **`respondWithError:`** Responds with an error message in JSON format, including the HTTP status code.
    b. **`respondWithJSON`**: Responds with JSON data, including the specified HTTP status code.

Overall, this code defines an HTTP server with handlers to manage book resources, allowing clients to perform CRUD operations (Create, Read, Update, Delete) on books through HTTP requests. The server uses the provided **bookService** to interact with the underlying data and respond to client requests with appropriate JSON data and status codes.

Now, we will proceed to establish the routes for directing incoming requests and managing responses.

Path: ~/books-app/internal/app/rest-books-server/router.go

```
package restbooksserver


import (

"github.com/orangeava/Modern-API-Design-with-gRPC/books-app/internal/
pkg/service"

"github.com/gorilla/mux"

)


func ProvideRouter(bookService service.BooksService) *mux.Router {

  r := mux.NewRouter()


  booksHandler := GetNewBooksHandler(bookService)


  r.HandleFunc("/books", booksHandler.GetBookList).Methods("GET")

  r.HandleFunc("/books", booksHandler.UpsertBookHandler).Methods("POST",
  "PUT")

  r.HandleFunc("/books/{isbn:[0-9]+}",     booksHandler.
  GetOrRemoveBookHandler).Methods("GET", "DELETE")


  return r

}
```

Here is a breakdown of the router code:

1. The preceding code defines a function called **ProvideRouter**, which is responsible for setting up and configuring the router using the **Gorilla Mux** package for handling HTTP routes.
2. It takes a parameter **bookService** of type **service.BooksService,** which represents the service responsible for managing books.
3. Inside the function, a new **router r** is created using **mux.NewRouter().**
4. An instance of the **BooksHandler** is created by calling the **GetNewBooksHandler** function with the **bookService** as a parameter. This handler will manage requests related to books.
5. **Route** handlers are then registered for various HTTP methods and paths using the **r.HandleFunc** method. Here is what each route does:
    a. **/books**: Handles HTTP GET requests for retrieving all books. It delegates the request to the **BooksHandler's GetBookList** method.
    b. **/books**: Handles HTTP POST and PUT requests for adding or updating a book. It delegates the request to the **BooksHandler's UpsertBookHandler** method.
    c. **/books/{isbn:[0-9]+}:** Handles HTTP GET and DELETE requests for a specific book identified by its ISBN. The ISBN is captured as a URL parameter. It delegates the request to the **BooksHandler's GetOrRemoveBookHandler** method.
6. Finally, the **router r** is returned, configured with all the defined routes, and can be used to handle incoming HTTP requests related to books.

The preceding code essentially sets up the routing infrastructure for the REST API, ensuring that different HTTP requests are directed to the appropriate handlers in the **BooksHandler.**

Now, let us delve into the implementation of a crucial package that facilitates configuration handling.

Path: ~/books-app/internal/pkg/configs/.go*

```
package configs


import (

  "flag"

  "io"
```

```
  "os"
  "sync"

  "github.com/hashicorp/go-multierror"
  "github.com/pkg/errors"
  "github.com/spf13/viper"
)

const (
  configFileKey = "configFile"
  defaultConfigFile = ""
  configFileUsage = "this is config file path"
)

var (
  once sync.Once
  cachedConfig *AppConfig
)

type ClientConfig struct {
  ClientName string `mapstructure:"clientName"`
  LogLevel string `mapstructure:"logLevel"`
  ServerAddress string `mapstructure:"serverAddress"`
}

type DatabaseConfig struct {
  Dbname string `mapstructure:"name"`
  Schema string `mapstructure:"schema"`
```

```
  Username string `mapstructure:"user"`
  Password string `mapstructure:"password"`
  Host string `mapstructure:"host"`
  Port int `mapstructure:"port"`
  LogMode bool `mapstructure:"logMode"`
  SslMode string `mapstructure:"sslMode"`
  Connection ConnectionPool `mapstructure:"connectionPool"`
  MigrationPath string `mapstructure:"migrationPath"`
}

type ConnectionPool struct {
  MaxOpenConnections int `mapstructure:"maxOpenConnections"`
  MaxIdleConnections int `mapstructure:"maxIdleConnections"`
  MaxIdleTime int `mapstructure:"maxIdleTime"`
  MaxLifeTime int `mapstructure:"maxLifeTime"`
  TimeOut int `mapstructure:"timeout"`
}

type ServerConfig struct {
  ServiceName string `mapstructure:"serviceName"`
  Host string `mapstructure:"host"`
  Port int `mapstructure:"port"`
  LogLevel string `mapstructure:"logLevel"`
}

type AppConfig struct {
  ServerConfig ServerConfig `mapstructure:"app"`
  DBConfig DatabaseConfig `mapstructure:"db"`
```

```
  ClientConfig ClientConfig `mapstructure:"client"`
}

func ProvideAppConfig() (c *AppConfig, err error) {
  once.Do(func() {
    var configFile string
    flag.StringVar(&configFile, configFileKey, defaultConfigFile,
    configFileUsage)
    flag.Parse()

    var configReader io.ReadCloser
    configReader, err = os.Open(configFile)
    defer configReader.Close() //nolint:staticcheck

    if err != nil {
      return
    }

    c, err = LoadConfig(configReader)
    if err != nil {
      return
    }

    cachedConfig = c
  })

  return cachedConfig, err
}
```

```
func LoadConfig(reader io.Reader) (*AppConfig, error) {
  var appConfig AppConfig

  viper.AutomaticEnv()
  viper.SetConfigType("yaml")

  keysToEnvironmentVariables := map[string]string{
    "app.port": "APP_PORT",
    "db.name": "DB_NAME",
    "db.user": "DB_USER",
    "db.host": "DB_HOST",
    "db.port": "DB_PORT",
    "db.password": "DB_PASSWORD",
  }

  err := bind(keysToEnvironmentVariables)
  if err != nil {
    return nil, err
  }

  if err := viper.ReadConfig(reader); err != nil {
    return nil, errors.Wrap(err, "Failed to load app config file")
  }

  if err := viper.Unmarshal(&appConfig); err != nil {
    return nil, errors.Wrap(err, "Unable to parse app config file")
  }

  return &appConfig, nil
```

```
}

func bind(keysToEnvironmentVariables map[string]string) error {
  var bindErrors error

  for key, environmentVariable := range keysToEnvironmentVariables {
    if err := viper.BindEnv(key, environmentVariable); err != nil {
      bindErrors = multierror.Append(bindErrors, err)
    }
}

  return bindErrors
}
```

This "`configs`" package handles configuration management for our application. Here is a breakdown of the code:

1. **Import Statements**: The code imports necessary packages for configuration management, including "`flag`" for command-line flag parsing, "`viper`" for configuration handling, and others like "`multierror`" and "`errors`" for error management.
2. **Constants and Variables**: Several constants and variables are defined, including:
    a. `configFileKey`: A key to identify the configuration file.
    b. `defaultConfigFile`: The default configuration file path.
    c. `configFileUsage`: A usage description for the configuration file.
    d. `once` and `cachedConfig`: These variables are used to ensure that configuration is loaded only once and cached for subsequent access.
3. **Configuration Structs**: The code defines several structs to represent different parts of the application configuration. These include:
    a. `ClientConfig`: Configuration related to client settings.
    b. `DatabaseConfig`: Configuration related to the database connection.
    c. `ConnectionPool`: Configuration for database connection pooling.

   d. `ServerConfig`: Configuration for the server, including host and port settings.

   e. `AppConfig`: The main application configuration struct that encompasses the preceding configurations.

4. **ProvideAppConfig Function**: This function provides the application configuration. It utilizes a `sync.Once` to ensure that configuration is loaded only once. It also uses the "`flag`" package to parse command-line arguments, allowing users to specify a custom configuration file. It then calls the `LoadConfig` function to load the configuration from the specified file.

5. **LoadConfig Function**: This function reads the configuration from a given reader (which can be a file or any other source). It uses the "`viper`" package to handle configuration loading and parsing. It also binds environment variables to configuration keys, allowing configuration values to be set via environment variables.

6. **bind Function**: This function binds environment variables to configuration keys based on a mapping defined in the `keysToEnvironmentVariables` map. This allows configuration values to be overridden by environment variables.

In summary, this code provides a structured way to manage application configuration using the "`viper`" package. It supports reading configuration from files and environment variables, ensuring that configuration values can be easily customized for different environments.

Now, let us delve into the implementation of another crucial package that facilitates database management and migrations.

Path: ~/books-app/internal/pkg/db/.go*

```
package db


import (

  "fmt"

  "log"

  "time"


  "github.com/orangeava/Modern-API-Design-with-gRPC/books-app/internal/
  pkg/configs"
```

```
  "github.com/pkg/errors"
  "gorm.io/driver/postgres"
  "gorm.io/gorm"
  "gorm.io/gorm/schema"
)

type DatabasePool interface {
  SetMaxOpenConns(n int)
  SetConnMaxLifetime(d time.Duration)
  SetMaxIdleConns(n int)
  SetConnMaxIdleTime(d time.Duration)
}

func ProvideDBConn(config *configs.DatabaseConfig) (*gorm.DB, error) {
  dbName := config.Dbname
  username := config.Username
  password := config.Password
  host := config.Host
  port := config.Port
  sslMode := config.SslMode
  connectionTimeOut := config.Connection.TimeOut

  args := fmt.Sprintf("host=%s port=%d user=%s dbname=%s password=%s
  sslmode=%s connect_timeout=%d", host, port, username, dbName,
  password, sslMode, connectionTimeOut)

  dbConnection, err := gorm.Open(postgres.Open(args), &gorm.Config{
      NamingStrategy: schema.NamingStrategy{
      TablePrefix: fmt.Sprintf("%s.", config.Schema),
```

```
    },
  })

  if err != nil {
    return nil, errors.WithMessagef(err, "GetDB.gorm.Open: failed to
    connect to db")
  }

  sqlDB, err := dbConnection.DB()
  if err != nil {
    return nil, errors.WithMessage(err, "Setup.db.DB")
  }

  ConfigureDatabasePool(sqlDB, config.Connection)

  if err := sqlDB.Ping(); err != nil {
    return nil, errors.WithMessage(err, "Setup.sqlDB.Ping")
  }

  log.Println("Created DB connection pool", sqlDB.Stats().
  OpenConnections,   sqlDB.Stats().MaxOpenConnections, sqlDB.Stats().
  InUse, sqlDB.Stats().Idle)

  return dbConnection, nil
}

func ConfigureDatabasePool(pool DatabasePool, connection configs.
ConnectionPool) {
  pool.SetMaxOpenConns(connection.MaxOpenConnections)
  pool.SetConnMaxLifetime(time.Second * time.Duration(connection.
  MaxLifeTime))
```

```
    pool.SetMaxIdleConns(connection.MaxIdleConnections)

    pool.SetConnMaxIdleTime(time.Second * time.Duration(connection.
    MaxIdleTime))

}
```

This preceding code is responsible for setting up and configuring a database connection pool using GORM (Go Object-Relational Mapping) and the PostgreSQL database driver. Here is an explanation of the code:

1. **Import Statements**: The code imports necessary packages for working with databases, including GORM, PostgreSQL driver, and various custom packages.
2. **`DatabasePool` Interface**: This interface defines methods for configuring the database connection pool. It includes methods for setting the maximum number of open connections, maximum connection lifetime, maximum idle connections, and maximum idle time.
3. **`ProvideDBConn` Function**: This function provides a GORM database connection based on the provided configuration. It takes a **`DatabaseConfig`** as input, which contains database connection details.
    a. It constructs the connection string (args) using the database configuration.
    b. It attempts to open a connection to the database using GORM's Open method, passing the PostgreSQL driver and configuration options.
    c. If successful, it retrieves the underlying SQL database connection (sqlDB) from GORM.
    d. It calls the ConfigureDatabasePool function to set the connection pool parameters based on the configuration.
    e. Finally, it checks the database connection's ping status and logs some connection pool statistics.
4. **`ConfigureDatabasePool` Function:** This function configures the database connection pool based on the provided DatabasePool interface and the connection pool configuration.
    a. It sets the maximum number of open connections (`MaxOpenConns`).
    b. It sets the maximum connection lifetime (`ConnMaxLifetime`).
    c. It sets the maximum number of idle connections (`MaxIdleConns`).
    d. It sets the maximum idle time for connections (`ConnMaxIdleTime`).

The code aims to establish a robust database connection pool with adjustable parameters based on the provided configuration. This connection pool is essential for efficiently managing database connections and optimizing database access within the application.

```
package migrations


import (

  "database/sql"

  "fmt"

  "log"

  "path/filepath"

  "strings"


  "github.com/orangeava/Modern-API-Design-with-gRPC/books-app/internal/
  pkg/configs"

  "github.com/golang-migrate/migrate/v4"

  "github.com/golang-migrate/migrate/v4/database/postgres"

  _ "github.com/golang-migrate/migrate/v4/source/file"

  "gorm.io/gorm"

)


const (

  cutSet = "file://"

  databaseName = "postgres"

)


type Migrator struct {

  pgDBMigrate *migrate.Migrate

}
```

```
func ProvideMigrator(config configs.DatabaseConfig, pgDB *gorm.DB)
(*Migrator, error) {
  dbConn, err := pgDB.DB()
  if err != nil {
    return nil, err
  }

  pgDBMigrate, err := initMigrate(dbConn, config.MigrationPath)
  if err != nil {
    return nil, err
  }

  return &Migrator{
    pgDBMigrate: pgDBMigrate,
  }, nil
}

func (m Migrator) RunMigrations() {
  m.RunMigrationsWith(m.pgDBMigrate, "Postgres Database")
}

func (m Migrator) RunMigrationsWith(migrateInstance *migrate.Migrate,
dBName string) {
  if err := migrateInstance.Up(); err != nil {
    if err == migrate.ErrNoChange {
      log.Printf("No change detected after running the migrations for
      %s", dBName)
      return
```

```
    }
    log.Println(fmt.Sprintf("Migration Failed for %s", dBName), err)
  }
  log.Printf("Migrations applied successfully to %s", dBName)
}

func initMigrate(dbConn *sql.DB, directory string) (*migrate.Migrate,
error) {
  driver, err := postgres.WithInstance(dbConn, &postgres.Config{})
  if err != nil {
    return nil, err
  }

  sourcePath, err := getSourcePath(directory)
  if err != nil {
    return nil, err
  }

  m, err := migrate.NewWithDatabaseInstance(sourcePath, databaseName,
  driver)
  if err != nil {
    return nil, err
  }
  return m, nil
}

func getSourcePath(directory string) (string, error) {
  directory = strings.TrimPrefix(directory, cutSet)
```

```
  absPath, err := filepath.Abs(directory)
  if err != nil {
    return "", err
  }
  return fmt.Sprintf("%s%s", cutSet, absPath), nil
}
```

The preceding code is responsible for managing database migrations in an application. Here is a breakdown of the code:

1. **Import Statements**: The code imports several packages required for database migrations, including **`"database/sql"`** for SQL database operations, **`"fmt"`** for formatted printing, **`"log"`** for logging, **`"path/filepath"`** for working with file paths, and various packages from **`"github.com"`** for database migrations and configuration management.
2. **Constants and Variables**:
    a. `cutSet`: A constant representing the prefix to cut from the migration directory path.
    b. `databaseName`: A constant specifying the name of the database, in this case, **`"postgres"`**.
3. `Migrator` **Struct**: This struct represents the database migrator and contains a field for the Postgres database migrator instance.
4. `ProvideMigrator` **Function**: This function provides a migrator instance. It takes a database configuration and a **GORM** (Go Object-Relational Mapping) database connection as input. It initializes and returns a migrator instance with the Postgres database migrator.
5. `RunMigrations` **Method**: This method runs the database migrations using the Postgres database migrator. It calls the RunMigrationsWith method with the specific migrator instance and the name of the database.
6. `RunMigrationsWith` **Method**: This method handles running the migrations with error handling. It checks if there were no changes in the migrations or if there was an error during migration and logs the corresponding messages.
7. `initMigrate` **Function**: This function initializes the migration instance for the Postgres database. It takes a SQL database connection and a migration directory as input. It creates a Postgres driver instance and then initializes the migration instance using the database driver.

8. **`getSourcePath` Function**: This function processes the migration directory path. It trims the **"`file://`"** prefix, obtains the absolute path, and returns the formatted source path required for migration.

In summary, this code sets up a migrator to manage database migrations for a Postgres database. It provides functions to run migrations and initializes the migration instance with the necessary configurations. This is a crucial part of maintaining the database schema when developing and deploying applications.

Now that we have all the necessary components in place for the REST books server to operate, let us integrate these components and launch the server.

Path: ~/books-app/internal/apps/rest-books-server/rest-books-server.go

```
package restbooksserver


import (

  "fmt"

  "log"

  "net/http"

  "time"


  "github.com/orangeava/Modern-API-Design-with-gRPC/books-app/internal/
  pkg/configs"

  "github.com/orangeava/Modern-API-Design-with-gRPC/books-app/internal/
  pkg/db"

  "github.com/orangeava/Modern-API-Design-with-gRPC/books-app/internal/
  pkg/db/migrations"

  "github.com/orangeava/Modern-API-Design-with-gRPC/books-app/internal/
  pkg/repo"

  "github.com/orangeava/Modern-API-Design-with-gRPC/books-app/internal/
  pkg/service"

  "gorm.io/gorm"

)
```

```
type App struct {
  dbConn *gorm.DB
}

func NewApp() *App {
  return &App{}
}

func (a *App) Start() {
  appConfig, err := configs.ProvideAppConfig()
  if err != nil {
    log.Fatal(err)
  }

  dbConn, err := db.ProvideDBConn(&appConfig.DBConfig)
  if err != nil {
    log.Fatal(err)
  }
  a.dbConn = dbConn

  migrator, err := migrations.ProvideMigrator(appConfig.DBConfig, dbConn)
  if err != nil {
    log.Fatal(err)
  }

  migrator.RunMigrations()

  bookRepo := repo.GetNewBookRepository(dbConn)
  bookSrv := service.GetNewBooksService(bookRepo)
```

```
  r := ProvideRouter(bookSrv)

  srv := http.Server{
    Addr: fmt.Sprintf("%s:%d", appConfig.ServerConfig.Host,     appConfig.
    ServerConfig.Port),
    Handler: r,
    WriteTimeout: 15 * time.Second,
    ReadTimeout: 15 * time.Second,
  }

  log.Println("Starting server")
  log.Fatal(srv.ListenAndServe())
}

func (a *App) Shutdown() {
  dbInstance, _ := a.dbConn.DB()
  _ = dbInstance.Close()
}
```

Path: ~/books-app/cmd/rest-books-server/main.go

```
package main

import (
  restbooksserver "github.com/orangeava/Modern-API-Design-with-gRPC/
  books-app/internal/apps/rest-books-server"
)

func main() {
  app := restbooksserver.NewApp()
```

```
    app.Start()


    app.Shutdown()
}
```

The preceding code defines the main application structure for the REST books server. Here is what it does:

1. It initializes the application by creating a new instance of the **App** structure.
2. In the **Start** method, **restbooksserver** reads the application configuration using **configs.ProvideAppConfig(),** which contains settings like the database connection details, server configuration, and more.
3. It establishes a database connection using the configuration obtained in the previous step. If there is an error, it logs a fatal error and exits.
4. It initializes a database migrator using **migrations.ProvideMigrator**, which handles database migrations to ensure the database schema is up to date.
5. It runs database migrations with **migrator.RunMigrations()** to apply any pending changes to the database schema.
6. It creates a repository for books using **repo.GetNewBookRepository** and a service for handling book-related operations using **service.GetNewBooksService**. These components are essential for processing incoming HTTP requests related to books.
7. It sets up a router using **ProvideRouter**, which defines the routes and handlers for the REST API.
8. It configures and starts an HTTP server using the settings provided in the application configuration, such as the host and port.
9. Finally, it logs the server's startup and runs it. If any errors occur during startup, they are logged as fatal errors.
10. The **Shutdown** method allows us to gracefully shut down the application by closing the database connection when needed.

In summary, this code initializes and starts the REST books server, including database connections, migrations, routing, and server configuration. It is the entry point for running the server.

Now, let us initiate the application and assess its functionality. To launch the application, we shall execute the following command in the terminal after navigating to the codebase directory:

```
go run books-app/cmd/rest-books-server/main.go -configFile=books-app/configs/rest-books-server.yaml
```

We can evaluate the endpoints using the following **curl** commands:

```
#!/bin/bash

# [REST] Fetch all books
curl --request GET --url http://localhost:8090/books | json_pp

# [REST] Fetch a book by isbn
curl --request GET --url http://localhost:8090/books/12346 | json_pp

# [REST] Add a book
curl --request POST \
--url http://localhost:8090/books \
--header 'Content-Type: application/json' \
--data '{
"isbn": "12348",
"name": "test book",
"publisher": "test publisher"
}'

# [REST] Update a book
curl --request PUT \
--url http://localhost:8090/books \
--header 'Content-Type: application/json' \
--data '{
```

```
"isbn": "12348",

"name": "test book",

"publisher": "new publisher"

}'


# [REST] Delete a book

curl --request DELETE --url http://localhost:8090/books/12348
```

We have the option to develop a client for the books server and evaluate its functionality.

The code for the rest books client can be viewed here: https://github.com/OrangeAVA/Modern-API-Design-with-gRPC/blob/main/books-app/internal/apps/rest-books-client/rest-books-client.go

The code in the preceding link defines a client application for interacting with the REST books server. Here is a breakdown of what it does:

1. The **App** structure is defined to hold the server address.
2. The **NewApp** function creates a new instance of the App structure.
3. In the **Start** method, it reads the application configuration to get the server address from **configs.ProvideAppConfig()**.
4. The **performClientOperations** method simulates various client operations:
   a. It creates a sample book in JSON format.
   b. Calls **AddBook** to add the book to the server.
   c. Updates the book and calls **UpdateBook** to send the updated data to the server.
   d. Calls **ListBooks** to retrieve a list of books from the server.
   e. Calls **FetchBook** to retrieve a specific book by ISBN.
   f. Calls **RemoveBook** to delete a book from the server.
5. The **AddBook** method sends an **HTTP POST** request to add a book to the server. It marshals the book data into JSON and sends it to the server using the HTTP client.
6. The **UpdateBook** method sends an **HTTP PUT** request to update a book on the server. It is similar to **AddBook** but uses the **HTTP PUT** method.

7. The **`ListBooks`** method sends an **`HTTP GET`** request to retrieve a list of books from the server.
8. The **`FetchBook`** method sends an **`HTTP GET`** request to retrieve a specific book by ISBN.
9. The **`RemoveBook`** method sends an **`HTTP DELETE`** request to remove a book from the server.

Each method logs any errors that occur during the HTTP requests.

In summary, this client application interacts with the REST books server by performing CRUD operations on books. It reads the server address from the configuration, sends HTTP requests with appropriate methods and data, and logs the server's responses or any errors. This client is a simulation and can be used for testing the server's REST API.

We conclude the development of CRUD operations APIs using REST. You can explore the full server implementation here: https://github.com/OrangeAVA/Modern-API-Design-with-gRPC/tree/main/books-app/internal/apps/rest-books-server and the client implementation here: https://github.com/OrangeAVA/Modern-API-Design-with-gRPC/tree/main/books-app/internal/apps/rest-books-client .

Next, we will proceed to implement RPCs with gRPC, leveraging several components located in the'**`pkg`** directory.

Implementing gRPC RPCs to perform CRUD operations

Just as we began with defining models for REST APIs, we need a similar structure to represent books. We will still continue to use DBBook because it aligns with our database. As you may recall from the previous chapter, we require **`protobuf`** messages for this purpose. Specifically, we will create a **Book** proto message and utilize the **`protoc`** compiler to auto-generate the code. However, in our current endeavor, we are taking it a step further. We need to define our RPCs (Remote Procedure Calls), essentially the endpoints for our gRPC service. These RPCs involve specifying the structure of the requests and responses. A group of RPCs collectively forms a service. Each RPC involves a request message and a corresponding response message. Following this, we utilize the **`protoc`** compiler to generate code and proceed to implement both the server-side and client-side interfaces. This step is pivotal in creating a robust and efficient gRPC-based API system.

Let us examine the structure of our book proto file. The contents of this proto file will provide us with a framework for what we intend to build. We will use the **protoc** compiler to automatically generate some boilerplate code, saving us from repetitive tasks. Then, our task will be to define the core functionality and data handling logic.

Path: ~/books-app/internal/pkg/proto/book.proto

```
syntax = "proto3";

package prot;
option go_package="./proto";

message Empty{}

message Book {
  int32 isbn = 1;
  string name = 2;
  string publisher = 3;
}

message AddBookResponse{
    string status = 1;
}

message ListBooksResponse{
    repeated Book books = 1;
}

message GetBookRequest{
    int32 isbn = 1;
}

message RemoveBookRequest{
```

```
    int32 isbn = 1;
}

message RemoveBookResponse{
    string status = 1;
}

message UpdateBookResponse{
    string status = 1;
}

service BookService{
  // Unary
  rpc AddBook(Book) returns (AddBookResponse) {};
  rpc ListBooks(Empty) returns (ListBooksResponse) {};
  rpc GetBook(GetBookRequest) returns (Book) {};
  rpc RemoveBook(RemoveBookRequest) returns (RemoveBookResponse) {};
  rpc UpdateBook(Book) returns (UpdateBookResponse) {};
}
```

Let us break down the key components of this protobuf file:

1. **Syntax Declaration**:

   ```
   syntax = "proto3";
   ```

   This line specifies that the protocol buffer file is written using version 3 of the protobuf syntax.

2. **Package Declaration**:

   ```
   package prot;
   ```

   This declares a package name for the protobuf definitions. It's common practice to use a package to organize related messages and service definitions.

3. **Option for Go Package**:

   ```
   option go_package=”./proto”;
   ```

   This option specifies the Go package name and the import path for generated Go code. The generated Go code will be placed in a package named **`“proto”`** in the current directory.

4. **Message Definitions**:

   Messages are used to define the structure of data that can be sent or received in gRPC requests and responses.

   a. **`Empty`**: This is an empty message with no fields. It is commonly used when an RPC method does not require any parameters or returns.

   b. **`Book`**: This message defines the structure of a Book object with three fields: ISBN, name, and publisher. Each field has a unique field number and a data type.

   c. **`AddBookResponse, ListBooksResponse, GetBookRequest, RemoveBookRequest, RemoveBookResponse, UpdateBookResponse`**: These messages define various request and response structures for the gRPC service methods.

5. **Service Definition**:

   ```
   service BookService{
     // Unary
     rpc AddBook(Book) returns (AddBookResponse) {};
     rpc ListBooks(Empty) returns (ListBooksResponse) {};
     rpc GetBook(GetBookRequest) returns (Book) {};
     rpc RemoveBook(RemoveBookRequest) returns (RemoveBookResponse)
     {};
     rpc UpdateBook(Book) returns (UpdateBookResponse) {};
   }
   ```

This section defines a gRPC service named **`BookService.`** It lists several RPC methods, including **`AddBook, ListBooks, GetBook, RemoveBook`**, and **`UpdateBook`**, each specifying the request and response message types.

Overall, this protobuf file serves as a contract for defining the message structures and service endpoints used in a gRPC-based application. The generated code from this protobuf file can be used by both the server and client to ensure that they communicate with each other using the same message formats and service definitions.

In order to generate code for the preceding protofile using protoc compiler, we can use the following command:

```
protoc --go_out=books-app/internal/pkg --go-grpc_out=books-app/internal/
pkg books-app/internal/pkg/proto/*.proto
```

Here is a breakdown of the command:

1. **--go_out=books-app/internal/pkg**: This part specifies the output directory for the generated Go code. In this case, it is set to **books-app/internal/pkg**. This means that the generated Go code will be placed in the **books-app/internal/pkg** directory.
2. **--go-grpc_out=books-app/internal/pkg**: This part specifies the output directory for the generated Go gRPC code. The **--go-grpc_out** flag is used to generate gRPC-related code. It is also set to **books-app/internal/pkg**, so the generated gRPC code will also be placed in the **books-app/internal/pkg** directory.
3. **books-app/internal/pkg/proto/*.proto**: This part specifies the input **.proto** files. The ***.proto** wildcard is used to indicate that all **.proto** files in the **books-app/internal/pkg/proto** directory should be processed.

So, when we run this command, it will take all the **.proto** files in the **books-app/internal/pkg/proto** directory, generate Go code from them, and place the generated code in the **books-app/internal/pkg** directory. This generated code will include both standard Go code and gRPC-related code necessary for implementing the defined services and messages in our **.proto** files.

To reiterate, the generated code produced by the **protoc** compiler for a protocol buffer (**.proto**) file will typically include the following components:

- **Message Types**: For each message defined in the **.proto** file, the generated code will include Go structs that represent those message types. These structs will have fields corresponding to the message fields, allowing us to create, manipulate, and serialize/deserialize message instances in our Go code. The generated structs for book.proto messages can be viewed here: https://github.com/OrangeAVA/Modern-API-Design-with-gRPC/blob/main/books-app/internal/pkg/proto/book.pb.go
- **Service Definitions**: If the **.proto** file defines RPC services, the generated code will include Go interfaces that define the service methods. These methods will typically mirror the RPCs defined in the **.proto** file.
- **Client Code**: If there are RPC client definitions in the **.proto** file, the generated code will include client implementations that allow us to make

RPC calls to a remote service. The generated interface for client code can be viewed at https://github.com/OrangeAVA/Modern-API-Design-with-gRPC/blob/398ac99960c2a5afa0edf8e5c9b13ed07f6874c9/books-app/internal/pkg/proto/book_grpc.pb.go#L24

- **Server Code**: If there are RPC server definitions in the `.proto` file, the generated code will include server implementations. These implementations define how the service should respond to RPC requests. The generated interface for server code can be viewed at https://github.com/OrangeAVA/Modern-API-Design-with-gRPC/blob/398ac99960c2a5afa0edf8e5c9b13ed07f6874c9/books-app/internal/pkg/proto/book_grpc.pb.go#L89
- **Serialization/Deserialization Code**: The generated code includes methods for serializing (marshaling) and deserializing (unmarshaling) message instances to/from binary or text format. This is essential for sending messages over a network or storing them.
- **gRPC Code**: Since we are using gRPC, the generated code will also include gRPC-specific components, such as gRPC server and client code, which handle the communication between gRPC clients and servers.
- **Additional Supporting Code**: Depending on the specifics of the `.proto` file and the generation options, the generated code might also include additional supporting code for things like error handling, context management, and more.

In summary, the generated code provides a foundation for working with the data structures and RPC services defined in the `.proto` file. It automates a lot of the boilerplate code required for serialization, deserialization, and communication, allowing us to focus on implementing the application's logic.

Complete generated code for `book.proto` can be viewed here: https://github.com/OrangeAVA/Modern-API-Design-with-gRPC/tree/main/books-app/internal/pkg/proto

Now let us see how we implement the server side interface.

Path: ~/books-app/internal/apps/grpc-books-server/.go*

The code for grpc books server can be found here: https://github.com/OrangeAVA/Modern-API-Design-with-gRPC/blob/main/books-app/internal/apps/grpc-books-server/grpc-books-server.go

The code in the aforementioned link defines a gRPC server for a book-related service. Let us break down the code functioning:

1. **Imports**: The code imports various packages needed for setting up the gRPC server, including packages related to configuration, database management, and gRPC itself.
2. **App Struct**: It defines a struct named **App**. This struct will be used to encapsulate the functionality of the gRPC server. It embeds the **`proto.UnimplementedBookServiceServer`** **interface**, which is auto-generated by the **protoc** compiler based on the service definition in the **`.proto`** file. This means that the compiler will not produce errors when we are compiling the APP (we will discuss forward compatibility in the future).
3. **`NewApp`** **Function:** This function creates and returns a new instance of the **App** struct.
4. **`Start`** **Method**: The **`Start`** method is used to start the gRPC server. Here is the step-by-step procedure:
   a. It fetches the application configuration from **`configs.ProvideAppConfig()`**.
   b. It establishes a database connection using **`db.ProvideDBConn`** and sets it as a field in the **App** struct.
   c. It initializes a **`bookRepo`** using the database connection.
   d. It sets up database migrations using the **`migrations.ProvideMigrator`** function.
   e. It prepares to listen on a network address (**`0.0.0.0`**) and port specified in the configuration.
   f. It creates a new gRPC server using **`grpc.NewServer`**.
   g. It registers the gRPC service implementation **`‘s’`** which is essentially the App struct instance and has the book server interface implemented and bound to it with the server using **`proto.RegisterBookServiceServer`**.
   h. It registers gRPC server reflection using **`reflection.Register`**, which provides information about gRPC services publicly on the server, and assists clients at runtime to construct RPC requests and responses without precompiled service information or for debugging and testing.
   i. Finally, it starts serving the gRPC requests on the specified network address and port.
5. **`Shutdown`** **Method**: The **`Shutdown`** method is used to gracefully shut down the gRPC server. It closes the database connection.

6. **Service Methods Implementation**: This code defines the actual implementation of the gRPC service methods that were declared in the **.proto** file. These methods allow clients to interact with the server for various book-related operations.
   a. **AddBook**: This method handles the addition of a book. It takes a proto.Book request, converts it to a database model (**model.DBBook**), adds the book to the database using the repository, and returns an **AddBookResponse** indicating success or failure status.
   b. **UpdateBook**: Similar to **AddBook**, this method handles updating book information. It takes a **proto.Book** request, converts it to a database model, updates the book in the database, and returns an **UpdateBookResponse**.
   c. **ListBooks**: This method lists all books. It retrieves books from the database using the repository, converts them to the **proto.Book** format, and returns a **ListBooksResponse** containing the list of books.
   d. **GetBook**: This method fetches information about a specific book by its ISBN. It takes a **proto.GetBookRequest** with an ISBN, retrieves the book from the database, and returns a **proto.Book** with the details of the book.
   e. **RemoveBook**: This method removes a book by its ISBN. It takes a **proto.RemoveBookRequest**, removes the book from the database, and returns a **proto.RemoveBookResponse** indicating success or failure status.

Just as we created an entry point for the REST books server in a main file, we follow the same approach for the gRPC server.

Path: ~/books-app/cmd/grpc-books-server/main.go

```
package main


import (

  grpcbooksserver "github.com/orangeava/Modern-API-Design-with-gRPC/
  books-app/internal/apps/grpc-books-server"

)


func main() {

  app := grpcbooksserver.NewApp()
```

```
  app.Start()

  app.Shutdown()
}
```

Now, let us initiate the gRPC server application and assess its functionality. To launch the application, we can execute the following command in the terminal after navigating to the codebase directory:

```
go run books-app/cmd/grpc-books-server/main.go -configFile=./books-app/configs/grpc-books-server.yaml
```

Testing gRPC endpoints (RPCs) differs from testing REST endpoints (APIs). Traditional tools like curl or **Postman** cannot be used for gRPC testing. Although some tools like **Postman** and **Insomnia** do offer gRPC support, we will demonstrate testing using **`grpcurl`**, a dedicated tool for gRPC, much like how we use curl for REST endpoints. **`grpcurl`** is a command-line utility designed for interacting with gRPC servers, akin to how **curl** is used for traditional HTTP servers.

We can evaluate the RPCs using the following **`grpcurl`** commands:

```
#!/bin/bash

# This command installs the grpcurl tool, which is used to make gRPC calls from the command line.

go install github.com/fullstorydev/grpcurl/cmd/grpcurl@latest

# Lists all available services on the gRPC server running at address 0.0.0.0:50051.

grpcurl -plaintext 0.0.0.0:50051 list

# Lists all the supported methods for the prot.BookService gRPC service

grpcurl -plaintext 0.0.0.0:50051 list prot.BookService
```

```
# Calls the ListBooks method of the prot.BookService gRPC service to get a list of all books.

grpcurl -plaintext 0.0.0.0:50051 prot.BookService/ListBooks

# Calls the GetBook method of the prot.BookService gRPC service to get a book with ISBN 12345.

grpcurl -plaintext -d '{"isbn": "12345"}' 0.0.0.0:50051 prot.BookService/GetBook

# Calls the AddBook method of the prot.BookService gRPC service to add a book with the given ISBN, name, and publisher.

grpcurl -plaintext -d '{"isbn": "12348", "name": "test name", "publisher": "test publisher"}' 0.0.0.0:50051 prot.BookService/AddBook

# Calls the UpdateBook method of the prot.BookService gRPC service to update a book with ISBN 12348, changing the publisher.

grpcurl -plaintext -d '{"isbn": "12348", "name": "test name", "publisher": "new publisher"}' 0.0.0.0:50051 prot.BookService/UpdateBook

# Calls the RemoveBook method of the prot.BookService gRPC service to remove a book with ISBN 12348.

grpcurl -plaintext -d '{"isbn": "12348"}' 0.0.0.0:50051 prot.BookService/RemoveBook
```

Another approach is to develop a gRPC client, similar to what we did for the REST API. Here is an example of how to implement it and communicate with the gRPC server.

```
package grpcbooksclient

import (
```

```
  "fmt"

  "log"

  "context"

    "github.com/orangeava/Modern-API-Design-with-gRPC/books-app/
    internal/pkg/configs"

  "github.com/orangeava/Modern-API-Design-with-gRPC/books-app/internal/
  pkg/proto"

  "google.golang.org/grpc"

)


type App struct {

  serverConn *grpc.ClientConn

  client proto.BookServiceClient

}


func NewApp() *App {

  return &App{}

}


func (a *App) Start() {

  appConfig, err := configs.ProvideAppConfig()

  if err != nil {

    log.Fatal(err)

  }


  servAddr := appConfig.ClientConfig.ServerAddress


  opts := grpc.WithTransportCredentials(insecure.NewCredentials())
```

```
  a.serverConn, err = grpc.Dial(servAddr, opts)
  if err != nil {
    log.Fatalf("could not connect: %v", err)
  }

  a.client = proto.NewBookServiceClient(a.serverConn)

  a.performClientOperations()
}

func (a *App) Shutdown() {
  a.serverConn.Close()
}

func (a *App) performClientOperations() {
  book := &proto.Book{
    Isbn: 12348,
    Name: "atomic habits",
    Publisher: "random house business books",
  }

  // add a book
  a.AddBook(book)

  // list books
  found := false
  books := a.ListBooks()
  for i, b := range books {
    fmt.Printf("[%d.] Name(%s), Isbn(%d), Publisher(%s)", i, b.Name,
```

```
    b.Isbn,   b.Publisher)
    if b.Isbn == book.Isbn &&
    b.Name == book.Name &&
    b.Publisher == book.Publisher {
      found = true
    }
  }
  if found {
    fmt.Println("Book sent through 'AddBook' request was verified to have
    been added while listing books.")
  }

  // fetch a book
  fetchedBook := a.FetchBook(12345)
  if fetchedBook.Isbn == 12345 &&
  fetchedBook.Name == "" &&
  fetchedBook.Publisher == "" {
    fmt.Println("Book added via migrations was successfully fetched.")
  }

  // update a book
  book.Name = "atomic habits vol-2"
  a.UpdateBook(book)

  // delete a book
  a.RemoveBook(int(book.Isbn))
}
```

```
func (a *App) AddBook(book *proto.Book) {
  resp, err := a.client.AddBook(context.Background(), book)
  if err != nil {
    log.Fatal(err)
  }

  log.Println(resp.Status)
}

func (a *App) ListBooks() []*proto.Book {
  resp, err := a.client.ListBooks(context.Background(), &proto.Empty{})
  if err != nil {
    log.Fatal(err)
  }

  return resp.Books
}

func (a *App) FetchBook(isbn int) *proto.Book {
  resp, err := a.client.GetBook(context.Background(), &proto.
  GetBookRequest{Isbn: int32(isbn)})
  if err != nil {
    log.Fatal(err)
  }

  return resp
}

func (a *App) RemoveBook(isbn int) {
```

```
  resp, err := a.client.RemoveBook(context.Background(), &proto.
  RemoveBookRequest{Isbn: int32(isbn)})
  if err != nil {
    log.Fatal(err)
  }

  log.Println(resp.Status)
}

func (a *App) UpdateBook(book *proto.Book) {
  resp, err := a.client.UpdateBook(context.Background(), book)
  if err != nil {
    log.Fatal(err)
  }

  log.Println(resp.Status)
}
```

This client code defines a gRPC client application **(App)** that communicates with a gRPC server providing book-related services. Here is a breakdown of its functionality:

1. **Initialization**:
   a. The **`NewApp()`** function initializes a new instance of the **App** struct.
   b. The **`Start()`** method is used to set up the client. It reads the application configuration, including the server address, and establishes a connection to the gRPC server. It also initializes the gRPC client for book services.
2. **Shutdown**: The **`Shutdown()`** method is responsible for closing the gRPC connection when the client is done.
3. **Client Operations**:
   a. The **`performClientOperations()`** method is where various client operations are performed.
   b. It starts by defining a book with some sample data.

  c. **AddBook()**: This method sends a request to the gRPC server to add a book using the provided book data.
  d. **ListBooks()**: This method requests a list of books from the server and prints information about each book. It also checks if the book added earlier through **AddBook()** is present in the list.
  e. **FetchBook()**: This method fetches a specific book by ISBN from the server and checks if it matches the expected book data.
  f. **UpdateBook()**: This method sends a request to update the information of a book.
  g. **RemoveBook()**: This method sends a request to delete a book from the server.
4. **RPC Methods**: The **AddBook()**, **ListBooks()**, **FetchBook()**, **UpdateBook()**, and **RemoveBook()** methods utilize the gRPC client to communicate with the server. They use the appropriate gRPC-generated client methods for these operations.

These methods make use of gRPC to communicate with the server and perform CRUD (Create, Read, Update, Delete) operations on books.

Overall, this code represents a gRPC client that interacts with the gRPC server to manage book-related data using the defined gRPC service methods.

Contrasting aspects of REST and gRPC implementations

The implementations of REST and gRPC in the preceding code base contrast in several ways:

Communication Protocol:

- **REST**: Utilized HTTP as the communication protocol, which is text-based and used standard methods like **GET, POST, PUT, and DELETE** for **CRUD** operations.
- **gRPC**: Used Protocol Buffers (**protobuf**) over HTTP/2, which is a binary and more efficient protocol. It generated strongly typed client and server code from proto definitions.

Data Serialization:

- **REST**: Relied on **JSON** for data serialization, which is human-readable but less efficient for parsing.

- **gRPC**: Used Protocol Buffers (**protobuf**) for data serialization, which is binary and more compact, making it faster to encode and decode data.

Service Definitions:

- **REST**: Involved defining custom endpoint routes for each API operation (for example , `/addBook, /listBooks`), which can lead to a large number of routes in the code.
- **gRPC**: Utilized a single service definition file (proto file) where all **RPC** methods are defined, resulting in a more structured and centralized API.

Code Generation:

- **REST**: Did not provide automatic code generation for clients or servers. We had to manually write HTTP request and response handling code.
- **gRPC**: Offers automatic code generation for client and server code based on the proto file, reducing the need for manual coding.

Complexity:

- **REST**: Simplicity in terms of protocol and readability. Well-suited for human interaction and debugging.
- **gRPC**: Slightly more complex due to Protocol Buffers and binary data, but more efficient and suitable for machine-to-machine communication.

Testing and Interaction:

- **REST**: Interactable using standard HTTP tools like cURL or web browsers. Testing is straightforward.
- **gRPC:** Required specialized tools like **grpcurl** for testing and interacting with the server. gRPC clients often need to be explicitly written.

In the **REST** implementation, we use the **mux** framework to define individual HTTP routes for each CRUD operation on books. The code is relatively straightforward and follows RESTful principles.

In the **gRPC** implementation, we define a single service interface with RPC methods in a proto file. The code is more centralized, and the gRPC server and client generate code based on this proto definition. Interaction with the server is demonstrated using the **grpcurl** tool.

In summary, the REST implementation is simpler and easier to start with, making it suitable for human-facing APIs and web services. On the other hand, the gRPC implementation offers efficiency, code generation, and performance benefits, making it ideal for machine-to-machine communication, microservices architectures, and scenarios where binary serialization is crucial. The choice between REST and gRPC depends on the specific requirements and trade-offs of the project.

Conclusion

We created a RESTful API server for managing books. We utilized the **Go** programming language with the **mux** framework, and implemented **CRUD** operations for books. We set up database migrations to manage the database schema. We defined and used RESTful endpoints to interact with the server. We provided clear documentation on how to test and interact with the REST API using tools like cURL. We also developed a RESTful API client to interact with the REST server. We made HTTP requests to the server for CRUD operations on books. We demonstrated how to test the REST endpoints using cURL commands. We showcased how to start the client application and perform various operations on books programmatically.

Similarly we created a gRPC server for managing books with the ability to add, list, fetch, update, and remove books. We utilized the **Go** programming language and the gRPC framework. We generated gRPC code from Protocol Buffers (proto) definitions using `protoc` compiler. In comparison to the previous chapter where we generated code for messages, in this chapter we ventured a step further and generated gRPC code as well. We implemented the gRPC service interface for book operations. We provided clear instructions on how to interact with the gRPC server using the `grpcurl` command-line tool. We demonstrated how to start the gRPC server and handle incoming gRPC requests. We also developed a gRPC client application to interact with the gRPC server. We established a connection to the gRPC server and generated client code from the proto definitions. We implemented client methods for adding, listing, fetching, updating, and removing books. We demonstrated how to perform these operations programmatically using the client application. We showcased how to initialize and shut down the client properly.

In summary, both the REST and gRPC implementations provided comprehensive solutions for managing books. They demonstrated how to set up server and client applications, perform CRUD operations, and interact with the server through either RESTful HTTP endpoints or gRPC services. The code examples included database management and clear instructions for testing and running the applications.

However, if we take a closer look, we should notice that our communication has been initiated only from one direction, specifically from the client to the server. In the context of RPC (Remote Procedure Call), this is known as the **Unary** communication pattern. In the realm of REST, there are no alternative communication patterns, so there is no specific terminology for this. However, gRPC offers a variety of communication patterns beyond Unary. In the next chapter, we will explore these different patterns in more detail.

Multiple Choice Questions

1. What is the primary difference between REST and gRPC?
    a. REST is synchronous, while gRPC is asynchronous.
    b. REST uses XML for data serialization, while gRPC uses JSON.
    c. REST relies on HTTP/HTTPS for communication, while gRPC uses its own protocol (HTTP/2-based).
    d. REST has no concept of services, while gRPC is service-oriented.
2. In the context of gRPC, what is a `service`?
    a. A microservice
    b. A remote procedure or method
    c. A database schema
    d. A REST API endpoint
3. What does "Unary" communication pattern mean in gRPC?
    a. One server communicates with multiple clients asynchronously.
    b. One client communicates with multiple servers synchronously.
    c. One client sends a single request and receives a single response from the server.
    d. Both the client and server send multiple requests and responses in parallel.
4. Which tool is commonly used for interacting with gRPC servers and is similar to "curl" for REST?
    a. grpcurl
    b. Postman
    c. Swagger
    d. Insomnia

5. What is the purpose of the "proto" files in gRPC?
    a. They contain the server's implementation code.
    b. They define the structure of the data exchanged between client and server.
    c. They store user authentication information.
    d. They are used for configuring the gRPC server.
6. Which protocol is commonly used for data serialization in gRPC?
    a. JSON
    b. XML
    c. Protocol Buffers (protobuf)
    d. YAML
7. In a gRPC client application, what does the "`WithInsecure()`" option signify when creating a connection to the server?
    a. It disables encryption and uses plaintext communication.
    b. It enforces strong encryption using TLS.
    c. It sets the communication timeout to zero.
    d. It specifies the server's public key.
8. What does **reflection** do in a gRPC server?
    a. It reflects the server's state to the client.
    b. It allows dynamic discovery of available services and methods.
    c. It encrypts all data exchanged between client and server.
    d. It ensures that the server is always running.
9. In the REST server code, what is the purpose of the `ProvideDBConn` function?
    a. To define the REST API routes.
    b. To establish a connection to the database.
    c. To serialize and deserialize data.
    d. To configure server settings.
10. In the gRPC server code, what does the `proto.UnimplementedBookService-Server` represent? (forward-compatibility)
    a. A placeholder for future service implementations.
    b. An error message indicating an incomplete implementation.

c. A predefined gRPC service provided by the framework.
d. A client connection to the gRPC server.

11. In the gRPC client code, what does the **`performClientOperations`** function do?
    a. Adds a book, lists books, fetches a book, updates a book, and removes a book.
    b. Lists books only.
    c. Adds a book and removes a book.
    d. Fetches a book and updates a book.
12. In the REST server code, what does the **`ConfigureDatabasePool`** function do?
    a. Configures the server's response headers.
    b. Sets the maximum number of open database connections.
    c. Defines the routes for REST endpoints.
    d. Manages client connections to the server.

Answers

1	c
2	b
3	c
4	a
5	b
6	c
7	a
8	b
9	b
10	a
11	a
12	b

CHAPTER 4

Communication patterns in gRPC

Introduction

In the previous chapter, we delved into the world of communication patterns by implementing both REST and gRPC to perform CRUD (Create, Read, Update, Delete) operations. We began by establishing the folder structure for a well-organized codebase. Then, we build REST APIs for CRUD operations, comprising a REST-based books server and client. Testing of REST APIs was demonstrated using familiar tools like curl. We shifted our focus to gRPC, we defined proto files, generated code with the **protoc** compiler, and constructed gRPC-based books servers and clients. We tested in the gRPC facilitated by grpcurl and gRPC clients. To provide clarity, we contrasted REST and gRPC, discussing their respective strengths and weaknesses.

Extending our exploration of communication patterns, this chapter delves deeper into the versatile capabilities of gRPC. Unlike REST, which primarily follows a single request-response cycle from the client to the server, gRPC offers a more expansive array of communication options. In gRPC, we can initiate communication patterns where requests stream from the client to the server, resulting in a single response. Alternatively, we can send a solitary request and receive a continuous stream of responses, or we can engage in bi-directional streaming, allowing for concurrent interactions between client and server. Throughout this chapter, we delve into real-world scenarios where each of these communication patterns is indispensable, illustrating their practical applications through hands-on implementations. This exploration enhances our comprehension of how gRPC excels in managing diverse communication requirements.

Conventionally, communication between clients and servers has often followed a straightforward single request and response cycle, catering to a wide range of use cases. However, this simplicity led to certain trade-offs and challenges, such as latency issues, limitations in throughput, and difficulties in handling compute-intensive tasks. Over time, alternative strategies emerged, including REST polling and websockets, to address some of these limitations. Nevertheless, these approaches also had their own set of constraints. Enter gRPC, a modern solution that not only effectively tackles these challenges but also offers a more robust approach, effectively bridging the gaps left by previous implementations.

Gone are the days of compromising on performance and efficiency; gRPC brings a comprehensive solution that streamlines communication across various use cases. It minimizes latency, optimizes throughput, and simplifies complex computations, providing a versatile and powerful toolset for contemporary application development. Through this chapter, we will explore the nuances of gRPC's communication patterns and understand how they serve as a game-changer in addressing real-world use cases, elevating communication between clients and servers to a new level of efficiency and flexibility.

Structure

In this chapter, we will discuss the following topics:

- Explaining Unary RPC
- Server-side streaming
    - Context
    - Discuss use cases
    - Implement fibonacci api using REST based polling
    - Implement fibonacci server-side streaming with gRPC
- Client-side streaming
    - Context
    - Discuss use cases
    - Implement find-average client-side streaming using gRPC

- Bi-Directional streaming
  - o Context
  - o Discuss use cases
  - o Implement find-max bi-directional streaming using gRPC

Explaining Unary RPC

In the preceding chapter, we delved into the unary RPC, which represents the classic communication pattern between client and server involving request and response. We effectively carried out CRUD operations on a book resource. Let's look at a concise explanation of the same. Unary RPC, short for Remote Procedure Call, is a fundamental communication pattern in gRPC. It refers to a simple client-server interaction where the client sends a single request to the server and receives a single response in return. This one-to-one request-response model is similar to traditional HTTP request-response communication used in RESTful APIs. In the context of gRPC, unary RPC represents a straightforward way for a client to communicate with a server, making it suitable for many types of use cases, such as fetching data or performing basic CRUD (Create, Read, Update, Delete) operations.

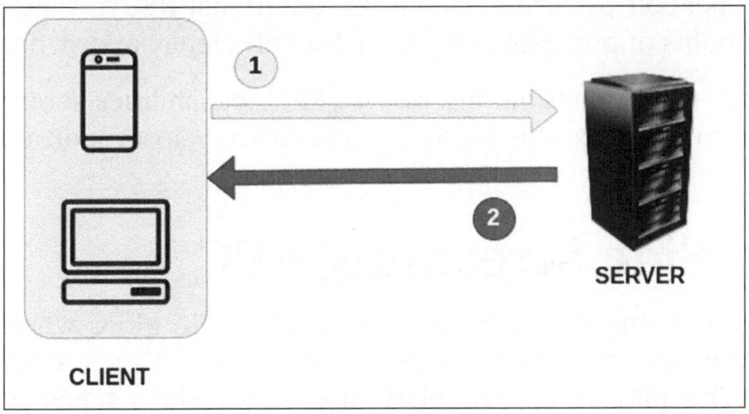

Figure 4.1: *Unary RPC communication between client and server*

The workflow of unary RPCs in gRPC follows a simple request-response pattern between a client and a server. Here's how it works:

- **Client Sends a Request**: The client initiates communication by sending a single request message to the server. This request message can contain data or instructions for the server, depending on the specific use case.

- **Server Processes the Request**: Upon receiving the request, the server processes it based on the defined gRPC service method associated with the request. The server may perform various operations, such as data retrieval, computation, or any other tasks, depending on the request's purpose.
- **Server Generates a Response**: After processing the request, the server generates a response message. This response message typically contains the result of the server's operations or any data requested by the client.
- **Server Sends the Response**: The server sends the response message back to the client.
- **Client Receives the Response**: The client receives the response from the server. The response can include data, status information, or any other relevant details based on the request.
- **Communication Concludes**: With the response received, the client has completed the unary RPC communication. The client can then use the response data or take further actions based on the server's reply.

Unary RPCs are suitable for use cases where a client needs to request specific information from a server or instruct the server to perform a particular action. This communication pattern is similar to traditional RESTful interactions but offers the benefits of protocol buffers, such as efficiency and strong typing.

However, what truly piques our interest is gRPC's capabilities in terms of diverse communication patterns. Our journey begins with a closer look at **Server-Side Streaming**.

Server-Side Streaming RPC

Server-side streaming is a communication pattern in gRPC where the server sends multiple responses to a single client request over a single long-lived connection. This pattern is particularly useful in various scenarios where the server has a series of data or events to share with the client.

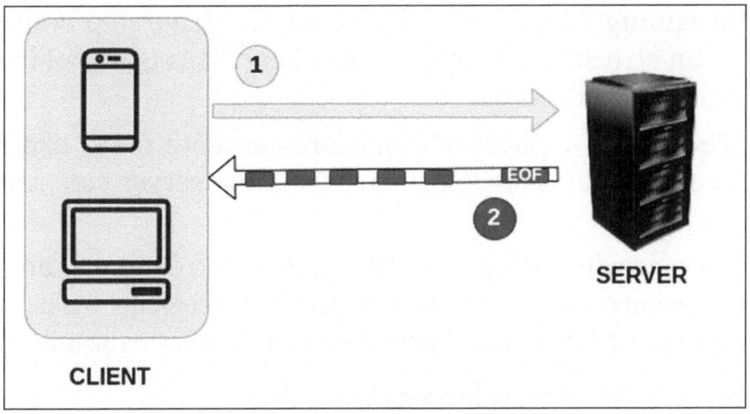

Figure 4.2: *Server-Side streaming RPC communication between client and server*

Key Features of Server-Side Streaming in gRPC:

- **Single Request, Multiple Responses**: In a server-side streaming RPC, the client sends a single request to the server, but the server can send an arbitrary number of responses back to the client. This contrasts with unary RPCs, where the server sends a single response for a single request.
- **Stream of Responses**: Server-side streaming allows the server to send a stream of responses to the client. This stream can represent a sequence of related data, events, or updates. The client reads these responses one by one as they arrive.
- **Efficient for Continuous Data**: This pattern is highly efficient for scenarios involving continuous data flows, real-time updates, or any situation where the server generates a series of related messages. It minimizes the overhead of opening and closing connections for each piece of data.
- **Flow Control:** gRPC supports flow control mechanisms, allowing the client to control the pace at which it consumes the streaming responses. This helps in managing resources efficiently, especially in situations where the server produces data faster than the client can consume it.

Common Use Cases for Server-Side Streaming:

- **Real-Time Updates**: For applications that require real-time updates, such as live sports scores, stock market data, online gaming, video streaming, or chat applications, server-side streaming allows the server to push updates to clients as soon as they are available.

- **Log Streaming**: In systems where logs are generated continuously, the server can stream log entries to the client. This is useful for monitoring and debugging purposes.
- **Data Feeds**: For applications that provide data feeds like social media feeds, news updates, or IoT sensor data, the server can stream the feed to clients in real-time.
- **Batch Processing Progress**: Server-side streaming can be used to provide progress updates during batch processing tasks, so the client can monitor the status and progress of a time-consuming operation.

Here's how server-side streaming works in gRPC:

1. **Service Definition**: First, we define a service (and messages) in Protocol Buffers (protobuf) that includes a method with a server-streaming RPC. For example:

   ```
   service MyService {
     rpc ServerStreamingMethod(MyRequest) returns (stream MyResponse);
   }
   ```

   In this example, **ServerStreamingMethod** is the server-side streaming method. It takes a single request of type **MyRequest** and returns a stream of **MyResponse** messages.

2. **Server Implementation**: On the server side (in our gRPC server application), we implement the **ServerStreamingMethod**. The server reads the request, processes it, and sends a stream of responses back to the client.

   ```
   func (s *MyServer) ServerStreamingMethod(req *pb.MyRequest, stream pb.MyService_ServerStreamingMethodServer) error {
       for i := 0; i < 10; i++ {
           response := &pb.MyResponse{Message: fmt.Sprintf("Response %d", i)}
           if err := stream.Send(response); err != nil {
               return err
           }
       }
       return nil
   }
   ```

In this Go example, the server sends 10 responses to the client over the streaming connection.

3. **Client Call**: On the client side (in our gRPC client application), we call the server-side streaming method and receive a stream of responses.

```
client := pb.NewMyServiceClient(conn)
request := &pb.MyRequest{...}

stream, err := client.ServerStreamingMethod(context.Background(),
request)
if err != nil {
    log.Fatalf("Error calling ServerStreamingMethod: %v", err)
}

for {
    response, err := stream.Recv()
    if err == io.EOF {
        break
    }
    if err != nil {
        log.Fatalf("Error receiving response: %v", err)
    }
    log.Printf("Received: %s", response.Message)
}
```

The client creates a stream and receives responses from the server until the server signals the end of the stream with an `EOF` (end-of-file) error.

Server-side streaming is useful when you need to send multiple related pieces of data from the server to the client, such as real-time updates, logs, or continuous data feeds. It's an efficient way to transfer data in a one-way flow from the server to the client.

Let's explore the previously mentioned use cases in more detail.

Use Case: Real-Time Updates

Real-time updates are a prominent use case for server-side streaming in gRPC. Real-time updates refer to the continuous and immediate delivery of new information or events to clients as they happen. This use case is relevant in a wide range of applications and industries. Let's explore real-world scenarios where this is beneficial:

- **Social Media Feeds**: On social media platforms like Facebook, Twitter, or Instagram, users expect to receive real-time updates on their feeds. When someone in their network posts a new message, shares a photo, or likes their content, these events trigger real-time updates. Server-side streaming in gRPC allows these platforms to push these updates to users as they occur.
- **Messaging Applications**: Messaging apps like WhatsApp, Slack, and Telegram rely heavily on real-time updates. When you're having a chat conversation, you want to see messages from your contact as soon as they're sent. Server-side streaming enables these apps to deliver incoming messages in real time.
- **Stock Market Data**: Investors and traders depend on real-time stock market data. Stock prices can change within milliseconds, and traders need immediate updates to make informed decisions. Server-side streaming is used to send real-time stock market data, ensuring that users receive up-to-the-second information.
- **Online Gaming**: Multiplayer online games require real-time updates to keep players synchronized. Actions performed by one player should be immediately visible to others. Whether it's a first-person shooter or a strategy game, server-side streaming ensures that game events are propagated in real time.
- **Live Sports Scores**: Sports enthusiasts rely on real-time updates for game scores, player statistics, and other game-related data. Sports apps and websites use server-side streaming to provide fans with continuous score updates and highlights.
- **Real-Time Collaboration**: Collaborative tools like Google Docs, Trello, and collaborative code editors, such as VS Code Live Share benefit from real-time updates. When multiple users collaborate on a document or project, changes made by one user should appear immediately to others.
- **Ride-Sharing Apps**: Ride-sharing services like Uber and Lyft use real-time updates to provide users with information about nearby drivers, estimated arrival times, and the progress of their ride. Passengers can track their driver's location in real time.
- **Internet of Things (IoT)**: IoT applications, such as smart home systems, weather stations, and industrial sensors, require real-time data

updates. Server-side streaming ensures that IoT devices can send data continuously to a central server or to user interfaces.

- **News and Content Aggregation**: News apps and content aggregation platforms use real-time updates to deliver breaking news, fresh articles, or the latest videos. Users get immediate access to the most recent content.
- **Video Streaming**: Platforms offering video streaming services, such as YouTube, Netflix, or live streaming platforms, utilize server-side streaming to deliver a continuous stream of video content to users in real time.

In these and many other scenarios, server-side streaming is essential for delivering information or events as they occur. It enhances user experiences by keeping users informed and engaged with real-time updates. It minimizes the need for users to manually refresh content or request updates, creating a more interactive and dynamic user experience.

Use Case: Log Streaming

In a log streaming use case, where log data from various sources is continuously collected and analyzed, server streaming in gRPC offers several key benefits:

- **Real-time Log Monitoring**: Server streaming allows log data to be continuously streamed from the server to the client. This enables real-time log monitoring, where logs are displayed as they are generated. Log administrators and DevOps teams can observe critical log events and troubleshoot issues in real time, minimizing system downtime and quickly addressing errors.
- **Efficient Log Aggregation**: Log streaming via gRPC allows logs from multiple sources to be aggregated into a single stream. This is particularly valuable in large-scale applications or microservices architectures. Centralized log aggregation simplifies log management, as log data from various sources can be consolidated into a single stream for analysis and storage.
- **Reduced Data Transfer Overhead**: Server streaming optimizes data transfer by sending log entries as they are generated rather than bundling them into large payloads. This approach reduces bandwidth and resource consumption, ensuring efficient log transmission over the network.
- **Dynamic Log Filters**: Server streaming can be enhanced with dynamic log filtering, where the client specifies the types of log events it wants to receive. Clients can filter logs based on log level, source, or specific

keywords, allowing them to focus on relevant log entries and ignore non-critical data.

- **Real-time Alerts and Notifications**: Log streaming can be paired with real-time alerting mechanisms. Whenever a log entry meets predefined criteria (for example, error messages, security breaches), the server can send notifications to clients. This proactive alerting ensures immediate attention to critical log events.
- **Historical Log Analysis**: While server streaming provides real-time access to log data, it can also support fetching historical logs. Clients can request logs within a specific time frame. Historical log analysis aids in identifying trends, diagnosing past issues, and maintaining compliance with data retention policies.
- **Scalability and Load Distribution**: Log streaming using gRPC is built for scalability. As log volumes grow, additional log sources and clients can be easily integrated into the system. Load distribution ensures that log data is efficiently handled even in high-traffic scenarios.
- **Resource Optimization**: Server streaming uses long-lived connections, reducing the overhead of repeatedly establishing new connections for each log entry. This connection reuse is more resource-efficient compared to traditional polling-based approaches.
- **Secure Data Transmission**: gRPC supports Transport Layer Security (TLS) for secure communication. Log data can be encrypted and authenticated, preventing unauthorized access and data tampering.
- **Third-Party Integration**: The server streaming architecture can be integrated with third-party log management and analysis tools. It allows logs to be exported or analyzed in external log monitoring systems, providing flexibility in log data usage.

In summary, server streaming in the context of log streaming is beneficial for real-time log monitoring, efficient aggregation and analysis of log data, proactive alerting, and dynamic log filtering. It enhances the scalability and resource optimization of log management systems while ensuring the secure and reliable transmission of log information. This approach is particularly valuable for mission-critical applications where log data plays a crucial role in maintaining system health and diagnosing issues.

Use Case: Batch Processing

In a batch processing use case, server streaming in gRPC offers several advantages that are particularly beneficial:

- **Efficient Data Transmission**: Server streaming allows the server to efficiently stream batches of processed data to the client without having to wait for the entire batch to complete. This reduces latency and provides more responsive feedback to clients.
- **Parallel Processing**: Server streaming enables the server to process data in parallel and stream the results as they become available. Clients can start processing streamed data while the server is still working on the remainder of the batch. This concurrent processing can significantly improve throughput.
- **Progressive Results**: As the server streams partial results, clients can work with this data without having to wait for the entire batch processing to finish. This is especially valuable in scenarios where real-time or near-real-time insights are required.
- **Scalability**: In batch processing, scalability is crucial. Server streaming can accommodate an increasing number of clients and data sources. As the number of clients grows, additional server instances can be deployed to handle the load, and each server can independently stream results.
- **Resource Optimization**: The server maintains long-lived connections with clients, reducing the overhead of repeated connection establishment for each batch. This reduces resource consumption on both the server and client sides, enhancing the overall system's efficiency.
- **Error Handling**: During batch processing, errors can occur. Server streaming allows the server to immediately notify clients of any errors, enabling rapid corrective action. Clients can react to errors in real-time, facilitating efficient troubleshooting and rerunning of specific processing steps.
- **Data-Intensive Operations**: In batch processing, operations can be data-intensive. Server streaming handles data transmission efficiently and is well-suited for use cases that involve large datasets. This approach ensures that large volumes of processed data are available to clients without overloading network resources.
- **Customized Processing**: Server streaming allows clients to define their processing steps based on intermediate results. Clients can adapt processing steps dynamically, enhancing the flexibility of batch processing pipelines.
- **Feedback-Driven Processing**: Clients can provide feedback to the server during processing. For example, they can request specific subsets of data

or adjust processing parameters. This interactive exchange of data and feedback is a valuable feature in data processing pipelines.

- **Data Aggregation and Transformation**: Batch processing often involves data aggregation and transformation. Clients can process and transform data as it arrives, facilitating various data processing operations.

In summary, server streaming in the batch processing use case enables efficient data transmission, parallel processing, progressive results, scalability, and resource optimization. It enhances the error-handling capabilities, particularly for data-intensive operations, and provides the flexibility to customize and adapt processing steps. The feedback-driven approach and support for data aggregation and transformation make it a powerful tool for managing large-scale batch processing workflows efficiently. This approach is particularly valuable in scenarios where timely insights from large datasets are essential.

Use case: Data Feeds

In data feeds use case, server streaming in gRPC offers several advantages that are particularly beneficial:

- **Real-Time Data Delivery**: Server streaming allows the server to continuously stream real-time data updates to clients as soon as they become available. This feature is essential for scenarios where receiving data as it happens is critical, such as financial market updates, IoT sensor data, or news feeds.
- **Low Latency**: Server streaming reduces the latency in data delivery since there's no need for clients to repeatedly request updates. Data is pushed to clients as soon as it's available, ensuring minimal delay.
- **Bandwidth Efficiency**: The server streaming approach is bandwidth-efficient because data is sent only once to multiple clients, reducing network congestion and resource consumption.
- **Scalability**: In data feeds, the number of clients can grow rapidly. Server streaming can accommodate large numbers of clients, and additional servers can be deployed to handle increased loads. The system scales efficiently to serve more clients.
- **Customized Subscriptions**: Clients can subscribe to specific data feeds of interest. They receive only the data they're interested in, reducing unnecessary data transmission and processing.
- **Error Handling**: Server streaming allows immediate notification of errors or disruptions in data feeds. Clients can respond to errors in real-time, take appropriate action, and ensure data consistency and integrity.

- **Data Transformation**: Clients can perform real-time data transformations and analysis on the incoming data streams. This feature is valuable in applications like real-time analytics or data filtering.
- **Filtering and Aggregation**: Server streaming provides the flexibility to filter, aggregate, or combine data streams, allowing clients to receive customized data. Clients can request aggregated data views or specific data subsets.
- **Real-Time Processing**: Clients can perform real-time processing on data feeds, making immediate decisions or generating alerts based on incoming data. This feature is critical in applications like fraud detection or predictive maintenance.
- **Feedback and Interaction**: Clients can provide feedback or interact with the server, dynamically adjusting their subscriptions or requesting specific data slices. This enables personalized and responsive data feeds.

In summary, server streaming in the data feeds use case enables real-time data delivery, low latency, bandwidth efficiency, scalability, and customized subscriptions. It enhances error handling, data transformation, filtering, and aggregation, allowing clients to perform real-time processing and receive tailored data feeds. The feedback and interaction capabilities make it a powerful tool for applications that rely on timely and personalized data updates. Server streaming is particularly valuable in scenarios where real-time data feeds are essential, such as financial services, IoT applications, and media content distribution.

Having explored the scenarios where gRPC's server-side streaming shines, it piques our curiosity to examine whether this can be achieved using conventional frameworks like REST with polling or WebSockets. To comprehend why gRPC might offer advantages, let's delve into a comparative analysis. This involves assessing factors such as real-time updates, log streaming, data feeds, and batch processing to understand the strengths and weaknesses of gRPC's server-side streaming in contrast to REST polling and WebSockets in different use cases. This exploration will provide a comprehensive view of the capabilities and limitations of these communication methods.

Polling in REST Framework:

In the context of REST (Representational State Transfer) architecture, polling is a client-server communication mechanism where the client repeatedly queries the server for updates or changes in resource status. This approach is used when the client needs to obtain real-time or near-real-time information about a resource, but the server does not automatically push updates to the client.

Instead, the client initiates requests at regular intervals to check for updates.

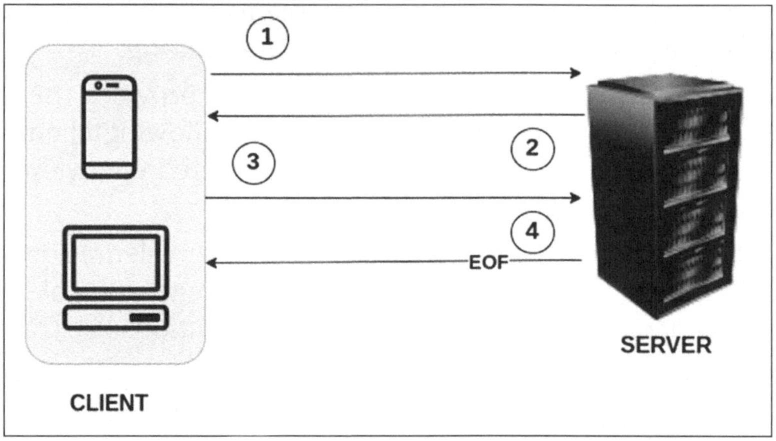

Figure 4.3: *REST polling communication between client and server*

Here's how polling works in the REST framework:

1. **Client Initiation**: The client initiates HTTP requests to the server at predetermined intervals or whenever it needs to check for updates. These requests typically involve HTTP GET requests to a specific resource endpoint.
2. **Server Response**: The server processes the client's request and responds with the current state or status of the requested resource. If there are no updates, the response may indicate that no changes have occurred.
3. **Client Repeats**: The client continues to poll the server periodically, repeating the request-response cycle to retrieve the latest information. The polling frequency is determined by the client's requirements or the nature of the resource being monitored.
4. **Handling Updates**: If the server detects updates or changes in the resource, it responds with the new data or status, which the client processes accordingly. The client is responsible for detecting differences between the current state and the previous state and taking appropriate actions.

Characteristics and Considerations:

- **Client-Driven**: In polling, the client is responsible for initiating communication. It decides when to check for updates, making it a client-driven approach.

- **Latency**: Polling introduces some level of latency since the client needs to wait for the next polling interval to receive updates. The frequency of polling affects the perceived real-time nature of the system.
- **Scalability**: Polling can put a burden on the server, especially if there are many clients polling frequently. Proper server optimization is necessary to handle large-scale polling.
- **Resource Efficiency**: Polling can be less efficient in terms of network and server resource usage compared to server push mechanisms like WebSockets.
- **Synchronization**: Clients need to implement logic for tracking the state of the resource and ensuring they do not miss any updates between polls.
- **Use Cases**: Polling is used in scenarios where real-time updates are required, but implementing server push mechanisms (like WebSockets) is not feasible. Common use cases include monitoring changes in data, checking for new messages or notifications, or tracking dynamic resource states.

Overall, polling in the REST framework is a practical way to achieve real-time or near-real-time communication between clients and servers when automatic updates are not possible or when the overhead of implementing server push mechanisms is not justified. It places the responsibility for timely updates on the client, which periodically queries the server for changes in resource state.

gRPC Server-Side Streaming versus REST Polling:

gRPC server-side streaming and REST polling are two different communication patterns, each with its own characteristics and use cases. Let's compare these two approaches:

Data Flow:

- **gRPC Server-Side Streaming**: In gRPC server-side streaming, the server sends a stream of data to the client over a single connection. The server can keep sending data to the client as it becomes available. The client can read from this stream continuously.
- **REST Polling**: In REST polling, the client initiates requests to the server at regular intervals or when it needs updates. The server responds to each request with the current state or changes.

Real-Time Updates:

- **gRPC Server-Side Streaming**: gRPC streaming provides a more real-time experience, as data is pushed from the server to the client as soon as it's available. This minimizes latency.
- **REST Polling**: REST polling introduces latency because the client has to wait for the next polling interval to receive updates. It may not be as real-time as gRPC.

Efficiency:

- **gRPC Server-Side Streaming**: gRPC is more efficient in terms of data transfer and resource usage because it maintains a single connection for the entire streaming session.
- **REST Polling**: REST polling can be less efficient, especially when clients poll frequently, as it requires opening and closing multiple HTTP connections.

Scalability:

- **gRPC Server-Side Streaming**: gRPC can handle a large number of clients efficiently due to its multiplexing and streaming capabilities.
- **REST Polling**: REST polling can become burdensome on the server, especially with many clients polling frequently, requiring server optimizations.

Complexity:

- **gRPC Server-Side Streaming**: Implementing gRPC server-side streaming requires defining streaming RPCs in the protocol buffer (protobuf) file, which can be more straightforward for developers.
- **REST Polling**: REST polling might require more complex client logic for handling state changes and missed updates between polling intervals.

Use Cases:

- **gRPC Server-Side Streaming**: Ideal for scenarios where the server needs to continuously push updates or a stream of data to clients. Use cases include real-time chat applications, live sports scores, or telemetry data from IoT devices.
- **REST Polling**: Commonly used when real-time updates are required but implementing server push mechanisms (like WebSockets) is not feasible. Use cases include monitoring changes in data, checking for new messages or notifications, or tracking dynamic resource states.

Latency Control:

- **gRPC Server-Side Streaming**: Provides lower latency, as data is pushed to the client as soon as it's available.
- **REST Polling**: Introduces some level of latency, as clients must wait for the next polling interval.

Resource Usage:

- **gRPC Server-Side Streaming**: More efficient in terms of network and server resource usage, as it maintains a persistent connection.
- **REST Polling**: Can be less efficient, especially with frequent polling, as it involves repeated connection establishment and data transfer.

In summary, gRPC server-side streaming is a more efficient and low-latency solution for scenarios where continuous data updates are required. REST polling is suitable when real-time updates are needed, but implementing more complex server push mechanisms is not practical. The choice between them depends on the specific requirements of the application.

Let's dive into the practical implementation of gRPC server-side streaming by building a Fibonacci service that streams the Fibonacci sequence from the server to the client. We chose the Fibonacci sequence because the recursive method for generating it becomes computationally intensive as the sequence length increases. This can lead to server response times exceeding a few seconds, which is not ideal. In fact, we aim for responses within 2-3 seconds. This scenario provides an excellent opportunity to showcase server-side streaming in action. The goal is to stream Fibonacci numbers to the client as soon as they're computed. We'll also compare this gRPC approach with the REST polling method for a better understanding of the differences.

The entire code base can be referred from here:

https://github.com/OrangeAVA/Modern-API-Design-with-gRPC/tree/main/chapter-4

We've opted for a simplified folder structure in this project since our main focus is to showcase various communication patterns.

Directory: */cmd*

This directory serves as the hub for entry points of all applications within this codebase. It includes distinct main applications, such as a gRPC-based fibonacci client and a gRPC-based fibonacci server. Each application is housed within its own subdirectory, and the subdirectory's name precisely matches the name of the corresponding executable (for example, **/cmd/grpc-fibonacci-server**).

Directory: */apps*

In this directory, you'll find the actual implementations of the applications. Each application resides in its respective subdirectory, and the name of the subdirectory directly corresponds to the name of the executable (for example, **/cmd/grpc-fibonacci-server**).

Directory: */proto*

Within this directory, you'll find the protobuf files and the accompanying auto-generated code essential for gRPC server and client operations.

Let's begin with the **REST Polling** implementation of the fibonacci server.

Path: ~/chapter-4/apps/rest-fibonacci-server/rest-fibonacci-server.go

The code for REST fibonacci server routing and middleware implementation can be viewed here:

https://github.com/OrangeAVA/Modern-API-Design-with-gRPC/blob/main/chapter-4/apps/rest-fibonacci-server/rest-fibonacci-server.go

Following is the code explanation for the same:

This code defines a simple REST Fibonacci server in Go. Here's a breakdown of its key components:

1. `App Struct`: This struct represents the main application. It contains an `asyncStores` map, which is used to store asynchronous Fibonacci calculations. It's initialized as an empty map when a new instance of the **App** is created.
2. `NewApp() Function`: This function creates and returns a new App instance, initializing the **asyncStores** map.
3. `Start() Function`: This function sets up the REST server. It creates a new Gorilla Mux router, applies a middleware for generating request IDs, and defines two routes for handling Fibonacci calculations.
    a. `/fibonacci/sync/{number:[0-9]+}:` This route is used for synchronous (blocking) Fibonacci calculations. The server will respond with the Fibonacci sequence for the provided number directly. The purpose of this API is to showcase the amount of time this takes for a higher number.

   b. **`/fibonacci/async/{number:[0-9]+}:`** This route is used for asynchronous Fibonacci calculations. The server initiates an asynchronous calculation and returns a request ID to the client. This API actually demonstrates REST polling.

   c. The server listens on port **8080** and prints a message to the console to indicate that it's running.

4. **`generateRequestIDMiddleware() Function`**: This is a middleware function that generates a unique request ID if one is not provided in the request's headers. It uses the **`github.com/google/uuid`** library to create a UUID and adds it to the request's headers with the key **`request-id`**. The purpose of employing this middleware to include a request ID in the request is to preserve state information for future requests. This enables the server to determine whether a new Fibonacci sequence calculation needs to be started or if it should continue with a previously initiated sequence. This is going to be a deterministic factor in deciding why to use gRPC server stream over REST polling.

This code sets up a basic REST server that can calculate Fibonacci numbers either synchronously or asynchronously, depending on the provided route. It uses Gorilla Mux for routing and includes a middleware to ensure each request has a unique identifier.

Path: ~/chapter-4/apps/rest-fibonacci-server/sync-handler.go

The code for REST fibonacci server sync handler implementation can be viewed here:

https://github.com/OrangeAVA/Modern-API-Design-with-gRPC/blob/main/chapter-4/apps/rest-fibonacci-server/sync-handler.go .

Following is the code explanation for the same:

This code defines an HTTP handler function, **`fibonacciSyncHandler`** for the REST Fibonacci server. It calculates Fibonacci numbers synchronously up to the specified number, and then it returns the result as a JSON response.

Here's how the code works:

1. The function extracts the value of the number from the URL path using the **Gorilla Mux** router.
2. It converts the number to an integer and performs error checking. If the conversion fails, it sends an HTTP error response with a 400 Bad Request status.

3. The function then calculates Fibonacci numbers up to the given number. It iterates through the numbers from 0 to **numFibonacci**, calling the **fib** function to calculate each Fibonacci number.
4. It records the time it took to perform the calculation using the **time** package.
5. It constructs a response containing the time taken and the list of Fibonacci numbers.
6. The response is marshaled to JSON, and the content type of the response is set to **application/json.**
7. Finally, the response is written to the HTTP response writer (w).

The **fib** function is a simple recursive implementation of Fibonacci sequence calculation.

In summary, this handler calculates Fibonacci numbers up to the specified value and sends the result as a JSON response, including the time taken for the calculation.

Path: ~/chapter-4/apps/rest-fibonacci-server/async-handler.go

The code for REST fibonacci server async handler implementation can be viewed here:

https://github.com/OrangeAVA/Modern-API-Design-with-gRPC/blob/main/chapter-4/apps/rest-fibonacci-server/async-handler.go.

Following is the code explanation for the same:

This code defines an HTTP handler function **fibonacciAsyncHandler** for the REST Fibonacci server, which calculates Fibonacci numbers asynchronously based on client requests. The server also streams the results to clients as they become available.

Here's how the code works:

1. The function extracts the value of the number from the URL path and validates it, just like in the synchronous handler.
2. It also extracts the **request-id** from the HTTP request headers. This identifier helps maintain the state of the ongoing calculation for each client. If no **request-id** is provided in the request, it responds with a 400 Bad Request status.
3. The code checks whether an **AsyncStore** exists for the given **request-id.** If not, it creates a new one, initiating an asynchronous Fibonacci

calculation for the specified number. A **goroutine** is launched to perform this computation concurrently.

4. The code periodically reads results from the **AsyncStore.** It retrieves the computed Fibonacci numbers, along with the current calculation progress (current) and the requested range (requested). The current value represents the last Fibonacci number computed, and requested is the target range.
5. If the current number equals the requested range, it indicates that the calculation is complete. In this case, the handler sets the **EndOfResponse** field in the response to true and removes the associated **AsyncStore** since the calculation has finished.
6. A response is constructed containing the **request-id,** the retrieved Fibonacci numbers, and whether it's the end of the response.
7. The response is marshaled to JSON, and the content type of the response is set to **application/json.**
8. The response is sent to the client.
9. An asynchronous function **fibAsync** is defined to compute Fibonacci numbers up to the specified range. It calculates and writes these numbers to the corresponding **AsyncStore.**

In summary, this handler allows clients to request Fibonacci numbers asynchronously and streams the results as they become available. The code maintains separate states for each client's calculation and delivers responses accordingly. This approach can significantly reduce latency when dealing with computationally intensive operations.

Path: ~/chapter-4/cmd/rest-fibonacci-server/main.go

```
package main


import restfibonacciserver "github.com/OrangeAVA/Modern-API-Design-with-gRPC/chapter-4/apps/rest-fibonacci-server"


func main() {

    app := restfibonacciserver.NewApp()

    app.Start()

}
```

This code is the entry point for the REST Fibonacci server. Here's a breakdown of what it does:

1. It imports the **`restfibonacciserver`** package, which contains the implementation of the REST server for computing Fibonacci numbers asynchronously.
2. In the **`main`** function, it creates an instance of the REST Fibonacci server application by calling the **`NewApp`** function from the imported package. This initializes the server application with any necessary configurations and data structures.
3. It then starts the server by invoking the **`Start`** method on the app object. This method sets up the HTTP server, initializes routes, and begins listening for incoming HTTP requests. The server will start and be accessible on port **`8080.`**

In summary, this code is the main entry point for the REST Fibonacci server, initializing and starting the server application defined in the **`restfibonacciserver`** package. The server is configured to compute Fibonacci numbers asynchronously and respond to client requests over HTTP.

Path: ~/chapter-4/apps/rest-fibonacci-client/rest-fibonacci-client.go

The code for the REST fibonacci client implementation can be viewed here:

https://github.com/OrangeAVA/Modern-API-Design-with-gRPC/blob/main/chapter-4/apps/rest-fibonacci-client/rest-fibonacci-client.go.

Following is the code explanation for the same:

This code defines a REST Fibonacci client application. Here's a breakdown of its functionality:

1. It imports necessary packages like **`flag`** for command-line argument parsing, **`fmt`** for formatting output, **`io/ioutil`** for reading response bodies, **`net/http`** for making HTTP requests, and **`time`** for time-related operations.
2. It defines command-line flags for configuring the client's behavior. The **`typeOfCall`** flag specifies whether the client should make synchronous or asynchronous calls to the server. The **`number`** flag is used to specify the Fibonacci number for which the sequence is to be generated.
3. In the **`init`** function, it sets the default values for the flags, providing a way to specify the type of call and the Fibonacci number when running the client.

4. The **App** struct is created to represent the client application.
5. The **NewApp** function initializes and returns a new App instance.
6. The **Start** method is the main function for the client application. It does the following:
   a. Parses the command-line flags to determine the type of call (synchronous or asynchronous) and the Fibonacci number.
   b. Constructs the base URL for the REST server.
   c. If the type of call is **sync,** it sends a synchronous GET request to the server to compute the Fibonacci sequence and displays the result.
   d. If the type of call is **async,** it enters a loop to repeatedly send asynchronous GET requests. It waits for responses and checks if the **endOfResponse** field in the JSON response indicates the end of the sequence. If so, it breaks out of the loop, it also extracts and stores the **request-id** header from the response for subsequent requests.
   e. Sleeps for 5 seconds between each asynchronous request to avoid overloading the server.
   f. The **sendRequest** function is used to send HTTP GET requests. It takes a URL and a map of headers as input, constructs the request, sends it to the server, and processes the response. If the response status code is not in the 2xx range, it returns an error.

In summary, this code defines a REST client application that can make synchronous and asynchronous requests to a REST server for computing Fibonacci sequences. The client takes command-line arguments to specify the type of call and the Fibonacci number and communicates with the server through HTTP requests.

Path: ~/chapter-4/cmd/rest-fibonacci-client/main.go

```
package main


import restfibonacciclient "github.com/OrangeAVA/Modern-API-Design-with-gRPC/chapter-4/apps/rest-fibonacci-client"


func main() {

   app := restfibonacciclient.NewApp()
```

```
    app.Start()
}
```

This code is the entry point for the Go application that serves as a REST client for a Fibonacci service. Here's a breakdown of what the code does:

- **Package Import**: The code imports the `restfibonacciclient` package, which contains the client implementation for the Fibonacci service. This allows the main function to use the client's functionality.
- **Main Function**: The `main` function is the entry point of the application. Within this function, the following steps are taken:
    - **App Initialization**: An instance of the `App` struct from the `restfibonacciclient` package is created by calling the `NewApp()` function. This instance represents the client application.
    - **Application Start**: The `Start()` method of the `App` instance is called. This method initiates the client application, which includes making requests to the Fibonacci service based on the provided command-line arguments.

In summary, this code serves as the starting point for the REST client application. It initializes the client, and upon execution, the client starts making requests to the Fibonacci service as specified by its implementation.

Now we shall start the REST fibonacci server using following command:

```
go run chapter-4/cmd/rest-fibonacci-server/main.go
```

Let's test, by invoking the REST fibonacci client, a few scenarios and draw out inferences:

1. **sync** API with a smaller limit:

   ```
   go run chapter-4/cmd/rest-fibonacci-client/main.go --typeOfCall sync --number 10
   // response
   Synchronous Fibonacci sequence result for 10: {"timeTaken":"0.000002 seconds","fibonacciNumbers":[0,1,1,2,3,5,8,13,21,34]}
   ```

   Please notice the `timeTaken` which is very miniscule.

2. **sync** API with a bigger limit:

   ```
   go run chapter-4/cmd/rest-fibonacci-client/main.go --typeOfCall sync --number 45
   // response
   ```

```
Synchronous Fibonacci sequence result for 45: {"timeTaken":"10.637090 seconds","fibonacciNumbers":[0,1,1,2,3,5,8,13,21,34,55,89,144,233,377,610,987,1597,2584,4181,6765,10946,17711,28657,46368,75025,121393,196418,317811,514229,832040,1346269,2178309,3524578,5702887,9227465,14930352,24157817,39088169,63245986,102334155,165580141,267914296,433494437,701408733]}
```

Please take note of the **timeTaken** which is significantly high, and this is not ideal for a request-response cycle. However, on the server side, it might not be possible to compute the results much faster. Therefore, the only solution is to make repeated requests to the server to fetch subsequent results.

3. **async** API with a bigger limit

```
go run chapter-4/cmd/rest-fibonacci-client/main.go --typeOfCall async --number 45

// response

Asynchronous Fibonacci result for 45: {"requestid":"2c445262-b1fe-4288-aa50-666f82def0c8","fibonacciNumbers":[],"endOfResponse":false}

Asynchronous Fibonacci result for 45: {"requestid":"2c445262-b1fe-4288-aa50-666f82def0c8","fibonacciNumbers":[0,1,1,2,3,5,8,13,21,34,55,89,144,233,377,610,987,1597, 2584,4181,6765,10946,17711,28657,46368,75025,121393,196418,317811,514229,832040,1346269,2178309,3524578,5702887,9227465,14930352,24157817,39088169,63245986,102334155,165580141,267914296],"endOfResponse":false}

Asynchronous Fibonacci result for 45: {"requestid":"2c445262-b1fe-4288-aa50-666f82def0c8","fibonacciNumbers":[433494437],"endOfResponse":false}

Asynchronous Fibonacci result for 45: {"requestid":"2c445262-b1fe-4288-aa50-666f82def0c8","fibonacciNumbers":[701408733],"endOfResponse":true}
```

It's important to observe that the client initiated several requests to the server, fetching portions of the Fibonacci sequence as they became available. Although the total time taken would have been the same as in **scenario #2**, this approach maintained the user engagement. The client stops polling based on the **"endOfResponse"** field received from the server.

Now let's look at how we can implement the same functionality with gRPC. Like every gRPC RPC implementation, we shall start by defining messages and services in a **proto** file and generate code using **protoc** compiler.

Path: ~/chapter-4/proto/fibonacci.proto

```
syntax = "proto3";


package proto;

option go_package="./proto";


message FibonacciRequest{

    int32 number = 1;

}


message SyncFibonacciResponse{

    string timeTaken = 1;

    repeated int32 fibonacciNumbers = 2;

}


message AsyncFibonacciResponse{

    int32 sequence = 1;

    int32 fibonacciNumber = 2;

}



service FibonacciService{

  // Unary

  rpc SyncFibonacci(FibonacciRequest) returns (SyncFibonacciResponse) {};
```

```
  // Server Streaming

  rpc AsyncFibonacci(FibonacciRequest) returns (stream
  AsyncFibonacciResponse) {};

}
```

This is a Protocol Buffers (proto3) definition for a gRPC service called **FibonacciService**. It includes the following message types and RPC methods:

- **`FibonacciRequest`**: This message contains a single field number, which is an int32. It is used as a parameter in both of the service's RPC methods to specify the number of Fibonacci numbers to generate.
- **`SyncFibonacciResponse:`** This message is returned by the SyncFibonacci RPC method. It includes two fields: **`timeTaken`**, which is a string representing the time taken for the operation, and **`fibonacciNumbers,`** which is a repeated (array) field containing a list of int32 values representing the generated Fibonacci numbers.
- **`AsyncFibonacciResponse`**: This message is used for server-side streaming. It contains two fields: sequence, an int32 representing the sequence position of the Fibonacci number, and **`fibonacciNumber`**, an int32 representing the actual Fibonacci number.
- **`FibonacciService`**: This is the service definition. It includes two RPC methods:
  - **`SyncFibonacci`**: This is a unary RPC method that takes a FibonacciRequest and returns a **`SyncFibonacciResponse.`**
  - **`AsyncFibonacci`**: This is a server-side streaming RPC method that also takes a **`FibonacciRequest`** but returns a stream of **`AsyncFibonacciResponse`** messages.

The service and message definitions are used for generating code in multiple programming languages, making it easier to implement and use gRPC-based services.

We can generate the code using **protoc** compiler with the following command:

```
protoc --go_out=chapter-4/proto --go-grpc_out=chapter-4/ chapter-4/proto/fibonacci.proto
```

The generated code for the preceding fibonacci.proto file can be viewed at the following links:

- https://github.com/OrangeAVA/Modern-API-Design-with-gRPC/blob/main/chapter-4/proto/fibonacci.pb.go

- https://github.com/OrangeAVA/Modern-API-Design-with-gRPC/blob/main/chapter-4/proto/fibonacci_grpc.pb.go

Path: ~/chapter-4/apps/grpc-fibonacci-server/grpc-fibonacci-server.go

The code for the gRPC fibonacci server implementation can be viewed here:

https://github.com/OrangeAVA/Modern-API-Design-with-gRPC/blob/main/chapter-4/apps/grpc-fibonacci-server/grpc-fibonacci-server.go.

The code explanation for the same is as follows:

This code defines a gRPC server for a Fibonacci service. The server has two main RPC methods:

1. **`SyncFibonacci`**: This is a unary RPC method. It takes a request containing the number of Fibonacci numbers to generate. The server calculates these numbers synchronously and sends the response, including the time taken and the Fibonacci numbers, back to the client.
2. **`AsyncFibonacci`**: This is a server-side streaming RPC method. It also takes the number of Fibonacci numbers to generate but calculates them asynchronously. As the numbers are generated, they are streamed to the client one by one, along with their sequence positions.

The server is initialized in the **`Start`** function, which binds it to a specified address and port, and the methods are registered with the gRPC server. The server listens for incoming client requests and handles them accordingly. This code allows clients to request Fibonacci numbers either synchronously or asynchronously using gRPC.

Path: ~/chapter-4/cmd/grpc-fibonacci-server/main.go

```
package main

import grpcfibonacciserver "github.com/OrangeAVA/Modern-API-Design-with-gRPC/chapter-4/apps/grpc-fibonacci-server"

func main() {
    app := grpcfibonacciserver.NewApp()
    app.Start()
}
```

This code is the entry point for the Go application that serves as a gRPC server for a Fibonacci service. Here's a breakdown of what the code does:

- **Package Import**: The code imports the `grpcfibonacciserver` package, which contains the server implementation for the Fibonacci service. This allows the main function to use the server's functionality.
- **Main Function**: The main function is the entry point of the application. Within this function, the following steps are taken:
    - o **App Initialization**: An instance of the **App** struct from the `grpcfibonacciserver` package is created by calling the `NewApp()` function. This instance represents the server application.
    - o **Application Start**: The `Start()` method of the App instance is called. This method initiates the server application, which includes starting the gRPC server and setting it up to handle incoming requests for the Fibonacci service.

In summary, this code serves as the starting point for the gRPC server application. It initializes the server, and upon execution, the server starts listening for incoming gRPC requests for the Fibonacci service, as specified by its implementation.

Path: ~/chapter-4/apps/grpc-fibonacci-client/grpc-fibonacci-client.go

The code for the gRPC fibonacci client implementation can be viewed here:

https://github.com/OrangeAVA/Modern-API-Design-with-gRPC/blob/main/chapter-4/apps/grpc-fibonacci-client/grpc-fibonacci-client.go.

The code explanation for the same is as follows:

This code is an example of a gRPC client implemented in Go for a service that generates Fibonacci sequences. Let's break down what the code does:

- **Initialization and Command Line Arguments**: The client initializes by reading command line arguments. It expects two arguments: **typeOfCall** and **number**. **typeOfCall** specifies whether to make synchronous or asynchronous calls, and **number** specifies the value for which to generate the Fibonacci sequence.
- **gRPC Connection**: The client connects to the gRPC server located at `localhost:50051` using an insecure connection. It creates a gRPC client to communicate with the server.
- **Synchronous Call**: If the `typeOfCall` is set to `sync` the client calls the `syncFibonacci` function to make a synchronous gRPC call. In this case,

the client sends a single request to the server, requesting the Fibonacci sequence for the specified number.

- **Asynchronous Call**: If the **typeOfCall** is set to **async** the client calls the **asyncFibonacci** function to make an asynchronous gRPC call. In this case, the client initiates a server streaming RPC, where it sends a single request and receives a stream of Fibonacci numbers.
- **Synchronous Call Function**: The **syncFibonacci** function sends a single request to the server and receives a response. It logs the Fibonacci sequence and the time taken to calculate it.
- **Asynchronous Call Function**: The **asyncFibonacci** function initiates the server streaming RPC and repeatedly reads messages from the stream until an end-of-stream (EOF) condition is reached. It logs each Fibonacci number as it's received.
- **Shutdown**: After completing the gRPC calls, the client closes the gRPC connection using the **Shutdown** function.

This code demonstrates how to use gRPC to make both synchronous and asynchronous calls to a server for generating Fibonacci sequences based on the user's choice of communication pattern.

Path: ~/chapter-4/cmd/grpc-fibonacci-client/main.go

```
package main


import grpcfibonacciclient "github.com/OrangeAVA/Modern-API-Design-with-gRPC/chapter-4/apps/grpc-fibonacci-client"


func main() {

    app := grpcfibonacciclient.NewApp()

    app.Start()


    app.Shutdown()

}
```

This code is the entry point for the Go application that acts as a gRPC client for the Fibonacci service. Let's break down what this code does:

- **Package Import**: The code imports the **`grpcfibonacciclient`** package, which contains the client implementation for the Fibonacci service. This allows the main function to use the client's functionality.
- **Main Function**: The main function is the entry point of the application. Within this function, the following steps are taken:
- **App Initialization**: An instance of the **`App`** struct from the **`grpcfibonacciclient`** package is created by calling the **`NewApp()`** function. This instance represents the client application.
- **Application Start**: The **`Start()`** method of the App instance is called. This method initiates the client application and sends gRPC requests to the Fibonacci service. Depending on the specific command-line parameters or configuration, it can make either synchronous or asynchronous requests to the service.
- **Application Shutdown**: After the client application has completed its tasks (in this case, making gRPC requests), it's a good practice to gracefully shut down any resources or connections. In this code, the **`Shutdown()`** method of the App instance is called. This method is responsible for closing any open gRPC connections or performing other cleanup operations.

In summary, this code is the starting point for a gRPC client application that interacts with the Fibonacci service. It initializes the client, sends gRPC requests to the server, and then properly shuts down the client application, ensuring that any resources are released gracefully.

Now we shall start the gRPC fibonacci server using the following command:

```
go run chapter-4/cmd/grpc-fibonacci-server/main.go
```

Let's test, by invoking the gRPC fibonacci client, a few scenarios and draw out inferences:

1. **`SyncFibonacci`** RPC with a smaller number:

   ```
   go run chapter-4/cmd/grpc-fibonacci-client/main.go --typeOfCall sync --number 10
   ```

   ```
   // response
   ```

   ```
   2023/10/18 13:48:15 Synchronous Fibonacci sequence result for 10: 0,1,1,2,3,5,8,13,21,34, and time taken was: 2.946e-06 seconds
   ```

   Please notice the **`timeTaken`** which is very miniscule.

2. **SyncFibonacci** RPC with a bigger number:

```
go run chapter-4/cmd/grpc-fibonacci-client/main.go --typeOfCall sync --number 45
```

```
// response
```

```
2023/10/18 13:49:45 Synchronous Fibonacci sequence result for 45: 0,1,1,2,3,5,8,13,21,34,55,89,144,233,377,610,987,1597,2584,4181,6765,10946,17711,28657,46368,75025,121393,196418,317811,514229,832040,1346269,2178309,3524578,5702887,9227465,14930352,24157817,39088169,63245986,102334155,165580141,267914296,433494437,701408733, and time taken was: 11.559436292000001 seconds
```

Please take note of the **`timeTaken`** which is significantly high here as well.

3. **`AsyncFibonacci`** RPC with a bigger number:

```
go run chapter-4/cmd/grpc-fibonacci-client/main.go --typeOfCall async --number 45
```

```
// response
```

```
2023/10/18 13:50:58 Response form fibonacci stream: sequence(0), fibonacci number(0)

2023/10/18 13:50:58 Response form fibonacci stream: sequence(1), fibonacci number(1)

2023/10/18 13:50:58 Response form fibonacci stream: sequence(2), fibonacci number(1)

2023/10/18 13:50:58 Response form fibonacci stream: sequence(3), fibonacci number(2)

2023/10/18 13:50:58 Response form fibonacci stream: sequence(4), fibonacci number(3)

2023/10/18 13:50:58 Response form fibonacci stream: sequence(5), fibonacci number(5)

2023/10/18 13:50:58 Response form fibonacci stream: sequence(6), fibonacci number(8)

2023/10/18 13:50:58 Response form fibonacci stream: sequence(7), fibonacci number(13)

2023/10/18 13:50:58 Response form fibonacci stream: sequence(8), fibonacci number(21)

2023/10/18 13:50:58 Response form fibonacci stream: sequence(9), fibonacci number(34)
```

```
2023/10/18 13:50:58 Response form fibonacci stream: sequence(10),
fibonacci number(55)
2023/10/18 13:50:58 Response form fibonacci stream: sequence(11),
fibonacci number(89)
2023/10/18 13:50:58 Response form fibonacci stream: sequence(12),
fibonacci number(144)
2023/10/18 13:50:58 Response form fibonacci stream: sequence(13),
fibonacci number(233)
2023/10/18 13:50:58 Response form fibonacci stream: sequence(14),
fibonacci number(377)
2023/10/18 13:50:58 Response form fibonacci stream: sequence(15),
fibonacci number(610)
2023/10/18 13:50:58 Response form fibonacci stream: sequence(16),
fibonacci number(987)
2023/10/18 13:50:58 Response form fibonacci stream: sequence(17),
fibonacci number(1597)
2023/10/18 13:50:58 Response form fibonacci stream: sequence(18),
fibonacci number(2584)
2023/10/18 13:50:58 Response form fibonacci stream: sequence(19),
fibonacci number(4181)
2023/10/18 13:50:58 Response form fibonacci stream: sequence(20),
fibonacci number(6765)
2023/10/18 13:50:58 Response form fibonacci stream: sequence(21),
fibonacci number(10946)
2023/10/18 13:50:58 Response form fibonacci stream: sequence(22),
fibonacci number(17711)
2023/10/18 13:50:58 Response form fibonacci stream: sequence(23),
fibonacci number(28657)
2023/10/18 13:50:58 Response form fibonacci stream: sequence(24),
fibonacci number(46368)
2023/10/18 13:50:58 Response form fibonacci stream: sequence(25),
fibonacci number(75025)
2023/10/18 13:50:58 Response form fibonacci stream: sequence(26),
fibonacci number(121393)
2023/10/18 13:50:58 Response form fibonacci stream: sequence(27),
fibonacci number(196418)
```

```
2023/10/18 13:50:58 Response form fibonacci stream: sequence(28),
fibonacci number(317811)
2023/10/18 13:50:58 Response form fibonacci stream: sequence(29),
fibonacci number(514229)
2023/10/18 13:50:58 Response form fibonacci stream: sequence(30),
fibonacci number(832040)
2023/10/18 13:50:58 Response form fibonacci stream: sequence(31),
fibonacci number(1346269)
2023/10/18 13:50:58 Response form fibonacci stream: sequence(32),
fibonacci number(2178309)
2023/10/18 13:50:58 Response form fibonacci stream: sequence(33),
fibonacci number(3524578)
2023/10/18 13:50:58 Response form fibonacci stream: sequence(34),
fibonacci number(5702887)
2023/10/18 13:50:58 Response form fibonacci stream: sequence(35),
fibonacci number(9227465)
2023/10/18 13:50:58 Response form fibonacci stream: sequence(36),
fibonacci number(14930352)
2023/10/18 13:50:58 Response form fibonacci stream: sequence(37),
fibonacci number(24157817)
2023/10/18 13:50:59 Response form fibonacci stream: sequence(38),
fibonacci number(39088169)
2023/10/18 13:50:59 Response form fibonacci stream: sequence(39),
fibonacci number(63245986)
2023/10/18 13:51:00 Response form fibonacci stream: sequence(40),
fibonacci number(102334155)
2023/10/18 13:51:01 Response form fibonacci stream: sequence(41),
fibonacci number(165580141)
2023/10/18 13:51:02 Response form fibonacci stream: sequence(42),
fibonacci number(267914296)
2023/10/18 13:51:05 Response form fibonacci stream: sequence(43),
fibonacci number(433494437)
2023/10/18 13:51:09 Response form fibonacci stream: sequence(44),
fibonacci number(701408733)
```

After implementing and thoroughly testing both REST polling and gRPC server-side streaming, it's worthwhile to highlight the significant distinctions in terms of functionality:

1. **Communication Method**:
   a. In REST polling, the client is responsible for repeatedly initiating requests to the server to retrieve data.
   b. In gRPC server-side streaming, the server proactively sends responses to the client as soon as they are available, without requiring the client to initiate multiple requests.
2. **Signaling End of Data**:
   a. In REST polling, the server often utilizes a custom field, such as **`'endOfResponse,`**' to signal the client to stop polling for more data.
   b. In gRPC server-side streaming, the framework inherently handles the end-of-data signal, typically utilizing the **End-of-File (EOF)** concept. There is no need for the server to explicitly maintain a field for this purpose.
3. **State Maintenance**:
   a. In REST polling, maintaining state across subsequent requests, particularly between the client and server, frequently involves the use of a request ID or similar mechanisms.
   b. In gRPC server-side streaming, the architecture is fundamentally different. There are no repeated requests; instead, a single request is established, and the server conveys responses through streams, simplifying state management.

In essence, gRPC's server-side streaming offers an elegant solution by allowing the server to proactively push data to clients as it becomes available, obviating the need for complex state management and repeated client requests, in stark contrast to the more traditional REST polling approach. This distinction makes gRPC particularly powerful for scenarios where real-time or event-driven data updates are essential.

Client-Side Streaming RPC

gRPC client-side streaming is one of the four types of RPC (Remote Procedure Call) patterns supported by gRPC, a high-performance, language-agnostic framework for building distributed systems. In client-side streaming, the client sends a sequence of messages to the server and receives a single response from the server. This is often used in scenarios where the client needs to send a stream of data to the server, and the server processes the data and returns a result once the entire stream is received.

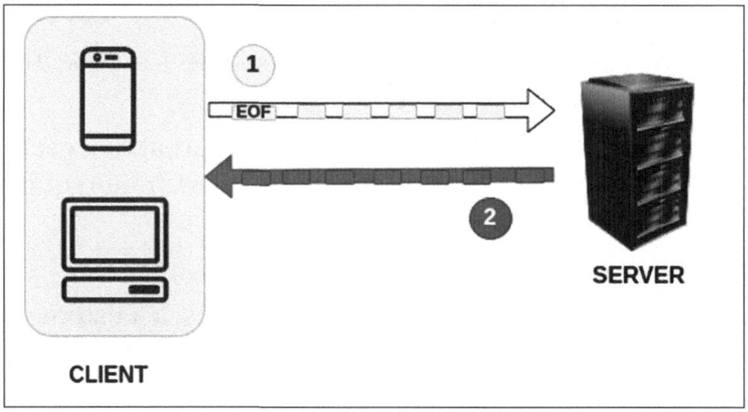

***Figure 4.4:** Client-Side streaming RPC communication between client and server*

Here's how gRPC client-side streaming works:

1. **Define the Protobuf Service**: We start by defining our service in a Protobuf file. The service should include a method that supports client-side streaming. For instance:

```
service MyService {
  rpc StreamData(stream MyRequest) returns (MyResponse);
}
```

2. **Generate Code**: Use the Protocol Buffers compiler **(protoc)** to generate client and server code from our Protobuf definitions.
3. **Server Implementation**: On the server side, we handle incoming client messages as they arrive, process them, and optionally send back responses.

```
package main


import (
  "context"
  "io"
  "log"
  "google.golang.org/grpc"
  pb "path-to-our-generated-code"
```

```
)

type server struct{}

func (s *server) StreamData(stream pb.MyService_StreamDataServer)
error {
  for {
    req, err := stream.Recv()
    if err == io.EOF {
      return stream.SendAndClose(&pb.MyResponse{Data:"Received
      !"}) // End of client stream
    }
    if err != nil {
      return err
    }
    log.Printf("Received message: %s", req.Data)

    // Process the request (e.g., store in a database, perform
    computations)
    // We can send responses back to the client using stream.Send()
  }
}

func main() {
  lis, err := net.Listen("tcp", "server-address")
  if err != nil {
    log.Fatalf("Failed to listen: %v", err)
  }

  s := grpc.NewServer()
  pb.RegisterMyServiceServer(s, &server{})

  if err := s.Serve(lis); err != nil {
```

```
    log.Fatalf("Failed to serve: %v", err)
  }
}
```

4. **Client Implementation**: In our client code, create a gRPC client for our service.

```
package main

import (
  "context"
  "log"
  "google.golang.org/grpc"
  pb "path-to-our-generated-code"
)

func main() {
  conn, err := grpc.Dial("server-address", grpc.WithInsecure())
  if err != nil {
    log.Fatalf("Failed to connect: %v", err)
  }
  defer conn.Close()

  client := pb.NewMyServiceClient(conn)

  // Create a stream
  stream, err := client.StreamData(context.Background())
  if err != nil {
    log.Fatalf("Error creating stream: %v", err)
  }

  // Send multiple messages to the server
  for i := 1; i <= 5; i++ {
    req := &pb.MyRequest{Data: "Message " + strconv.Itoa(i)}
```

```
        if err := stream.Send(req); err != nil {
          log.Fatalf("Error sending message: %v", err)
        }
      }

      // Close the send stream
     response, err := stream.CloseAndRecv()
      if err != nil {
        log.Fatalf("Error closing send stream: %v", err)
      }
    log.Printf("response :%+v\n", response)

      // Receive and process the server's response
      for {
        resp, err := stream.Recv()
        if err == io.EOF {
          break // End of stream
        }
        if err != nil {
          log.Fatalf("Error receiving response: %v", err)
        }
        log.Printf("Received response: %s", resp.Data)
      }
    }
```

In this example, the client sends a sequence of messages to the server, and the server processes them as they arrive. This pattern is useful for scenarios like uploading files, sending sensor data, or any situation where the client needs to send a stream of data to the server.

Use Cases for gRPC Client-Side Streaming:

- **Upload Large Files**: When a client needs to upload large files, it can stream the file's contents to the server in smaller chunks. The server processes the incoming data in real-time and may begin processing before the entire file is uploaded.

- **Data Feeds**: Clients can send a continuous stream of data to the server, such as sensor data, log entries, or financial market data. The server processes and reacts to this incoming stream.
- **Real-time Dashboards**: Clients can continuously send metrics or updates to the server, which processes the data and provides real-time updates to dashboards or monitoring systems.
- **Collaborative Editing**: In collaborative applications, multiple clients can send their edits to a shared document, and the server processes these edits and sends updates to all clients.
- **Live Chat Applications**: Clients can send and receive real-time messages in a chat application. The server processes and relays messages among clients.
- **Data Stream Aggregation**: Clients can aggregate data from various sources and send it to a central server, which aggregates and analyzes the data in real-time.
- **Voice or Video Communication**: Clients can stream audio or video data to the server, facilitating real-time communication with other clients or participants.

gRPC client-side streaming provides efficient and low-latency communication for these and other use cases where clients need to send a continuous or large volume of data to the server. It is a powerful feature for building real-time and collaborative applications.

Now, let's explore the hands-on application of gRPC client-side streaming through the creation of an Average service. This service involves the client sending a continuous stream of numbers to the server as requests, and, in return, it anticipates receiving the average of these numbers as a response.

We shall use the same folder structure as we used for server side streaming.

Now let's look at how we can implement the client-side streaming with gRPC. Like every gRPC RPC implementation, we shall start by defining messages and services in a **`proto`** file and generate code using **`protoc`** compiler.

Path: ~/chapter-4/proto/average.proto

```
syntax = "proto3";


package proto;
```

```
option go_package="./proto";

message AverageRequest{
    int32 number = 1;
}

message AverageResponse{
    int32 average = 2;
}


service AverageService{
  // Client Streaming
  rpc FindAverage(stream AverageRequest) returns (AverageResponse) {};
}
```

We can generate the code using **protoc** compiler with the following command:

```
protoc --go_out=chapter-4/proto --go-grpc_out=chapter-4/ chapter-4/proto/average.proto
```

The generated code for the preceding fibonacci.proto file can be viewed at the links given here:

- https://github.com/OrangeAVA/Modern-API-Design-with-gRPC/blob/main/chapter-4/proto/average.pb.go
- https://github.com/OrangeAVA/Modern-API-Design-with-gRPC/blob/main/chapter-4/proto/average_grpc.pb.go

Path: ~/chapter-4/apps/grpc-average-server/grpc-average-server.go

Please head over to 'https://github.com/OrangeAVA/Modern-API-Design-with-gRPC/blob/main/chapter-4/apps/grpc-average-server/grpc-average-server.go' view the gRPC average server implementation. Following is the code explanation for the same:

This code defines a gRPC server for an `AverageService` that calculates the average of a series of numbers streamed by the client. Here's a breakdown of the code:

1. **App struct**: This is the application struct that implements the **AverageServiceServer** interface generated from the Protocol Buffers definition. It has methods for starting the server and handling the **FindAverage** RPC call.
2. **NewApp()**: This is a constructor function for the **App** struct. It returns a new instance of the **App.**
3. **Start()**: This method starts the gRPC server. It listens on a specified port (**50052** in this case) and registers the **AverageService** on the server.
4. Inside the **FindAverage** method, the server processes the client's streaming requests:
   a. **sum** and **count** variables are initialized to keep track of the sum of the numbers and the count of numbers received from the client.
   b. The method enters a loop to continually receive requests from the client.
   c. **stream.Recv()** is used to receive a request from the client. If the request stream reaches its end (io.EOF), the server calculates the average and sends it back to the client using **stream.SendAndClose().**
   d. If there's an error while reading the client stream, it logs an error message.
   e. For each valid request received, the server updates the sum and count accordingly.

This server efficiently calculates the average of a stream of numbers sent by the client and returns it when the client's stream ends.

Path: ~/chapter-4/cmd/grpc-average-server/main.go

```
package main


import grpcaverageserver "github.com/OrangeAVA/Modern-API-Design-with-gRPC/chapter-4/apps/grpc-average-server"


func main() {

    app := grpcaverageserver.NewApp()

    app.Start()

}
```

This code serves as the entry point for a gRPC server that handles the computation of an average. Here's a breakdown of the code:

- **main function**: This is the starting point of the program. It creates an instance of the gRPC server application, starts the server, and waits for incoming client requests.
- `grpcaverageserver`: This is an imported package containing the implementation of the gRPC server. Specifically, it defines the `NewApp()` function, which creates a new instance of the server application.
- `app := grpcaverageserver.NewApp()`: This line initializes the gRPC server application by calling the `NewApp()` constructor function defined in the imported package. This function creates an instance of the server and sets it up.
- `app.Start()`: After creating the server instance, this line invokes the `Start()` method of the server application. The `Start()` method configures and starts the gRPC server, making it ready to receive and process incoming requests.

In summary, this code is the entry point for a gRPC server for computing averages. It creates the server, initializes it using the `NewApp()` function, and starts it using `app.Start()`. Once the server is running, it can accept incoming gRPC client requests for average calculations.

Path: ~/chapter-4/apps/grpc-average-client/grpc-average-client.go

The code for the gRPC average client implementation can be viewed here:

https://github.com/OrangeAVA/Modern-API-Design-with-gRPC/blob/main/chapter-4/apps/grpc-average-client/grpc-average-client.go.

Following is the code explanation for the same:

This code defines a gRPC client that streams a series of numbers to a server and expects to receive an average in response. Here's how it works:

- `numbers`: This is a command-line flag that allows the user to provide a list of comma-separated numbers. The client will use these numbers for computing the average.
- `App struct`: This is the application struct that manages the gRPC client's functionality. It includes methods for starting the client, performing client-streaming to the server, and shutting down the client.
- `NewApp()`: This is a constructor function for the **App** struct. It creates and returns a new instance of the client application.

- **`Start()`**: This method initializes the gRPC client and sends a stream of numbers to the server:
  - o The command-line flag -numbers is parsed to get the user-provided list of numbers.
  - o The client connects to the server at the specified address (**`localhost:50052`**) using an insecure connection (we should typically use a secure connection in a production environment).
  - o The **`averageServiceClient`** is created to interact with the server.
  - o The user-provided numbers are parsed and stored in the **`numberArr`** slice.
  - o The **`doClientStreaming`** function is called with the client and the list of numbers.
- **`Shutdown()`**: This method is used to close the client's connection to the server gracefully.
- **`doClientStreaming()`**: This function is responsible for streaming numbers to the server and handling the server's response:
  - o It creates an array of gRPC requests (**`AverageRequest`**) based on the user-provided numbers.
  - o A gRPC stream is initiated using the **`FindAverage`** method, and requests are sent one by one to the server.
  - o A brief pause (1 second) is introduced between sending each request, simulating a streaming scenario.
  - o After sending all requests, the client closes the stream using **`stream.CloseAndRecv()`**. This action sends a termination signal to the server.
  - o The client then receives the server's response, which should contain the computed average.
  - o The response is logged for the user to see.

This client allows users to send a stream of numbers to the server, which then calculates and returns the average once all numbers have been sent. The code demonstrates how to perform client-side streaming in gRPC, where the client can send multiple requests to the server over a single connection.

Path: ~/chapter-4/cmd/grpc-average-client/main.go

```
package main
```

```
import grpcaverageclient "github.com/OrangeAVA/Modern-API-Design-with-gRPC/chapter-4/apps/grpc-average-client"

func main() {
    app := grpcaverageclient.NewApp()
    app.Start()

    app.Shutdown()
}
```

This code sets up a gRPC client for the Average service, parses user input, establishes a connection to the gRPC server, sends the list of numbers to the server for calculating the average, and then performs a clean shutdown of the client application. It demonstrates how gRPC client applications can be structured and run.

We can start the average server with the following command:

```
go run chapter-4/cmd/grpc-average-server/main.go
```

Now let's tests the behavior by invoking the client:

```
go run chapter-4/cmd/grpc-average-client/main.go --numbers 23,36,89,76,112

//client request streams
2023/10/18 15:15:11 sending request: number:23
2023/10/18 15:15:12 sending request: number:36
2023/10/18 15:15:13 sending request: number:89
2023/10/18 15:15:14 sending request: number:76
2023/10/18 15:15:15 sending request: number:112
// server response
2023/10/18 15:15:16 FindAverage response: average:67
```

Upon closer examination, we provide a set of numbers separated by commas to the client using the **numbers** flag. The client then sequentially processes these numbers and forwards a continuous stream of requests to the server. Meanwhile, the server patiently awaits the arrival of all requests before computing the final average.

It's essential to understand that the server isn't bound to hold up the entire process until all client requests are completed. It has the flexibility to calculate the average as soon as individual requests arrive. Nevertheless, the server only sends the aggregated response when it has processed all incoming client requests.

Bi-Directional Streaming RPC

Bidirectional streaming is one of the four types of RPC (Remote Procedure Call) patterns supported by gRPC, a high-performance, language-agnostic framework for building distributed systems. In bidirectional streaming, both the client and server can send a stream of messages to each other over a single gRPC connection. This bidirectional communication enables real-time, interactive scenarios where both sides can independently send and receive data.

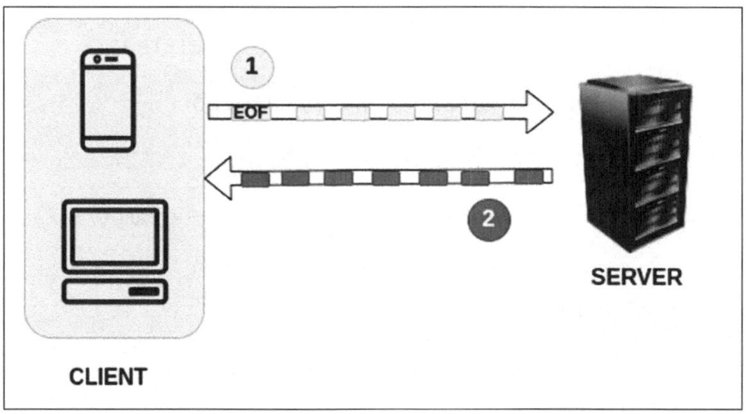

***Figure 4.5**: Bi-Directional streaming RPC communication between client and server*

Here's how bidirectional streaming works in gRPC:

1. **Client and Server Create Streams**: The client initiates the RPC by creating a streaming call to the server. Both the client and server establish their own data streams within the same gRPC connection. These streams enable bidirectional communication.
2. **Both Sides Send Messages**: After setting up the streams, both the client and server can send messages to each other independently. The messages are sent asynchronously, so there's no strict order of when they arrive.

3. **Continuous Communication**: The client and server can keep sending messages as needed, creating a continuous and interactive communication channel. This is particularly useful for scenarios where real-time, back-and-forth communication is required.
4. **No Set Endpoint**: In bidirectional streaming, there is no set "start" or "end" to the communication. Both sides can send and receive messages throughout the lifetime of the RPC. They can close the streams and end the communication when it's no longer needed.

Use Cases for gRPC Bidirectional Streaming:

- **Chat Applications**: Bidirectional streaming is well-suited for chat applications where users need to send and receive messages in real-time. The client and server can continuously exchange messages in both directions.
- **Multiplayer Games**: In online multiplayer games, players and the game server can communicate via bidirectional streaming. Players send input commands, and the server sends game state updates back to the players.
- **Collaborative Applications**: Applications that support real-time collaboration, such as collaborative document editing or whiteboarding, can use bidirectional streaming to synchronize changes among users.
- **Monitoring and Notifications**: For monitoring systems, the server can push real-time updates or notifications to connected clients, and clients can send commands or queries back to the server.
- **Interactive Dashboards**: In real-time dashboards, data can be continuously streamed from the server to clients, and clients can send queries or configuration updates back to the server.
- **Voice and Video Conferencing**: Bidirectional streaming can be used for voice and video conferencing applications, where audio and video data is continuously exchanged between clients and the conferencing server.

Bidirectional streaming provides a powerful mechanism for building real-time, interactive, and collaborative applications that require continuous communication between clients and servers. It is an important feature for use cases where bidirectional data exchange is essential.

Websockets:

WebSockets are a communication protocol that provides full-duplex communication channels over a single TCP connection. Unlike the traditional HTTP protocol, which follows a request-response pattern, WebSockets allow for continuous, bidirectional data exchange between a client and a server. This real-time, low-latency communication is particularly well-suited for applications that require instant updates, such as chat applications, online gaming, financial trading platforms, and collaborative tools. WebSockets are designed to reduce the overhead of repeatedly establishing new connections, making them efficient for scenarios where frequent data exchange is essential. In summary, WebSockets offer a persistent, two-way communication channel that is ideal for interactive and real-time web applications.

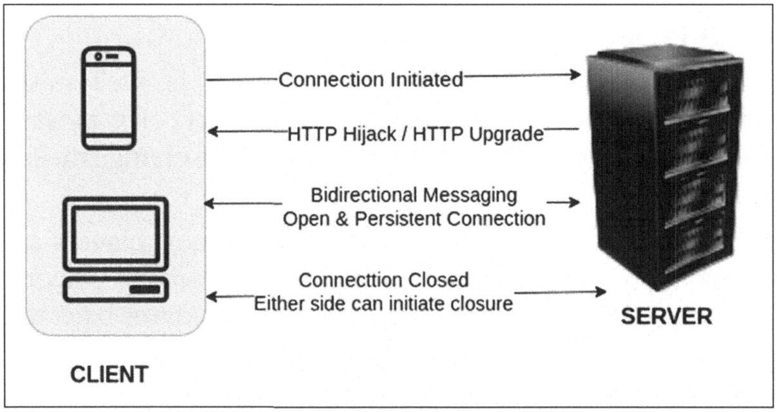

Figure 4.6: *Websockets bi-directional communication between client and server*

gRPC Server-Side Streaming versus WebSockets:

gRPC bi-directional streaming and WebSockets are both powerful communication protocols that enable real-time, bidirectional data exchange between clients and servers. However, they have different use cases, features, and implementations. Let's compare the two:

- **Protocol and Implementation**:
  - **gRPC Bi-Directional Streaming**: gRPC is a framework that uses HTTP/2 as the underlying protocol. Bi-directional streaming in gRPC is based on HTTP/2's multiplexing, allowing multiple streams over a single connection.
  - **WebSockets**: WebSockets is its own protocol designed for real-time, full-duplex communication. It's not based on HTTP and usually runs over a dedicated WebSocket connection.
- **Use Cases**:
  - **gRPC Bi-Directional Streaming**: gRPC is particularly suited for microservices architectures and scenarios where you need high-

performance, language-agnostic communication. It's often used in scenarios like chat applications, collaborative tools, and IoT devices.

  - **WebSockets**: WebSockets are commonly used for web applications that require real-time features, such as chat, online gaming, live notifications, and collaborative editing.

- **Complexity**:
  - **gRPC Bi-Directional Streaming**: gRPC is relatively more complex to set up, especially in scenarios where you need to handle service definitions and code generation. However, it provides strong typing and code generation for multiple languages.
  - **WebSockets**: WebSockets are simpler to implement, especially in web applications, where most modern browsers have built-in support. There is less emphasis on strict typing.

- **Message Serialization**:
  - **gRPC Bi-Directional Streaming**: gRPC typically uses Protocol Buffers (ProtoBuf) for message serialization, providing efficient and compact binary serialization.
  - **WebSockets**: WebSockets don't mandate a specific serialization format. They are often used with JSON, which is more human-readable but less efficient compared to ProtoBuf.

- **Security**:
  - **gRPC Bi-Directional Streaming**: gRPC enforces strong authentication and supports features like SSL/TLS encryption and token-based authentication.
  - WebSockets: Security must be handled at the application level. While you can secure WebSocket connections, it requires additional work.

- **Performance**:
  - **gRPC Bi-Directional Streaming**: gRPC, with its use of HTTP/2, has excellent performance characteristics, including multiplexing, binary serialization, and efficient connection handling.
  - **WebSockets**: WebSockets provide good performance, but it may not be as efficient as gRPC for high-frequency data exchange.

- **Ecosystem and Language Support**:
  - **gRPC Bi-Directional Streaming**: gRPC has strong language support and an ecosystem, making it a great choice in microservices environments where various programming languages are used.

    - **WebSockets**: WebSockets are more web-centric and commonly used in JavaScript-based web applications.
- **Ease of Setup**:
    - **gRPC Bi-Directional Streaming**: Setting up gRPC can be more involved due to the need for service definitions and code generation.
    - **WebSockets**: WebSockets are relatively easier to set up, especially in web applications where many frameworks provide WebSocket support.
- **Scalability:**
    - **gRPC Bi-Directional Streaming**: Scales effectively in scenarios with a large number of concurrent connections due to its underlying protocol features.
    - **WebSockets**: Scalability considerations may involve handling multiple connections and efficiently managing server resources.
- **Browser Support:**
    - **gRPC Bi-Directional Streaming:** While gRPC itself may not be directly supported in web browsers, it can be used in conjunction with HTTP/2, which is well-supported by modern browsers. However, client-side implementations may involve additional considerations.
    - WebSockets: WebSockets are specifically designed for real-time communication in web browsers. They have built-in support in modern browsers, making them a natural choice for web-centric applications.

In summary, the choice between gRPC bi-directional streaming and WebSockets depends on your specific use case and requirements. gRPC is an excellent choice for microservices and performance-critical applications, while WebSockets are well-suited for web applications that need real-time, interactive features. Both technologies have their strengths and can be the right tool for different jobs.

Next, we will delve into the practical use of gRPC bidirectional streaming by developing a **Max** service. This service orchestrates simultaneous communication between the client and server. The client continually dispatches numbers in a stream of requests, while the server replies with the maximum value among the numbers received so far. This back-and-forth interaction persists until the client transmits a termination signal.

We shall use the same folder structure as we used for server and client-side streaming.

Now let's look at how we can implement the bi-directional streaming with gRPC. Like every gRPC RPC implementation, we shall start by defining messages and services in a **proto** file and generate code using **protoc** compiler.

Path: ~/chapter-4/proto/max.proto

```
syntax = "proto3";


package proto;

option go_package="./proto";


message MaxRequest{

    int32 number = 1;

}


message MaxResponse{

    int32 max = 1;

}



service MaxService{

  // Bi-Directional Streaming

  rpc FindMax(stream MaxRequest) returns (stream MaxResponse) {};

}
```

This code defines a gRPC service for calculating the maximum value from a stream of numbers. Here's a breakdown of the key elements:

- **Syntax and Package Declaration**:
  - o **`syntax = "proto3";`**: Indicates the Protocol Buffers version used.
  - o **`package proto;`**: Defines the package name for the generated code.
  - o **`option go_package = "./proto";`**: Specifies the Go package name for the generated code.

- **Message Definitions**:
  - o `MaxRequest`: This message represents a single number sent from the client to the server. It contains an int32 field named number.
  - o `MaxResponse`: This message represents the maximum value calculated by the server in response to the client's stream of numbers. It contains an int32 field named max.
- **Service Definition**:
  - o `MaxService`: Declares a gRPC service named MaxService.
  - o **`rpc FindMax(stream MaxRequest) returns (stream MaxResponse) {}`**: Defines an RPC method called **`FindMax`**. This method uses bidirectional streaming, indicated by the stream keyword both for input (`MaxRequest`) and output (`MaxResponse`). It allows the client and server to send and receive a stream of messages in real-time, and the server responds with the maximum value calculated from the received numbers.

In summary, this Protocol Buffers file outlines the message structures and service method required for bidirectional streaming communication between a client and server to find the maximum value from a continuous stream of numbers.

We can generate the code using **`protoc`** compiler with the following command:

```
protoc --go_out=chapter-4/proto --go-grpc_out=chapter-4/ chapter-4/
proto/max.proto
```

The generated code for the preceding fibonacci.proto file can be viewed at following links:

- https://github.com/OrangeAVA/Modern-API-Design-with-gRPC/blob/main/chapter-4/proto/max.pb.go
- https://github.com/OrangeAVA/Modern-API-Design-with-gRPC/blob/main/chapter-4/proto/max_grpc.pb.go

Path: ~/chapter-4/apps/grpc-max-server/grpc-max-server.go

The code for the gRPC max server implementation can be viewed here:

'https://github.com/OrangeAVA/Modern-API-Design-with-gRPC/blob/main/chapter-4/apps/grpc-max-server/grpc-max-server.go.

Following is the code explanation for the same:

This code defines a gRPC server for a **Max** service. The **Max** service calculates and returns the maximum value from a continuous stream of numbers sent by a client. Here's an explanation of the key components:

- **Server Initialization**:
  - o **`serverPort`** specifies the port (**`50053`**) at which the gRPC server will listen for incoming connections.
  - o **`servAddr`** is the server's address.
- **gRPC Server Initialization**:
  - o A new gRPC server is created with the specified options.
  - o The **`MaxService`** is registered with this server. This service is implemented by the **`App`** struct, which is created using **`NewApp().`**
- **`Start`** **Method**:
  - o The **`Start`** method initiates the gRPC server by listening on the specified address.
  - o It also registers the service reflection, which allows tools like **`grpcurl`** to interact with the service using reflection.
- **`FindMax`** **Method**:
  - o This method is responsible for finding and streaming the maximum number to the client.
  - o It uses bidirectional streaming, indicated by the **`MaxService_FindMaxServer`** parameter.
  - o It initializes a max variable to -1 as there may not be any numbers received initially.
  - o It continuously reads requests from the client using **`stream.Recv().`**
  - o If the end of the stream is reached (indicated by io.EOF), the method returns without error.
  - o If there's an error while reading the client stream, an error is logged.
  - o The maximum number is updated if a new number is greater than the current maximum.
  - o After a 2-second delay, the maximum number is sent back to the client using **`stream.Send().`**

In summary, this code sets up a gRPC server that listens for client connections on port **`50053.`** The server implements the **`MaxService`** service, which uses bidirectional streaming to calculate and send the maximum number from a continuous stream of client-provided numbers. The server responds with the maximum value after processing each number.

Path: ~/chapter-4/cmd/grpc-max-server/main.go

```
package main


import grpcmaxserver "github.com/OrangeAVA/Modern-API-Design-with-gRPC/chapter-4/apps/grpc-max-server"


func main() {
    app := grpcmaxserver.NewApp()
    app.Start()
}
```

This code initializes and starts the gRPC server for the **Max** service, which is defined in the **grpcmaxserver** package. The server is started by calling the Start method of the App instance. This code represents the server's entry point, and once executed, it will listen for incoming gRPC requests and handle them accordingly.

Path: ~/chapter-4/apps/grpc-max-client/grpc-max-client.go

The code for the gRPC max client implementation can be viewed here:

https://github.com/OrangeAVA/Modern-API-Design-with-gRPC/blob/main/chapter-4/apps/grpc-max-client/grpc-max-client.go.

Following is the code explanation for the same:

This code is for a gRPC client that communicates with a "Max" service using bidirectional streaming. The client sends a stream of numbers to the server and receives the maximum number calculated by the server in real-time. Here's a breakdown of the code:

1. **Initialization**:
    a. The init function sets up a command-line flag, **numbers**, which allows us to provide a list of comma-separated numbers.
2. **App Struct**:
    a. The **App** struct contains the gRPC client connection.

3. **NewApp Function**:
   a. `NewApp()` initializes and returns a new App instance.
4. **Start Method**:
   a. The `Start` method is the main function to interact with the gRPC server.
   b. It parses the command-line flags and establishes a connection with the gRPC server running on `localhost:50053`.
   c. It creates an instance of the `MaxServiceClient` to interact with the server.
5. **Processing Numbers**:
   a. The numbers provided via the **numbers** flag are parsed and stored in the `numberArr` slice.
6. **`doBidirectionalStreaming` Function**:
   a. This function is responsible for bidirectional streaming with the gRPC server.
   b. It creates a list of requests, one for each number in the `numberArr`.
   c. A bidirectional streaming connection is established using `c.FindMax(context.Background())`.
7. **Goroutines:**
   a. Two goroutines are used to handle sending and receiving messages simultaneously.
   b. The first goroutine sends each request to the server at one-second intervals, simulating the real-time nature of the communication.
   c. The second goroutine listens for responses from the server and logs the maximum number received.
   d. The `<-waitChan` statement blocks the program until both goroutines finish.

In summary, this code sets up a gRPC client that streams a list of numbers to the server. The server calculates the maximum number in real-time and streams the maximum back to the client. This bidirectional streaming communication is managed by two goroutines: one for sending and one for receiving, and it demonstrates a practical use case of bidirectional streaming in gRPC.

Path: ~/chapter-4/cmd/grpc-max-client/main.go

```
package main
```

```
import grpcmaxclient "github.com/OrangeAVA/Modern-API-Design-with-gRPC/
chapter-4/apps/grpc-max-client"

func main() {
    app := grpcmaxclient.NewApp()
    app.Start()

    app.Shutdown()
}
```

This code initializes and starts the gRPC client for the **Max** service, which is defined in the **grpcmaxclient** package. The client interacts with the server to send and receive numbers while continuously calculating and receiving the maximum number in the stream. The **Shutdown** method ensures proper termination of the client application.

We can start the max server with the following command:

```
go run chapter-4/cmd/grpc-max-server/main.go
```

Now let's tests the behavior by invoking the client:

```
go run chapter-4/cmd/grpc-max-client/main.go --numbers 321,142,654,11,987

// client request and client response
2023/10/18 15:47:09 sending message: number:321
2023/10/18 15:47:10 sending message: number:142
2023/10/18 15:47:11 sending message: number:654
2023/10/18 15:47:11 response received: 321
2023/10/18 15:47:12 sending message: number:11
2023/10/18 15:47:13 sending message: number:987
2023/10/18 15:47:13 response received: 321
```

```
2023/10/18 15:47:15 response received: 654
2023/10/18 15:47:17 response received: 654
2023/10/18 15:47:19 response received: 987
```

Upon closer examination, it becomes evident that the client's requests and the server's responses are intricately intertwined, occurring simultaneously and interdependently. This interwoven nature makes it challenging to separate them into distinct phases. This is a fundamental characteristic of bidirectional streaming in gRPC, where the client and server engage in a continuous and interactive exchange of data, blurring the lines between request and response, and enabling a dynamic and synchronized communication process.

Conclusion

In our exploration of communication paradigms, we've encountered four distinct methods for data exchange between clients and servers. Server-side streaming enables the server to send multiple responses to a single client request, making it ideal for scenarios like real-time data feeds. Client-side streaming, on the other hand, empowers clients to send a stream of data to the server incrementally, making it suitable for use cases such as uploading large files. Bidirectional streaming, or duplex streaming, facilitates two-way communication between clients and servers, allowing both sides to send multiple requests and responses asynchronously. This method is vital for interactive applications like real-time chat. In contrast, REST polling relies on clients repeatedly sending requests to the server to retrieve data, often using request-id or similar mechanisms to maintain state across subsequent requests. The choice of these methods depends on the specific needs of the application, ranging from real-time streaming and interactive communication to more traditional polling scenarios.

As we move forward into the next chapter, we will explore advanced gRPC concepts, such as gRPC interceptors, which are akin to middleware in traditional web applications. We'll also cover server-side and client-side interceptors, providing insights into how they can enhance communication processes. Additionally, we'll delve into essential topics like deadlines and cancellation, panic handling, and stack tracing. This knowledge will further enrich our understanding of gRPC and equip us with the tools to design robust and efficient APIs for a wide array of applications.

Multiple Choice Questions

1. In which type of gRPC streaming is the client sending a single request and receiving multiple responses from the server?
   a. Server-Side Streaming
   b. Client-Side Streaming
   c. Bidirectional Streaming
   d. Unary Streaming
2. What is the key feature of client-side streaming in gRPC?
   a. Client sends a single request and receives a single response.
   b. Client sends multiple requests and receives a single response.
   c. Client sends a single request and receives multiple responses.
   d. Client and server communicate in real-time.
3. In server-side streaming, how does the communication flow between the client and server?
   a. Client sends a single request and receives multiple responses
   b. Client sends multiple requests and receives a single response
   c. Both client and server send multiple requests and responses
   d. Client and server exchange data in real-time
4. Which gRPC streaming type is suitable for scenarios where the client and server need to maintain a continuous, interactive connection?
   a. Server-Side Streaming
   b. Client-Side Streaming
   c. Bidirectional Streaming
   d. Unary Streaming
5. In a bidirectional streaming scenario, how do the client and server communicate?
   a. Client sends a single request and receives multiple responses
   b. Client sends multiple requests and receives a single response
   c. Both client and server send multiple requests and responses
   d. Client and server communicate asynchronously

6. What is the primary use case for server-side streaming in gRPC?
   a. Real-time chat applications
   b. File uploads from the client to the server
   c. Calculating an average from multiple client values
   d. Retrieving a continuous stream of data from the server
7. Which gRPC streaming type is suitable for scenarios where the client needs to upload a large file to the server?
   a. Server-Side Streaming
   b. Client-Side Streaming
   c. Bidirectional Streaming
   d. Unary Streaming
8. In bidirectional streaming, what is the key advantage?
   a. Server can send responses at any time
   b. Server has full control of the communication
   c. The client has full control of the communication
   d. Both client and server have separate communication channels
9. In client-side streaming, what is the typical use case?
   a. Real-time monitoring of server events
   b. Uploading a large file to the server
   c. Sending a single request and receiving multiple responses
   d. Bidirectional communication for chat applications
10. In which gRPC streaming type is it common for the server to process client requests as they arrive and send responses as soon as they are ready?
    a. Server-Side Streaming
    b. Client-Side Streaming
    c. Bidirectional Streaming
    d. Unary Streaming
11. Which gRPC streaming type is most suitable for a chat application where users need to send and receive messages in real-time?
    a. Server-Side Streaming
    b. Client-Side Streaming

   c. Bidirectional Streaming
   d. Unary Streaming

12. What is the primary characteristic of gRPC bidirectional streaming?
    a. Client and server maintain separate communication channels
    b. The server responds to client requests in real-time
    c. Client and server communicate sequentially
    d. It allows for the exchange of multiple requests and responses in parallel

Answers

1	a
2	b
3	a
4	c
5	c
6	d
7	b
8	a
9	b
10	a
11	c
12	d

CHAPTER 5
Advanced gRPC Concepts

Introduction

In the preceding chapter, we explored gRPC communication patterns and delved deeper into its versatile capabilities. Unlike REST, which primarily follows a single request-response cycle, gRPC introduces an expansive array of communication options. We explored scenarios where communication involves streaming requests from the client to the server, resulting in a single response, or sending a solitary request and receiving a continuous stream of responses. Additionally, we explored bi-directional streaming that allows concurrent interactions between client and server. Hands-on implementations showcased the practical applications of these patterns, demonstrating how gRPC excels in managing diverse communication requirements. Through these discussions, we've deepened our grasp of how gRPC excels in meeting real-world use cases, enhancing the efficiency and flexibility of communication between clients and servers.

In this chapter, we embark on an exploration of the sophisticated features that gRPC offers, designed to bolster its effectiveness in orchestrating communication between clients and servers. The journey begins with a nuanced examination of interceptors, a pivotal aspect of gRPC that bears similarity to the middleware concept. We draw parallels between these two, elucidating the integral role interceptors play in shaping the processing of requests and responses. As we navigate through the intricacies, we dissect the realm of Unary and Streaming interceptors, providing tangible examples such as a logging interceptor, which enhances transparency, and a recovery interceptor, crucial for handling unexpected panics.

Transitioning towards building resilience into our gRPC communication, we confront challenges such as cascading failures that could potentially disrupt system integrity. We delve into the indispensable facets of context and deadlines, understanding how they form the backbone of robust communication. Practical implementations follow suit as we decode the implementation of essential patterns. We unveil the significance of timeouts to streamline communication in scenarios where swift responses are imperative. The implementation of retry patterns enhances reliability, ensuring robustness in the face of transient failures. The intricate concept of circuit breakers is explored, offering an effective mechanism to prevent service degradation during turbulent circumstances.

As we explore advanced gRPC concepts, we'll gain a deep understanding of the tools and strategies available to us. By learning to use timeouts, retries, and circuit breakers, we'll be ready to build communication systems that are not only strong and efficient but also flexible enough to handle real-world challenges. We'll wrap up with a clear overview of these advanced gRPC features, strengthening our ability to create robust communication networks.

Structure

In this chapter, we will cover the following topics:

- Interceptors
  - Draw parallels with middlewares
  - Unary and Streaming interceptors
  - Implement logging interceptor
  - Implement recovery interceptor
- Resilient gRPC communication
  - Cascading failures
  - Context and Deadlines
  - Implement timeout pattern
  - Implement retry pattern
  - Implement circuit breaker pattern

Interceptors

In the gRPC realm, interceptors are a powerful and flexible mechanism that allows developers to intercept and manipulate the processing of Remote Procedure Calls (RPCs) on both the client and server sides. They provide a way to augment, transform, or otherwise modify the behavior of the communication between the client and server.

Interceptors are analogous to middlewares in web frameworks and serve as a chain of functions that get executed around the execution of an RPC. They can be employed for various purposes such as logging, authentication, monitoring, error handling, and more. In essence, interceptors enable the implementation of cross-cutting concerns without tightly coupling them to the business logic of the service.

There are two main types of interceptors:

- **Unary Interceptors**: These interceptors are executed for unary RPCs, which involve a single request and a single response.
- **Streaming Interceptors**: These interceptors are applied to streaming RPCs, which involve a stream of requests or responses.

Developers can implement custom interceptors to cater to the specific needs of their application. This flexibility and extensibility make interceptors a crucial component for building robust and adaptable gRPC services.

Comparisons with middlewares

Interceptors in gRPC share similarities with middlewares in web frameworks, and both serve as a means to intercept and modify the behavior of requests and responses in a flexible and reusable manner. Here are some key similarities between interceptors and middlewares:

Chain of Execution:

- **Interceptors**: In gRPC, interceptors are organized as a chain of functions that get executed around the processing of RPCs. Each interceptor in the chain has the opportunity to handle the request and response.
- **Middlewares**: In web frameworks, middlewares are functions or components arranged in a chain, where each middleware has the ability to process the HTTP request and response in sequence.

Cross-Cutting Concerns:

- **Interceptors**: They allow developers to implement cross-cutting concerns, such as logging, authentication, monitoring, and error handling, without tightly coupling these concerns to the core logic of the service.
- **Middlewares**: Similarly, middlewares provide a way to address cross-cutting concerns in web applications, allowing developers to encapsulate functionalities like authentication, caching, and error handling.

Reusability:

- **Interceptors**: They promote code reusability by enabling the modular implementation of functionalities that can be applied to multiple RPCs or services.
- **Middlewares**: Likewise, middlewares encourage the reuse of components across different routes or endpoints in web applications.

Extensibility:

- **Interceptors**: Developers can extend the functionality of gRPC services by introducing custom interceptors tailored to their specific requirements.
- **Middlewares**: Web frameworks often provide an extensible middleware system, allowing developers to create and incorporate custom middleware components.

Separation of Concerns:

- **Interceptors**: They contribute to the separation of concerns by allowing developers to address specific aspects of RPC processing in isolated interceptor functions.
- **Middlewares**: Similarly, middlewares aid in separating concerns in web applications, maintaining a clean separation between business logic and auxiliary functionalities.

In summary, interceptors in gRPC and middlewares in web frameworks share the fundamental goal of providing a flexible and modular way to extend and enhance the behavior of services while promoting code organization and maintainability.

While interceptors in gRPC and middlewares in web frameworks share similarities, they also have key differences that stem from the distinct characteristics and requirements of these two communication paradigms. Here are some differences between interceptors and middlewares:

Communication Paradigm:

- **Interceptors**: gRPC is a RPC framework designed for efficient communication between services. Interceptors in gRPC are tailored to the needs of RPC-based communication, where clients make calls to remote services, and both the request and response are structured and strongly typed.
- **Middlewares**: Web frameworks, on the other hand, are designed for handling HTTP requests and responses in a stateless and often text-based manner. Middlewares are built around the HTTP protocol and are focused on the needs of web applications.

Message Structure:

- **Interceptors**: gRPC deals with structured binary messages, typically defined by Protocol Buffers. Interceptors operate on these structured messages, allowing manipulation of RPC-related metadata and message content.
- **Middlewares**: Middlewares commonly deal with HTTP messages, which are often text-based and include headers and bodies. Middlewares can modify HTTP headers, request bodies, and response bodies.

Service Invocation Model:

- **Interceptors**: gRPC follows a strong typing system and supports various RPC types, including unary RPCs, server streaming, client streaming, and bidirectional streaming. Interceptors are designed to handle these different invocation models.
- **Middlewares**: Middlewares typically focus on the request-response cycle of web applications. They may handle scenarios like authentication, logging, and caching in the context of HTTP requests and responses.

Transport Protocol:

- **Interceptors**: gRPC can use HTTP/2 as its transport protocol, providing advantages like multiplexing and header compression. Interceptors leverage features specific to the HTTP/2 protocol.
- **Middlewares**: Web frameworks often support multiple transport protocols, including HTTP/1.1 and HTTP/2. Middlewares work with the characteristics of these protocols.

Context Handling:

- **Interceptors**: gRPC uses the context. Context for handling deadlines, cancellations, and carrying metadata throughout the lifecycle of an RPC. Interceptors interact with this context.
- **Middlewares**: Context handling in web frameworks is often associated with the HTTP request context, which includes information like request headers, parameters, and cookies.

In summary, while both interceptors and middlewares provide a way to intercept and augment the processing of requests and responses, their differences arise from the specific requirements and contexts of gRPC and web frameworks. Interceptors are tailored to the structured, RPC-based nature of gRPC communication, while middlewares are designed for the more flexible and text-based world of HTTP in web applications.

In the context of REST APIs, and more broadly, in any web framework based on HTTP 1.1, middlewares assume a crucial role in providing the enumerated advantages. Now, let's explore some code snippets of a REST web server that reveal how middlewares are employed to establish context. Subsequently, we can delve into the implementation of corresponding gRPC interceptors.

Here is the definition and integration of a **logger middleware** within a REST web server:

```
package main


import (

    "log"

    "net/http"

    "time"

)


// LoggerMiddleware is a middleware that logs details of incoming requests.

func LoggerMiddleware(next http.Handler) http.Handler {

    return http.HandlerFunc(func(w http.ResponseWriter, r *http.Request)
    {

        start := time.Now()
```

```
        // Call the next handler in the chain.
        next.ServeHTTP(w, r)

        // Log the request details.
        log.Printf(
            "%s %s %s %s",
            r.Method,
            r.RequestURI,
            r.RemoteAddr,
            time.Since(start),
        )
    })
}

func main() {
    router := http.NewServeMux()

    // Attach the LoggerMiddleware to the router.
    router.Handle("/", LoggerMiddleware(http.HandlerFunc(func(w http.
    ResponseWriter, r *http.Request) {
        w.Write([]byte("Hello, World!"))
    })))

    // Start the server.
    http.ListenAndServe(":8080", router)
}
```

The preceding code defines a simple **HTTP server** in **Go** that utilizes a **middleware** pattern to implement **logging**. Let's break down the key components:

1. **`LoggerMiddleware` Function**:
   a. The **`LoggerMiddleware`** function is a middleware that takes an **`http.Handler (next)`** and returns a new **`http.Handler`**.
   b. It logs details of incoming requests, including the HTTP method, request URI, remote address, and the time it takes to process the request.
   c. After logging, it calls the next handler in the chain.
2. **`Main` Function**:
   a. The main function creates a new **`http.ServeMux`** (a basic HTTP request multiplexer).
   b. It attaches the **`LoggerMiddleware`** to the router, ensuring that every request passes through this middleware.
   c. The main handler is a simple **"`Hello, World!`"** response.
3. **Server Start**:
   a. The server is started using **`http.ListenAndServe`** on port **8080**.

In essence, this code demonstrates how middleware can be implemented to perform additional operations before and after handling an HTTP request. The **`LoggerMiddleware`** provides a way to log details about each incoming request, offering insights into the server's activity.

Here is the definition and integration of a **recovery middleware** within a REST web server:

```
package main

import (
    "fmt"
    "net/http"
)

// RecoveryMiddleware is a middleware that recovers from panics and returns a 500 Internal Server Error.
func RecoveryMiddleware(next http.Handler) http.Handler {
    return http.HandlerFunc(func(w http.ResponseWriter, r *http.Request)
```

```
    {
        defer func() {
            if err := recover(); err != nil {
                // Log the panic and send a generic response.
                fmt.Println("Recovered from panic:", err)
                http.Error(w, "Internal Server Error", http.
                StatusInternalServerError)
            }
        }()

        // Call the next handler in the chain.
        next.ServeHTTP(w, r)
    })
}

func main() {
    router := http.NewServeMux()

    // Attach the RecoveryMiddleware to the router.
    router.Handle("/", RecoveryMiddleware(http.HandlerFunc(func(w http.
    ResponseWriter, r *http.Request) {
        // Simulate a panic for demonstration purposes.
        panic("Something went wrong!")

        w.Write([]byte("Hello, World!")) // This won't be executed due
        to panic.
    })))

    // Start the server.
```

```
    http.ListenAndServe(":8080", router)
}
```

The preceding code defines an **HTTP server** in **Go** that includes a **middleware** for **recovering** from panics. Here's a breakdown of the code:

1. **`RecoveryMiddleware` Function**:
    a. The `RecoveryMiddleware` function is a middleware that takes an `http.Handler (next)` and returns a new `http.Handler`.
    b. It uses a **deferred function** (`defer`) to recover from panics. If a panic occurs in the next handler or subsequent middleware, this deferred function will catch it.
    c. If a panic is caught, it logs the panic details and sends a generic `"Internal Server Error"` response with a status code of 500.
    d. After the deferred function, it calls the next handler in the chain.
2. **Main Function**:
    a. The `main` function creates a new `http.ServeMux`.
    b. It attaches the `RecoveryMiddleware` to the router, ensuring that every request passes through this middleware.
    c. The **main** handler is a function that simulates a panic for demonstration purposes. Note that the line `w.Write([]byte("Hello, World!"))` won't be executed due to the preceding panic.
3. **Server Start**:
    a. The server is started using `http.ListenAndServe` on port **8080**.

In summary, this code demonstrates how to implement a recovery middleware in Go. The `RecoveryMiddleware` provides a safety net for handling panics in a web server, preventing them from crashing the entire application and responding with a meaningful error message instead.

Next, we will proceed to implement gRPC interceptors, utilizing the books application introduced in *Chapter 3: Getting started with gRPC.*

Implementing logging interceptor

Before delving into the implementation of a logging interceptor, let's explore the creation of a logging package. This package will serve as a foundation for our logging interceptor, offering a comprehensive solution. Moreover, this fully featured logging package can also be employed for REST middlewares, providing structured logs rather than relying on basic one-liners.

For more information, please view the logger package implementation at: https://github.com/OrangeAVA/Modern-API-Design-with-gRPC/blob/main/books-app/internal/pkg/logger/logger.go

The logger package code defines a logging package that utilizes the **Zap** logging library for structured logging. Here are the key components:

1. **Global Logger Initialization (Init function)**:
   a. Initializes the logger using the `zap` package with a specified configuration.
   b. Configuration includes settings for log encoding, log levels, output paths (stdout in this case), and encoder configurations.
   c. Configures time encoding to a custom format or uses the default.
   d. Redirects standard Go log calls to the **Zap** logger.
2. **Logging Functions**:
   a. Provides a **Sugar** logger, which is a structured, human-friendly logger provided by **Zap**.
   b. Exposes a `WithContext` function that enhances the logger with additional request-specific fields. This is particularly useful for associating logs with specific requests in a web server environment.
   c. The `WithContext` function adds the `request ID` as a field to the logger if it is available in the context.
3. **Concurrency Control (`onceInit`)**:
   a. Utilizes the `sync.Once` type to ensure that the logger is initialized only once.
4. **Default Values**:
   a. By default, the logger is configured to output logs in **JSON** format to the standard output (`stdout`).
   b. The log level is set to `Debug.`
   c. If the logger initialization encounters an error, it is logged using the standard Go logger (`glog`).

This `logging` package is designed to be used throughout a Go application, providing a consistent and structured approach to logging. It offers the flexibility to configure log levels, output paths, and other settings. The `WithContext` function is particularly useful for associating contextual information, such as request IDs, with log entries, aiding in debugging and tracing.

It is now opportune to leverage the previously introduced logger package and construct a logger interceptor.

Here is what our gRPC logger interceptor function declaration looks like:

```
func AddLogging(logger *zap.Logger, uInterceptors *[]grpc.
UnaryServerInterceptor, sInterceptors *[]grpc.StreamServerInterceptor) {

    // attach logger instance to unary interceptor array

    // attach logger instance to stream interceptor array

}
```

The function, **AddLogging**, serves to incorporate a logging mechanism into gRPC interceptors. It takes, as parameters, a logger of the Zap logger type and two arrays: **uInterceptors** for Unary Server Interceptors and **sInterceptors** for Stream Server Interceptors. The purpose is to append the logger instance to these interceptor arrays, thereby integrating logging capabilities into both unary and streaming server interceptors. This ensures that the logger is seamlessly integrated into the gRPC server operations, facilitating detailed and structured logging for both unary and streaming requests.

Before directly associating the logger instance with the arrays of unary and stream interceptors, let's explore the implementations of specific helper methods:

```
func codeToLevel(code codes.Code) zapcore.Level {

    if code == codes.OK {

        // It is DEBUG

        return zap.DebugLevel

    }

    return grpc_zap.DefaultCodeToLevel(code)

}
```

The **codeToLevel** function is designed to convert a gRPC status code (**codes.Code**) into the corresponding Zap logger level (**zapcore.Level**). The function checks if the provided gRPC code is equal to **codes.OK,** indicating a successful operation. If so, it returns the **zap.DebugLevel**, considering success as a debug-level log entry. If the gRPC code is anything other than **codes.OK,** it utilizes the

grpc_zap.DefaultCodeToLevel function to get the default Zap logger level based on the provided gRPC status code. This ensures that log levels are appropriately set based on the nature and outcome of the gRPC operation.

```
func extractFields(fullMethod string) map[string]interface{} {

   return make(map[string]interface{})

}
```

The **extractFields** function is a placeholder or a stub that is meant to be filled with logic to extract fields from a gRPC request. Currently, it does not perform any extraction and returns an empty map of type **map[string]interface{}.**

The function takes a parameter **fullMethod (type: string),** which is the full gRPC method name. In gRPC, the full method name includes both the service and the method names, separated by a slash ("/"). For example, "YourService/YourMethod".

The function returns a map of type **map[string]interface{}.** This map is intended to contain extracted fields from the gRPC request, and these fields could be used for logging or other purposes.

```
func messageProducer(ctx context.Context, msg string, level zapcore.
Level, code codes.Code, err error, duration zapcore.Field) {

   ctxzap.AddFields(ctx, zap.String(request.RequestIDKey, request.
   GetContextRequestID(ctx)))

   ctxzap.Extract(ctx).Check(level, msg).Write(

      zap.Error(err),

      zap.String("grpc.code", code.String()),

      duration,

   )

}
```

The **messageProducer** function is a utility function for producing log messages using the **Zap** logging library in a gRPC context. Here's a breakdown of its parameters and functionality:

1. **ctx (type: context.Context)**: The context object associated with the gRPC request. It is used to retrieve information like the request ID.

2. **`msg (type: string)`**: The log message that describes the event or action being logged.
3. **`level (type: zapcore.Level)`**: The logging level (for example, Debug, Info, Warn, Error).
4. **`code (type: codes.Code)`**: The gRPC status code associated with the event.
5. **`err (type: error)`**: The error associated with the event, if any.
6. **`duration (type: zapcore.Field)`**: A field representing the duration of the event for logging the time it took for an operation.

The function performs the following steps:

1. It adds a field to the context, specifically the request ID retrieved from the context. This information is then added to the log entries to associate logs with specific requests.
2. It uses **`ctxzap.Extract(ctx).Check(level, msg)`** to create a log entry with the specified log level and message.
3. It writes additional fields to the log entry, including the error (**`zap.Error(err)`**), the gRPC status code (**`zap.String("grpc.code", code.String())`**), and the duration field.

In summary, the **`messageProducer`** function is a utility for producing structured log messages in the context of a gRPC request. The logs include details such as the request ID, log level, message, error, gRPC status code, and duration.

By employing the aforementioned helper methods, we've integrated our logging package with both unary and stream interceptors:

```
func AddLogging(logger *zap.Logger, uInterceptors *[]grpc.
UnaryServerInterceptor, sInterceptors *[]grpc.StreamServerInterceptor) {

    // Shared options for the logger, with a custom gRPC code to log
    level function.

    o := []grpc_zap.Option{

        grpc_zap.WithLevels(codeToLevel),

        grpc_zap.WithMessageProducer(messageProducer),

    }
```

```
    // Make sure that log statements internal to gRPC library are logged
    using the zaplogger as well.
    grpc_zap.ReplaceGrpcLoggerV2(logger)

    *uInterceptors = append(*uInterceptors, grpc_
    ctxtags.UnaryServerInterceptor(grpc_ctxtags.
    WithFieldExtractor(extractFields)))
    *uInterceptors = append(*uInterceptors, grpc_zap.
    UnaryServerInterceptor(logger, o...))

    *sInterceptors = append(*sInterceptors, grpc_ctxtags.
    StreamServerInterceptor(grpc_ctxtags.WithFieldExtractor(grpc_
    ctxtags.CodeGenRequestFieldExtractor)))
    *sInterceptors = append(*sInterceptors, grpc_zap.
    StreamServerInterceptor(logger, o...))

}
```

Now, let's integrate the interceptor with the server. Let's explore how we can accomplish this.

If we revisit *Chapter 3, Getting started with gRPC*, where we established the books-app gRPC server, the server definition resembled the following:

```
opts := []grpc.ServerOption{}
s := grpc.NewServer(opts...)
proto.RegisterBookServiceServer(s, a)
reflection.Register(s)

if err := s.Serve(lis); err != nil {
    log.Fatalf("Failed to serve: %v", err)
}
```

However, we now associate our interceptor(s) with the server by providing them as server options:

```
opts := []grpc.ServerOption{}
middlewareOpts := middleware.ProvideGrpcMiddlewareServerOpts()
opts = append(opts, middlewareOpts...)

s := grpc.NewServer(opts...)
proto.RegisterBookServiceServer(s, a)
reflection.Register(s)

if err := s.Serve(lis); err != nil {
    log.Fatalf("Failed to serve: %v", err)
}
```

The function **ProvideGrpcMiddlewareServerOpts** offers us a convenient way to set up common gRPC server interceptor, such as logging, by combining them with the standard gRPC server options. The approach follows the chaining of interceptors, a common pattern in gRPC middleware design. Let's look at how this is achieved:

```
package middleware

import (
   "github.com/OrangeAVA/Modern-API-Design-with-gRPC/books-app/
   internal/pkg/logger"
   "google.golang.org/grpc"
)

func AddInterceptors(opts []grpc.ServerOption, uInterceptors []grpc.
UnaryServerInterceptor, sInterceptors []grpc.StreamServerInterceptor) []
grpc.ServerOption {
   opts = append(opts, grpc.ChainUnaryInterceptor(uInterceptors...))
   opts = append(opts, grpc.ChainStreamInterceptor(sInterceptors...))
   return opts
```

```
}

// Add grpc default middleware like logging
func ProvideGrpcMiddlewareServerOpts() []grpc.ServerOption {
    // gRPC server startup options
    opts := []grpc.ServerOption{}

    uInterceptors := []grpc.UnaryServerInterceptor{}
    sInterceptors := []grpc.StreamServerInterceptor{}

    // add middlewares
    AddLogging(logger.Log, &uInterceptors, &sInterceptors)

    opts = AddInterceptors(opts, uInterceptors, sInterceptors)

    return opts
}
```

The **`middleware`** package provides functions for adding gRPC server interceptors, specifically unary and stream interceptors. Here's an explanation of the key functions:

1. **`func AddInterceptors(opts []grpc.ServerOption, uInterceptors []grpc.UnaryServerInterceptor, sInterceptors []grpc.StreamServerInterceptor) []grpc.ServerOption`**: This function takes in gRPC server options, unary server interceptors, and stream server interceptors. It appends the unary and stream interceptors to the server options using **`grpc.ChainUnaryInterceptor`** and **`grpc.ChainStreamInterceptor`**, respectively. The modified server options are then returned.
2. **`func ProvideGrpcMiddlewareServerOpts() []grpc.ServerOption`**: This function initializes gRPC server options and empty slices for unary and stream interceptors. It then adds a logging interceptor using the **`AddLogging`** function. Finally, it calls **`AddInterceptors`** to combine the server options with the interceptor and returns the resulting gRPC server options.

It is now time to see the benefit of adding **logger** interceptors.

Test logging interceptor

1. Comment out the code where we added the interceptors as server options and bound with the server to see the results before adding the log interceptor:

```
// middlewareOpts := middleware.ProvideGrpcMiddlewareServerOpts()
// opts = append(opts, middlewareOpts...)
```

2. Command to start the server:

```
go run books-app/cmd/grpc-books-server/main.go -configFile="./books-app/configs/grpc-books-server.yaml"
```

3. Following are the logs generated at the start of the gRPC books server:

```
host=localhost port=5432 user=postgres dbname=books_db password=mysecretpassword sslmode=disable connect_timeout=30
2023/11/16 20:44:57 Created DB connection pool 1 30 0 1
2023/11/16 20:44:57 No change detected after running the migrations for Postgres Database
starting books gRPC server at 0.0.0.0:50051
```

4. Command to fetch books from the gRPC books server:

```
grpcurl -plaintext 0.0.0.0:50051 prot.BookService/ListBooks
```

5. Output:


```
{
  "books": [
    {
      "isbn": 12345,
      "name": "da vinci code",
      "publisher": "doubleday"
    },
    {
      "isbn": 12346,
      "name": "the best laid plans",
      "publisher": "harper"
    },
    {
```

```
        "isbn": 12347,
        "name": "modern api design using grpc",
        "publisher": "ava orange"
      }
    ]
  }
```

There are no additional logs on the server.

6. Now, let's enable the interceptors by uncommenting the code we commented in step #1, and then repeat steps #2 to #4 again.
7. Change in server logs:

```
host=localhost port=5432 user=postgres dbname=books_db password=mysecretpassword sslmode=disable connect_timeout=30
{"level":"INFO","timestamp":"2023-11-16T15:21:37Z","caller":"db/db.go:54","msg":"Created DB connection pool 1 30 0 1"}
{"level":"INFO","timestamp":"2023-11-16T15:21:37Z","caller":"migrations/migrator.go:49","msg":"No change detected after running the migrations for Postgres Database"}
starting books gRPC server at 0.0.0.0:50051
{"level":"INFO","timestamp":"2023-11-16T15:21:37Z","caller":"grpclog/component.go:36","msg":"[core][Server #1] Server created","system":"grpc","grpc_log":true}
{"level":"INFO","timestamp":"2023-11-16T15:21:37Z","caller":"grpclog/component.go:36","msg":"[core][Server #1 ListenSocket #2] ListenSocket created","system":"grpc","grpc_log":true}
{"level":"INFO","timestamp":"2023-11-16T15:21:59Z","caller":"grpc-books-server/handlers.go:42","msg":"listing books"}
{"level":"DEBUG","timestamp":"2023-11-16T15:21:59Z","caller":"middleware/logger.go:32","msg":"finished unary call with code OK","grpc.start_time":"2023-11-16T20:51:59+05:30","system":"grpc","span.kind":"server","grpc.service":"prot.BookService","grpc.method":"ListBooks","peer.address":"127.0.0.1:47578","request-id":"","grpc.code":"OK","grpc.time_ms":11.846}
{"level":"DEBUG","timestamp":"2023-11-16T15:21:59Z","caller":"middleware/logger.go:32","msg":"finished streaming call with code OK","grpc.start_time":"2023-11-16T20:51:59+05:30","system":"grpc","span.kind":"server","grpc.service":"grpc.reflection.
```

```
v1.ServerReflection","grpc.method":"ServerReflectionInfo","peer.address":"127.0.0.1:47578","request-id":"","grpc.code":"OK","grpc.time_ms":16.709}
```

Now, observe that information about the request is visible in the server logs, providing valuable insights for debugging and monitoring purposes.

Implementing Recovery Interceptor

A recovery interceptor is crucial in gRPC servers to handle and recover from panics. In a server-client communication model, if an unexpected panic occurs on the server side due to a runtime error, it can lead to the termination of the entire server process. This abrupt termination can be detrimental to the availability and reliability of the server, especially in production environments.

The recovery interceptor serves as a safety net by intercepting and recovering from panics. When a panic occurs within the server's execution context, the recovery interceptor catches it, logs relevant information, and ensures that the server continues to function rather than crashing. It helps prevent cascading failures, allowing the server to gracefully handle unexpected errors and maintain overall system stability.

In essence, the recovery interceptor is a defensive mechanism that contributes to the robustness and fault tolerance of gRPC servers.

We won't need a separate recovery package, as we did with the logger package. Instead, let's directly explore how to construct a recovery interceptor:

```
package middleware


import (

    "context"

    "runtime/debug"


    "github.com/OrangeAVA/Modern-API-Design-with-gRPC/books-app/
    internal/pkg/logger"

    grpc_recovery "github.com/grpc-ecosystem/go-grpc-middleware/recovery"

    "google.golang.org/grpc"

    "google.golang.org/grpc/codes"
```

```
    "google.golang.org/grpc/status"
)

// to handle panic and log stack trace
// also returns error from panic to send error-message to gateway
func PanicTracer(ctx context.Context, p interface{}) error {
    logger.WithContext(ctx).Errorf("Stack Trace: %s", string(debug.
    Stack()))
    return status.Errorf(codes.Unknown, "Panic triggered: %v", p)
}

func AddRecovery(uInterceptors *[]grpc.UnaryServerInterceptor,
sInterceptors *[]grpc.StreamServerInterceptor) {

    opts := []grpc_recovery.Option{
        grpc_recovery.WithRecoveryHandlerContext(PanicTracer),
    }

    *uInterceptors = append(*uInterceptors, grpc_recovery.
    UnaryServerInterceptor(opts...))
    *sInterceptors = append(*sInterceptors, grpc_recovery.
    StreamServerInterceptor(opts...))
}
```

This code implements a recovery middleware for gRPC servers using the **grpc_recovery** package. It includes a panic tracer function **PanicTracer**, which logs the stack trace in case of a panic and returns an error message that can be sent to the client via gRPC status.

The **PanicTracer** function takes a context and a recovered panic as parameters. It uses the logger from the internal package to log the stack trace and then constructs an error message using the gRPC **status** package. This error message includes information that a panic was triggered and the recovered panic value.

The **AddRecovery** function configures recovery options, including the previously defined **PanicTracer**, and then appends the unary and stream recovery interceptors with these options to the corresponding interceptor slices.

In summary, this code provides a recovery mechanism for gRPC servers, enhancing their robustness by logging stack traces in case of panics and sending appropriate error messages to clients.

We will now update the method to add recovery functionality to both unary and stream interceptors:

```
// Add grpc default middleware like logging and recovery

func ProvideGrpcMiddlewareServerOpts() []grpc.ServerOption {

    // gRPC server startup options

    opts := []grpc.ServerOption{}


    uInterceptors := []grpc.UnaryServerInterceptor{}

    sInterceptors := []grpc.StreamServerInterceptor{}


    // add middlewares

    AddLogging(logger.Log, &uInterceptors, &sInterceptors)

AddRecovery(&uInterceptors, &sInterceptors)


    opts = AddInterceptors(opts, uInterceptors, sInterceptors)


    return opts

}
```

It is now time to see the benefit of adding **recovery** interceptors.

Test recovery interceptor

1. Comment out the code where we added the interceptors as server options and bound with the server:

    ```
    // middlewareOpts := middleware.ProvideGrpcMiddlewareServerOpts()

    // opts = append(opts, middlewareOpts...)
    ```

2. Let's introduce a known malicious code that will create a panic in the books server's fetch books method:

```
func (a *App) ListBooks(ctx context.Context, _ *proto.Empty) (*proto.ListBooksRespose, error) {
    log.Println("listing books")
    panic("fatal error while listing book")

    // books, err := a.bookRepo.GetAllBooks()
    // if err != nil {
    //  return nil, err
    // }

    // b, err := json.Marshal(books)
    // if err != nil {
    //  return nil, fmt.Errorf("error while marshalling books", err.Error())
    // }

    // pbBooks := []*proto.Book{}
    // err = json.Unmarshal(b, &pbBooks)
    // if err != nil {
    //  return nil, fmt.Errorf("error while unmarshalling books", err.Error())
    // }

    // return &proto.ListBooksRespose{Books: pbBooks}, nil
}
```

3. Command to start the server:

```
go run books-app/cmd/grpc-books-server/main.go -configFile="./books-app/configs/grpc-books-server.yaml"
```

4. Following are the logs generated at the start of the gRPC books server:

```
host=localhost port=5432 user=postgres dbname=books_db password=mysecretpassword sslmode=disable connect_timeout=30
```

```
2023/11/16 21:01:42 Created DB connection pool 1 30 0 1
2023/11/16 21:01:42 No change detected after running the migrations
for Postgres Database
starting books gRPC server at 0.0.0.0:50051
```

5. Command to fetch books from the gRPC books server:

```
grpcurl -plaintext 0.0.0.0:50051  prot.BookService/ListBooks
```

6. Output:

```
ERROR:
  Code: Unavailable
  Message: error reading from server: EOF
```

7. Server has stopped working now:

```
host=localhost    port=5432    user=postgres    dbname=books_db
password=mysecretpassword sslmode=disable connect_timeout=30
2023/11/16 21:01:42 Created DB connection pool 1 30 0 1
2023/11/16 21:01:42 No change detected after running the migrations
for Postgres Database
starting books gRPC server at 0.0.0.0:50051
2023/11/16 21:02:59 listing books
panic: fatal error while listing book

goroutine 35 [running]:
github.com/OrangeAVA/Modern-API-Design-with-gRPC/books-app/
internal/apps/grpc-books-server.(*App).ListBooks(0xc645e0?,
{0xc000432f30?, 0x5097a6?}, 0x0?)
/home/hitesh/Documents/personal/codebases/Modern-API-Design-with-
gRPC/books-app/internal/apps/grpc-books-server/handlers.go:42
+0x8f
github.com/OrangeAVA/Modern-API-Design-with-gRPC/books-app/
internal/pkg/proto._BookService_ListBooks_Handler({0xcb3be0?,
0xc000224530}, {0xe44d28, 0xc000432f00}, 0xc00029b260, 0x0)
/home/hitesh/Documents/personal/codebases/Modern-API-Design-with-
gRPC/books-app/internal/pkg/proto/book_grpc.pb.go:155 +0x169
google.golang.org/grpc.(*Server).processUnaryRPC(0xc000372000,
{0xe49538, 0xc00027a4e0}, 0xc0002c4120, 0xc0003324b0, 0x13ccf78,
0x0)
```

```
/home/hitesh/go/pkg/mod/google.golang.org/grpc@v1.58.2/server.
go:1376 +0xde7

google.golang.org/grpc.(*Server).handleStream(0xc000372000,
{0xe49538, 0xc00027a4e0}, 0xc0002c4120, 0x0)

/home/hitesh/go/pkg/mod/google.golang.org/grpc@v1.58.2/server.
go:1753 +0x9e7

google.golang.org/grpc.(*Server).serveStreams.func1.1()

/home/hitesh/go/pkg/mod/google.golang.org/grpc@v1.58.2/server.
go:998 +0x8d

created by google.golang.org/grpc.(*Server).serveStreams.func1 in
goroutine 14

/home/hitesh/go/pkg/mod/google.golang.org/grpc@v1.58.2/server.
go:996 +0x165

exit status 2

make: *** [Makefile:90: main-grpc-serve] Error 1
```

8. Now, let's enable the interceptors and redo the steps #3 to #5.
9. Output (it is now more informative):

```
ERROR:
  Code: Unknown
  Message: Panic trigg

ered: fatal error while listing book
```

10. Even though there was a panic, the server now has logged the panic details and stack trace while remaining active:

```
host=localhost port=5432 user=postgres dbname=books_db
password=mysecretpassword sslmode=disable connect_timeout=30

{"level":"INFO","timestamp":"2023-11-16T15:35:10Z","caller":"db/
db.go:54","msg":"Created DB connection pool 1 30 0 1"}

{"level":"INFO","timestamp":"2023-11-16T15:35:10Z","caller":"mi-
grations/migrator.go:49","msg":"No change detected after running
the migrations for Postgres Database"}
```

```
starting books gRPC server at 0.0.0.0:50051
```

{"level":"INFO","timestamp":"2023-11-16T15:35:10Z","caller":"grpclog/component.go:36","msg":"[core][Server #1] Server created","system":"grpc","grpc_log":true}

{"level":"INFO","timestamp":"2023-11-16T15:35:10Z","caller":"grpclog/component.go:36","msg":"[core][Server #1 ListenSocket #2] ListenSocket created","system":"grpc","grpc_log":true}

{"level":"INFO","timestamp":"2023-11-16T15:35:14Z","caller":"grpc-books-server/handlers.go:41","msg":"listing books"}

{"level":"ERROR","timestamp":"2023-11-16T15:35:14Z","caller":"middleware/recovery.go:17","msg":"Stack Trace: goroutine 38 [running]:\nruntime/debug.Stack()\n\t/usr/local/go/src/runtime/debug/stack.go:24 +0x5e\ngithub.com/OrangeAVA/Modern-API-Design-with-gRPC/books-app/internal/pkg/middleware.PanicTracer({0xe99808?, 0xc0004c93e0?}, {0xc0a0e0, 0xe8cc50})\n\t/home/hitesh/Documents/personal/codebases/Modern-API-Design-with-gRPC/books-app/internal/pkg/middleware/recovery.go:17 +0x45\ngithub.com/grpc-ecosystem/go-grpc-middleware/recovery.recoverFrom({0xe99808?, 0xc0004c93e0?}, {0xc0a0e0?, 0xe8cc50?}, 0xc14dab8c83f06ae5?)\n\t/home/hitesh/go/pkg/mod/github.com/grpc-ecosystem/go-grpc-middleware@v1.4.0/recovery/interceptors.go:61 +0x30\ngithub.com/grpc-ecosystem/go-grpc-middleware/recovery.UnaryServerInterceptor.func1.1()\n\t/home/hitesh/go/pkg/mod/github.com/grpc-ecosystem/go-grpc-middleware@v1.4.0/recovery/interceptors.go:29 +0x75\npanic({0xc0a0e0?, 0xe8cc50?})\n\t/usr/local/go/src/runtime/panic.go:914 +0x21f\ngithub.com/OrangeAVA/Modern-API-Design-with-gRPC/books-app/internal/apps/grpc-books-server.(*App).ListBooks(0x148e180?, {0xc0003c1770?, 0xb90a9d?}, ...}

{"level":"ERROR","timestamp":"2023-11-16T15:35:14Z","caller":"middleware/logger.go:32","msg":"finished unary call with code Unknown","grpc.start_time":"2023-11-16T21:05:14+05:30","system":"grpc","span.kind":"server","grpc.service":"prot.BookService","grpc.method":"ListBooks","peer.address":"127.0.0.1:43956","request-id":"","error":"rpc error: code = Unknown desc = Panic triggered: fatal error while listing book","grpc.code":"Unknown","grpc.time_ms":0.613,"stacktrace":.....}

{"level":"DEBUG","timestamp":"2023-11-16T15:35:14Z","caller":"middleware/logger.go:32","msg":"finished streaming call with

```
code      OK","grpc.start_time":"2023-11-16T21:05:14+05:30","sys-
tem":"grpc","span.kind":"server","grpc.service":"grpc.reflection.
v1.ServerReflection","grpc.method":"ServerReflectionInfo","peer.ad-
dress":"127.0.0.1:43956","request-id":"","grpc.code":"OK","grpc.
time_ms":5.44}
```

From the described scenarios, we have successfully tested our interceptor implementations and confirmed their functionality.

Resilient gRPC communication

Before delving into advanced concepts for constructing resilient gRPC communication, it's worth noting that we've introduced modifications to the books application. Additionally, we've incorporated two new gRPC servers: the **Review Server** and the **Book Info Server**.

Review Server

This server is designed to handle operations related to book reviews. It responds to client requests for adding and retrieving reviews associated with specific books.

Let's begin by examining the proto-service definitions. Here, we've introduced a new service along with its own set of RPCs:

```
service ReviewService {
   // Unary RPC to submit a book review
  rpc SubmitReviews(SubmitReviewRequest) returns (SubmitReviewResponse);

   // Unary RPC to fetch all book reviews
 rpcGetBookReviews(GetBookReviewsRequest)returns(GetBookReviewsResponse);
}
```

The **ReviewService** in the gRPC service definition specifies two Unary RPC methods:

1. **SubmitReviews**:
    a. **Request**: It takes a **SubmitReviewRequest** as input, presumably containing information about a book review that a client wishes to submit.

   b. **Response**: It returns a **`SubmitReviewResponse`**, indicating the outcome or any relevant information about the submission.

2. **GetBookReviews**:

   a. **Request**: It expects a **`GetBookReviewsRequest`**, which likely includes details about the book for which the client wants to retrieve reviews.

   b. **Response**: The server responds with a **`GetBookReviewsResponse`**, containing the reviews associated with the specified book.

In essence, clients can use these two methods to interact with the **`ReviewService`**. They can submit new reviews and retrieve existing reviews for a particular book. These Unary RPCs follow a simple request-response model, where each client request corresponds to a single server response.

Let's also look at the message structures as well:

```
message Review {
  string reviewer = 1;
  string comment = 2;
  int32 rating = 3;
}

message SubmitReviewRequest {
  int32 isbn = 1;
  string reviewer = 2;
  string comment = 3;
  int32 rating = 4;
}

message SubmitReviewResponse {
  string status = 1;
}

message GetBookReviewsRequest {
```

```
  int32 isbn = 1;

}


message GetBookReviewsResponse {

  repeated Review reviews = 1;

}
```

The complete implementation of the review service can be viewed at: https://github.com/OrangeAVA/Modern-API-Design-with-gRPC/tree/main/books-app/internal/apps/grpc-review-server

Here is a detailed breakdown of the handler's code:

1. **GetBookReviews**:
    a. **Purpose**: Retrieves all reviews for a given book.
    b. **Implementation**:
        i. Logs a message indicating that book reviews are being fetched.
        ii. Calls the **`GetAllReviews`** method of the bookRepo to get reviews from the repository.
        iii. Converts the retrieved reviews from the internal model to the gRPC proto format.
        iv. Returns a response containing the list of reviews in proto format.
2. **SubmitReviews**:
    a. **Purpose**: Submits a new review for a book.
    b. **Implementation**:
        i. Logs a message indicating that a book review is being submitted.
        ii. Creates a new **`DBReview`** based on the information provided in the gRPC request.
        iii. Calls the **`AddReview`** method of the **`bookRepo`** to add the new review to the repository.
        iv. Returns a response indicating the success of the review submission.

These methods are part of the **App** struct and handle the gRPC service methods related to book reviews. The implementation involves interaction with the book repository (**`bookRepo`**) and the conversion between the internal model and the gRPC proto format.

The review server setup closely resembles the approach taken for the book server and the review server runs on **50052** port.

Book Info Server

The Book Info Server specializes in providing information about various books. Clients can query book details and associated reviews about a particular book.

Let's begin by examining the proto-service definitions. Here, as well, we've introduced a new service along with its own set of RPCs:

```
message GetBookInfoRequest {
  int32 isbn = 1;
}

message GetBookInfoResponse {
  int32 isbn = 1;
  string name = 2;
  string publisher = 3;
  repeated Review reviews = 4;
}

service BookInfoService {
  // Unary RPC to get book information with reviews by ID
  rpc GetBookInfoWithReviews(GetBookInfoRequest) returns
  (GetBookInfoResponse);
}
```

In this gRPC service definition, we have two messages and one service. The **GetBookInfoRequest** message contains an integer field **isbn**, which serves as the unique identifier for a book. The **GetBookInfoResponse** message includes information about a book, such as its **ISBN**, **name**, **publisher**, and a **list of reviews**. The **BookInfoService** service provides a single RPC method named **GetBookInfoWithReviews**, which is a unary RPC that takes a **GetBookInfoRequest** and returns a **GetBookInfoResponse**. This RPC is designed to retrieve detailed information about a book, including its reviews, based on the provided **ISBN**.

The complete implementation of the book info service can be viewed at: https://github.com/OrangeAVA/Modern-API-Design-with-gRPC/tree/main/books-app/internal/apps/grpc-book-info-server

While the book info server setup (running on port **50053**) is similar to the setup of the book server and review server, the implementation of the **GetBookInfoWithReviews** is what we need to analyze.

```
package grpcbooksserver

import (
    "context"
    "log"

    "github.com/OrangeAVA/Modern-API-Design-with-gRPC/books-app/
    internal/pkg/proto"
)

func (a *App) GetBookInfoWithReviews(ctx context.Context, req *proto.
GetBookInfoRequest) (*proto.GetBookInfoResponse, error) {
    log.Println("fetching book and reviews")

    book, err := a.bookServerClient.GetBook(ctx, &proto.
    GetBookRequest{Isbn: req.GetIsbn()})
    if err != nil {
        return nil, err
    }

    resp, err := a.reviewServerClient.GetBookReviews(ctx, &proto.
    GetBookReviewsRequest{Isbn: req.GetIsbn()})
    if err != nil {
        return nil, err
    }
```

```
    return &proto.GetBookInfoResponse{
        Isbn:      req.GetIsbn(),
        Name:      book.Name,
        Publisher: book.Publisher,
        Reviews:   resp.GetReviews(),
    }, nil
}
```

The **GetBookInfoWithReviews** function is an implementation of the **GetBookInfoWithReviews RPC** method for the **BookInfoService** service. This method is designed to fetch detailed information about a book, including its reviews. The function takes a **context.Context** and a ***proto.GetBookInfoRequest** as parameters, representing the context of the request and the request payload, respectively.

Inside the function, it logs a message indicating that it is fetching information about a book and its reviews. It then uses the **bookServerClient** to get information about the book by calling the **GetBook** RPC method and stores the result in the book variable. Next, it uses the **reviewServerClient** to get the reviews for the same book by calling the **GetBookReviews** RPC method and stores the result in the **resp** variable.

Finally, the function constructs and returns a ***proto.GetBookInfoResponse** with the book's **ISBN**, **name**, **publisher**, and the **reviews** obtained from the resp. In case of any errors during these operations, the function returns an error.

Let's now run all these servers and see how they work in tandem.

Start the books server:

```
go run books-app/cmd/grpc-books-server/main.go -configFile="./books-app/configs/grpc-books-server.yaml"
```

Start the reviews server:

```
go run books-app/cmd/grpc-review-server/main.go -configFile="./books-app/configs/grpc-review-server.yaml"
```

Start the book info server:

```
go run books-app/cmd/grpc-book-info-server/main.go -configFile=”./books-app/configs/grpc-book-info-server.yaml”
```

Fetch book details with ISBN (12347) from the books server

Command:

```
grpcurl -plaintext -d ‘{“isbn”: “12345”}’ 0.0.0.0:50051 prot.BookService/GetBook
```

Output:

```
{
  “isbn”: 12347,
  “name”: “modern api design using grpc”,
  “publisher”: “ava orange”
}
```

Submit a review for the book with ISBN (12347) to reviews server:

Command:

```
grpcurl -plaintext -d ‘{“isbn”: “12347”, “reviewer”: “reviewer-7231”, “comment”: “practical book”, “rating”: “4”}’ 0.0.0.0:50052 prot.ReviewService/SubmitReviews
```

Output:

```
{
  “status”: “review for book(12347) submitted successfully”
}
```

Fetch book and reviews for the book with ISBN (12347) from the book info server:

Command:

```
grpcurl -plaintext -d ‘{“isbn”: “12347”}’ 0.0.0.0:50053 prot.BookInfoService.GetBookInfoWithReviews
```

Output:


```
{
  "isbn": 12347,
  "name": "modern api design using grpc",
  "publisher": "ava orange",
  "reviews": [
    {
      "reviewer": "hitesh pattanayak",
      "comment": "good book",
      "rating": 5
    },
    {
      "reviewer": "another person",
      "comment": "great book",
      "rating": 4
    },
    {
      "reviewer": "reviewer-7231",
      "comment": "practical book",
      "rating": 4
    }
  ]
}
```


It's essential to highlight that the **Book Info** server has a direct dependency on both the **Books** and **Reviews** servers. This interdependence is a crucial consideration due to the inherent tight coupling between these services. The significance lies in the potential occurrence of what is termed as **cascading failures**. In a cascading failure scenario, if either the Books or Reviews service encounters unexpected issues or malfunctions, it can propagate issues to the Book Info service, leading to a domino effect of failures. This phenomenon underscores the need for robust error handling and resilience mechanisms within the system architecture to mitigate the impact of potential failures and maintain overall system reliability.

Cascading failures

Cascading failures refer to a situation in a distributed system where a failure in one component triggers failures in other interconnected components, creating a chain reaction of issues throughout the system. This phenomenon can have severe consequences for the overall stability and reliability of the system. Here's a detailed breakdown of cascading failures:

- **Dependency Chain**: In a distributed system, services often depend on one another to perform various tasks. When one service fails, especially if it's a critical or foundational service, it disrupts the workflow of other services that depend on it.
- **Propagation of Failures**: A failure in a service can propagate to its dependent services, causing them to fail as well. This propagation can continue through multiple layers of dependencies, creating a domino effect.
- **Increased Load and Stress**: As failures propagate, the load on other services may increase as they attempt to compensate for the failed components. This increased load can lead to performance degradation and further stress on the system.
- **Resource Exhaustion**: The additional load and stress on surviving components may lead to resource exhaustion. This could include running out of memory, exceeding processing capacity, or reaching connection limits.
- **Unpredictable Behavior**: Cascading failures often result in unpredictable and chaotic behavior across the system. Services may respond to failures in unexpected ways, and the system may enter an unstable state.
- **Global Outages**: In extreme cases, cascading failures can lead to a global outage where a significant portion of the system becomes unavailable.
- **Recovery Challenges**: Recovering from cascading failures can be challenging because simply restarting failed services may not be sufficient. System administrators need to identify the root cause, fix the underlying issues, and carefully orchestrate the recovery process.

- **Resilience Measures**: To prevent or mitigate cascading failures, distributed systems need to incorporate resilience measures. This includes implementing fallback mechanisms, introducing redundancy, and employing strategies like circuit breakers.
- **Monitoring and Alerting**: Effective monitoring and alerting systems are crucial to detect issues early and initiate proactive responses before failures cascade.
- **Isolation of Services**: Designing services with proper isolation ensures that failures in one service don't have a widespread impact on the entire system.

Understanding and addressing the challenges associated with cascading failures is fundamental in building robust and resilient distributed systems. It involves a combination of architectural best practices, diligent monitoring, and effective response strategies to maintain the overall health and reliability of the system.

In the sets of services described in the context of the books application (**Books Server, Reviews Server, and Book Info Server**), cascading failures could be a concern due to the interdependencies between these services. Let's break down the potential scenarios where cascading failures might occur:

- **Tight Service Coupling**: The Book Info Server depends on both the Books Server and Reviews Server. If either the Books Server or Reviews Server faces a failure, it can directly impact the Book Info Server's ability to fulfill requests.
- **Dependency Chain**: Consider a scenario where the Reviews Server experiences downtime or becomes unresponsive. Since the Book Info Server relies on the Reviews Server to fetch reviews, this failure could propagate to the Book Info Server.
- **Resource Exhaustion**: A failure in the Books Server could lead to increased traffic on the Reviews Server as clients attempt to obtain book reviews. This increased load might lead to resource exhaustion in the Reviews Server, affecting its performance.
- **Global Outages**: If a critical failure occurs in the Books Server, it could trigger a chain reaction affecting not only the Reviews Server but also any other services that depend on the Books Server. This could potentially lead to a global outage, impacting the entire application.
- **Recovery Challenges**: Recovering from a cascading failure might involve restarting multiple services and ensuring that they come back online

in a coordinated manner. Identifying the root cause of the failure and implementing fixes could be complex.

- **Unpredictable Behavior**: Cascading failures can lead to unpredictable behavior, making it challenging to anticipate how the system will respond under certain failure conditions.

Mitigating Cascading Failures:

1. **Fallback Mechanisms**: Implementing fallback mechanisms can help services gracefully degrade when a dependent service is unavailable. We can have retry and timeout mechanisms in place for this.
2. **Circuit Breakers**: Implementing circuit breakers can prevent further requests from being sent to a failing service, giving it time to recover.

Context and Deadlines

In Go, the **`context`** package is used to carry deadlines, cancellations, and other request-scoped values across API boundaries and between processes. The **`context`** package provides a way to pass deadlines to functions that perform I/O or other tasks that may take a variable amount of time.

Here's an overview of **context** and **deadlines** in Go:

Context

A **`context.Context`** is an object that carries deadlines, cancellations signals, and other request-scoped values across API boundaries and between processes. It's often used in networking code and is especially useful in managing the lifecycle of operations.

```
package main

import (
   "context"
   "fmt"
   "time"
)

func main() {
```

```
    // Creating a context with a timeout of 2 seconds

    ctx, cancel := context.WithTimeout(context.Background(), 2*time.
    Second)

    defer cancel() // Always call cancel to release resources associated
    with the context


    // Passing the context to a function

    doSomething(ctx)

}


func doSomething(ctx context.Context) {

    select {

    case <-ctx.Done():

        fmt.Println("Operation canceled or timed out.")

        return

    case <-time.After(3 * time.Second):

        fmt.Println("Operation completed successfully.")

    }

}
```

Deadlines

A deadline is a timestamp that represents the maximum allowed time for a specific operation to complete. If the operation doesn't complete within the specified deadline, the associated context is canceled.

```
package main


import (

    "context"

    "fmt"

    "time"
```

```
)

func main() {
   // Creating a context with a deadline of 5 seconds
   ctx, cancel := context.WithDeadline(context.Background(), time.
   Now().Add(5*time.Second))
   defer cancel()

   // Passing the context to a function
   doSomething(ctx)
}

func doSomething(ctx context.Context) {
   select {
   case <-ctx.Done():
      fmt.Println("Operation canceled or deadline exceeded.")
      return
   case <-time.After(3 * time.Second):
      fmt.Println("Operation completed successfully.")
   }
}
```

In both examples, the **context.WithTimeout** and **context.WithDeadline** functions create a new context with an associated cancel function. The cancel function should be called to release resources when the operation is complete or canceled.

These are simplified examples, and in real-world scenarios, you might see the use of **context** in functions that involve network requests, database queries, or other potentially long-running operations. The **select** statement is used to handle multiple channels concurrently, including the cancellation signal from the context.

Mitigating cascading failures with Timeout pattern

Let's see how we can mitigate the probable cascading failure using the **Timeout** pattern.

To do this, we need to simulate a situation where either the reviews or books service or both take more time to give response than expected.

Simulating a delay in reviews service's `GetBookReviews` method:

```
func (a *App) GetBookReviews(ctx context.Context, req *proto.GetBookReviewsRequest) (*proto.GetBookReviewsResponse, error) {
   log.Println("fethcing book reviews")

   // Simulate a potentially long-running operation.
   select {
   case <-time.After(3 * time.Second): // Simulating a delay
      reviews := a.bookRepo.GetAllReviews(int(req.GetIsbn()))

      protoReviews := make([]*proto.Review, 0)

      for _, r := range reviews {
         protoReview := &proto.Review{Reviewer: r.Reviewer, Comment: r.Comment, Rating: int32(r.Rating)}
         protoReviews = append(protoReviews, protoReview)
      }

      return &proto.GetBookReviewsResponse{Reviews: protoReviews}, nil
   case <-ctx.Done():
      // Operation was canceled or timed out.
      return nil, ctx.Err()
   }
```

```
}
```

In the given code snippet, the **`GetBookReviews`** function simulates a potentially long-running operation using the **`time.After`** function to introduce a delay. This is a common pattern to mimic operations that might take some time, such as fetching data from an external service or a database.

Here's a breakdown of the delay simulation portion:

- **`time.After(3 * time.Second)`**: This creates a channel that sends the current time after a specified duration. In this case, it simulates a delay of 3 seconds.
- **`select`**: The **`select`** statement is used to wait on multiple communication operations. In this context, it's waiting for either the simulated delay to complete or for the **`ctx.Done()`** channel to close.
- If the simulated delay completes first, the actual logic for fetching book reviews is executed.
- If the context is canceled (either due to a timeout or cancellation), **`ctx.Done()`** will close, and the corresponding case will be selected. In this case, it returns **nil** and the error associated with the canceled context (**`ctx.Err()`**).

This pattern allows the function to be responsive to cancellation signals from the context, ensuring that the operation doesn't continue unnecessarily if the client cancels the request or if a timeout occurs.

Similarly, simulating a delay in the books service's **`GetBook`** method as well:

```
func (a *App) GetBook(ctx context.Context, req *proto.GetBookRequest)
(*proto.Book, error) {

    log.Println("fetching book")


    // Simulating a potentially long-running operation.

    select {

    case <-time.After(3 * time.Second): // Simulating a delay

        book := a.bookRepo.GetBook(int(req.Isbn))


        return &proto.Book{
```

```
            Isbn:      int32(book.Isbn),
            Name:      book.Name,
            Publisher: book.Publisher,
        }, nil
    case <-ctx.Done():
        // Operation was canceled or timed out.
        return nil, ctx.Err()
    }

}
```

Now, let's see how we can handle the delay in response situations from the books and reviews services in the book info server's **`GetBookInfoWithReviews`** method:

```
func (a *App) GetBookInfoWithReviews(ctx context.Context, req *proto.
GetBookInfoRequest) (*proto.GetBookInfoResponse, error) {
    log.Println("fetching book and reviews")

    newCtx, cancel := context.WithTimeout(ctx, 5*time.Second)
    defer cancel()

    book, err := a.bookServerClient.GetBook(newCtx, &proto.
    GetBookRequest{Isbn: req.GetIsbn()})
    if err != nil {
        return nil, err
    }

    resp, err := a.reviewServerClient.GetBookReviews(newCtx, &proto.
    GetBookReviewsRequest{Isbn: req.GetIsbn()})
    if err != nil {
```

```
        return nil, err
    }

    return &proto.GetBookInfoResponse{
        Isbn:      req.GetIsbn(),
        Name:      book.Name,
        Publisher: book.Publisher,
        Reviews:   resp.GetReviews(),
    }, nil
}
```

The **GetBookInfoWithReviews** function demonstrates the use of a timeout with the **context.WithTimeout** function. This is employed to set a deadline for the operations within the function, ensuring that they don't take longer than the specified duration.

Here's the breakdown of the timeout portion:

- **context.WithTimeout(ctx, 5*time.Second)**: This creates a new context (**newCtx**) derived from the original context (**ctx**) but with a deadline set 5 seconds into the future. This means that any operations initiated with this new context must complete within 5 seconds.
- **defer cancel()**: The **defer** statement ensures that the **cancel** function is called when the surrounding function returns. This is important for releasing resources associated with the context, even if the function encounters an error or returns early.

The operations following the creation of **newCtx** (calls to **a.bookServerClient.GetBook** and **a.reviewServerClient.GetBookReviews**) will be bound by the timeout set in this context. If the total time of these operations exceeds 5 seconds, they will be canceled, and the function will return with an error.

This pattern helps prevent operations from blocking indefinitely and allows the function to be more responsive to potential delays or failures in the underlying services.

Mitigating Cascading Failures with Retry pattern

Let's see how we can mitigate the probable cascading failure using the **Retry** pattern.

To do this, we need to simulate a situation where either the reviews or books service or both fail intermittently.

```
func (a *App) GetBookReviews(_ context.Context, req *proto.
GetBookReviewsRequest) (*proto.GetBookReviewsResponse, error) {

    log.Println("fethcing book reviews")


    // Simulate a potentially failing operation.

    if time.Now().Second()%2 == 0 {

        return nil, fmt.Errorf("failed to fetch book")

    }


    reviews := a.bookRepo.GetAllReviews(int(req.GetIsbn()))


    protoReviews := make([]*proto.Review, 0)


    for _, r := range reviews {

        protoReview := &proto.Review{Reviewer: r.Reviewer, Comment:
        r.Comment, Rating: int32(r.Rating)}

        protoReviews = append(protoReviews, protoReview)

    }


    return &proto.GetBookReviewsResponse{Reviews: protoReviews}, nil

}
```

A potential failing scenario is introduced to simulate the occurrence of errors during the execution of the `GetBookReviews` function. The failing condition is triggered based on the current second of the system time. Let's break down this portion:

- **`time.Now().Second()%2 == 0`**: This condition checks if the current second of the system time is an even number. It introduces a deterministic element to simulate failure half of the time.
- **`return nil, fmt.Errorf("failed to fetch book")`**: If the condition is true, meaning the current second is even, the function returns an error. This error message, "failed to fetch book," is a simulated representation of a failure in fetching book reviews.

The purpose of introducing such a failing scenario is to mimic real-world situations where services may encounter intermittent issues or failures. This allows developers to test how well their systems handle errors and implement appropriate error-handling mechanisms. In this case, it provides an opportunity to observe how the calling code responds to a failure during the book reviews fetching process.

The same code has been also added in the books service's **`GetBook`** method:

```
func (a *App) GetBook(_ context.Context, req *proto.GetBookRequest) (*proto.Book, error) {
    log.Println("fetching book")

    // Simulate a potentially failing operation.
    if time.Now().Second()%2 == 0 {
        return nil, fmt.Errorf("failed to fetch book")
    }

    book := a.bookRepo.GetBook(int(req.Isbn))

    return &proto.Book{
        Isbn:      int32(book.Isbn),
        Name:      book.Name,
        Publisher: book.Publisher,
```

```
    }, nil
}
```

Let's now see how the failing scenarios are being handled using retries in the book info server:

```
func (a *App) GetBookInfoWithReviews(ctx context.Context, req *proto.
GetBookInfoRequest) (*proto.GetBookInfoResponse, error) {
    log.Println("fetching book and reviews")

    ctx, cancel := context.WithTimeout(context.Background(), 5*time.
    Second)
    defer cancel()

    // Define a retryable function for getting a book.
    retryableGetBook := func() (interface{}, error) {
        return a.bookServerClient.GetBook(ctx, &proto.
        GetBookRequest{Isbn: req.GetIsbn()})
    }

    // Execute the retryableGetBook function with retry logic.
    result, err := WithRetry(ctx, retryableGetBook, 3, 2*time.Second)
    if err != nil {
        return nil, err
    }

    book, ok := result.(*proto.Book)
    if !ok {
        return nil, fmt.Errorf("could not fetch book with isbn(%v)", req.
        GetIsbn())
    }
```

```
    // Define a retryable function for getting reviews.
    retryableGetReviews := func() (interface{}, error) {
        return a.reviewServerClient.GetBookReviews(ctx, &proto.
        GetBookReviewsRequest{Isbn: req.GetIsbn()})
    }

    // Execute the retryableGetReviews function with retry logic.
    result, err = WithRetry(ctx, retryableGetReviews, 3, 3*time.Second)
    if err != nil {
        return nil, err
    }

    resp, ok := result.(*proto.GetBookReviewsResponse)
    if !ok {
        return nil, fmt.Errorf("could not fetch reviews for book with
        isbn(%v)", req.GetIsbn())
    }

    return &proto.GetBookInfoResponse{
        Isbn:      req.GetIsbn(),
        Name:      book.Name,
        Publisher: book.Publisher,
        Reviews:   resp.GetReviews(),
    }, nil
}
```

The retry logic is implemented using the **`WithRetry`** function to handle potential transient failures during the fetching of book information and reviews. Let's break down how retry is handled:

- **`retryableGetBook`**: This is a closure function representing the operation to get a book using the gRPC client. It is designed to be retried in case of failures.
- **`WithRetry`**: This is a utility function that executes the provided retryable function with retry logic. It takes parameters like the context, the retryable function, maximum retry attempts, and the interval between retries.
- **`result, err := WithRetry(...)`**: The **`WithRetry`** function is invoked to execute the **`retryableGetBook`** function with retry logic. The result of the operation and any error encountered during retries are captured.
- **`book, ok := result.(*proto.Book)`**: If the result is successfully type-asserted to a **`proto.Book`**, it means that the book retrieval was successful. Otherwise, an error is returned.

Let's look at the implementation of **`WithRetry`** function:

```
// WithRetry executes a function with retry logic.

func WithRetry(ctx context.Context, retryFunc RetryableFunc, maxAttempts int, retryInterval time.Duration) (interface{}, error) {

    var result interface{}

    var err error


    for attempt := 1; attempt <= maxAttempts; attempt++ {

        select {

        case <-ctx.Done():

            // Operation was canceled.

            return nil, ctx.Err()

        default:

            // [No-Op] Continue with the retry.

        }


        result, err = retryFunc()
```

```
        if err == nil {
            // Operation succeeded, break the loop.
            break
        }

        // Log or handle the error (optional).
        fmt.Printf("Attempt %d failed: %v\n", attempt, err)

        // Wait before the next retry.
        time.Sleep(retryInterval)
    }

    return result, err
}
```

Here's how it works:

- The function takes four parameters:
    - **ctx**: The context for the operation.
    - **retryFunc**: The function to be executed with retry logic. This function must conform to the **RetryableFunc** type, which means it should return a result and an error.
    - **maxAttempts**: The maximum number of attempts to execute **retryFunc**.
    - **retryInterval**: The interval between retry attempts.
- Inside the function, it iterates over the specified number of **maxAttempts.**
- It checks if the context has been canceled. If it has, the function returns with the context error.
- If the context is still active, it executes the **retryFunc.**
- If **retryFunc** returns with no error, indicating success, the function breaks the loop and returns the result.
- If **retryFunc** returns an error, the function logs the error and waits for the specified **retryInterval** before retrying the operation.

Overall, this function provides a mechanism for executing a function with retry logic, allowing for resilience against transient errors.

The same pattern is then applied for fetching reviews. This retry mechanism is crucial in handling transient failures, ensuring that the system attempts to fetch the required information multiple times before declaring a failure, which improves the resilience of the service against temporary issues.

Mitigating Cascading Failures with Circuit Breaker Pattern

Let's see how we can mitigate the probable cascading failure using the **Circuit Breaker** pattern.

To do this, we need to simulate a situation where either the reviews or books service or both fail intermittently. Since we have already implemented failed scenarios in the case of the **Retry** pattern in both books and reviews servers, we will reuse them here as well.

Unlike timeouts and retries, where we made use of Go's in-built out-of-the-box features, in the case of a circuit breaker, we need to come up with some custom implementation.

```
package grpcbooksserver


import (

   "context"

   "fmt"

   "time"

)


type CircuitBreaker struct {

   threshold    int

   failureCount int

   open         bool

}
```

```
// NewCircuitBreaker creates a new CircuitBreaker.
func NewCircuitBreaker(threshold int) *CircuitBreaker {
    return &CircuitBreaker{
        threshold: threshold,
        open:      false,
    }
}

// Execute executes a function using the circuit breaker pattern.
func (cb *CircuitBreaker) Execute(ctx context.Context, fn func()
(interface{}, error)) (interface{}, error) {
    if cb.open {
        return nil, fmt.Errorf("circuit breaker is open")
    }

    result, err := fn()

    if err != nil {
        cb.failureCount++

        if cb.failureCount >= cb.threshold {
            cb.open = true
            go func() {
                // Automatically attempt to close the circuit after a timeout.
                <-time.After(5 * time.Second)
                cb.open = false
                cb.failureCount = 0
            }()
```

```
        }
    } else {
        // Reset the failure count on successful execution.
        cb.failureCount = 0
    }

    return result, err
}
```

Here's how the circuit breaker works:

- **Initialization**: The **NewCircuitBreaker** function creates a new instance of the circuit breaker with a specified failure threshold.
- **Execution**: The **Execute** method takes a function fn as an argument and executes it. If the function encounters an error, the failure count is incremented. If the failure count exceeds the threshold, the circuit is opened, and an automatic attempt to close the circuit is scheduled after a timeout. If the function executes successfully, the failure count is reset.
- **Circuit State**: The **open** flag indicates whether the circuit is open or closed. If the circuit is open, subsequent calls to **Execute** will return an error without executing the provided function.

This basic circuit breaker implementation helps prevent the system from continuously attempting to execute a failing operation, giving it time to recover before retrying. The circuit breaker opens when a certain number of consecutive failures occur and automatically attempts to close after a specified timeout.

Let's now see how the failing scenarios are being handled using a circuit breaker in the book info server.

```
func (a *App) GetBookInfoWithReviews(ctx context.Context, req *proto.GetBookInfoRequest) (*proto.GetBookInfoResponse, error) {
    log.Println("fetching book and reviews")

    // Set a deadline for the entire operation.
    ctx, cancel := context.WithTimeout(ctx, 5*time.Second)
    defer cancel()
```

```
// Define a function for getting a book.
getBookFunc := func() (interface{}, error) {
   return a.bookServerClient.GetBook(ctx, &proto.
   GetBookRequest{Isbn: req.GetIsbn()})
}

// Execute getBookFunc function using the circuit breaker.
result, err := a.cb.Execute(ctx, getBookFunc)

if err != nil {
   return nil, err
}

// Display the result.
book, ok := result.(*proto.Book)
if !ok {
   return nil, fmt.Errorf("could not fetch book with isbn(%v)", req.
   GetIsbn())
}

// Define a function for getting book reviews.
getBookReviewsFunc := func() (interface{}, error) {
   return a.reviewServerClient.GetBookReviews(ctx, &proto.
   GetBookReviewsRequest{Isbn: req.GetIsbn()})
}

// Execute getBookReviewsFunc function using the circuit breaker.
result, err = a.cb.Execute(ctx, getBookReviewsFunc)
```

```
    if err != nil {
        return nil, err
    }

    // Display the result.
    resp, ok := result.(*proto.GetBookReviewsResponse)
    if !ok {
        return nil, fmt.Errorf("could not fetch book reviews with
        isbn(%v)", req.GetIsbn())
    }

    return &proto.GetBookInfoResponse{
        Isbn:      req.GetIsbn(),
        Name:      book.Name,
        Publisher: book.Publisher,
        Reviews:   resp.GetReviews(),
    }, nil
}
```

A circuit breaker is used to manage the execution of two functions: one for fetching book information (`getBookFunc`) and another for fetching book reviews (`getBookReviewsFunc`). Let's break down the code:

Here's how the circuit breaker is utilized:

- **Function Definitions**: Two functions (`getBookFunc` and `getBookReviewsFunc`) are defined. Each function represents an operation that may encounter failures.
- **Execution Using Circuit Breaker**: The Execute method of the circuit breaker (`a.cb.Execute`) is called for each function. This ensures that the functions are executed under the circuit breaker's control. If the circuit is open (due to previous failures), the functions are not executed, and an error is returned immediately.
- **Handling Results**: The results of the executed functions are checked.

If an error occurs during execution, it is returned immediately. If the execution is successful, the results are cast to their respective types (`*proto.Book` for book information and `*proto.GetBookReviewsResponse` for reviews).

- **Returning the Combined Result**: Finally, the book information and reviews are combined into a `proto.GetBookInfoResponse`, which is returned.

This approach with the circuit breaker helps prevent the continuous execution of functions that may be failing, providing a level of fault tolerance and resilience in the face of potential failures in dependent services.

Conclusion

In this chapter, we delved into the advanced concepts of gRPC, focusing on interceptors and their role in enhancing the resilience of gRPC communication. We drew parallels between interceptors and middlewares, showcasing how they facilitate modular and reusable components in handling both unary and streaming operations. The implementation of a logging interceptor provided insights into capturing and structuring logs for debugging and monitoring. Similarly, the recovery interceptor demonstrated a crucial aspect of handling panics and ensuring graceful degradation in the face of failures.

The chapter then shifted its focus to building resilient gRPC communication. The discussion around cascading failures highlighted the potential challenges arising from tight dependencies between services. Context and deadlines were explored, emphasizing their significance in managing the lifecycle of requests and setting boundaries for execution.

To address potential issues related to long-running operations, the timeout pattern was introduced, showcasing how deadlines can be set to prevent operations from exceeding acceptable time limits. The retry pattern was discussed as a strategy to handle transient failures, allowing for automatic retries of failed operations.

The chapter concluded with an exploration of the circuit breaker pattern, a vital tool in preventing cascading failures. The code implementation illustrated how a circuit breaker can be employed to intelligently manage the execution of functions, providing a layer of protection against repeated failures and promoting fault tolerance in distributed systems.

Overall, this chapter provided a comprehensive understanding of advanced gRPC concepts and their practical implementations, offering valuable insights into building robust and resilient communication systems.

In the upcoming chapter, we will delve into the crucial topic of load balancing in the context of gRPC servers. We will explore the fundamental reasons why load balancing is essential for distributed systems and how it plays a pivotal role in ensuring optimal performance, resource utilization, and reliability. Load balancing, while universally important, presents unique challenges in the realm of gRPC servers, and we will dissect the intricacies that make it a nuanced task. The chapter will navigate through various strategies employed to tackle this challenge, with a focus on client-side load balancing and look-aside load balancing. By the end of the chapter, you will gain insights into the significance of load balancing in gRPC environments and acquire practical knowledge on how to implement effective load balancing strategies to enhance the overall efficiency and resilience of distributed systems.

Multiple Choice Questions

1. What is the primary purpose of interceptors in gRPC?
   a. Handling user authentication
   b. Modifying request and response data
   c. Managing database connections
   d. Defining protocol buffers
2. How are interceptors in gRPC similar to middlewares in web frameworks?
   a. Both handle client-side logic
   b. Both are used for load balancing
   c. Both modify request and response cycles
   d. Both focus on server-side operations
3. In gRPC, what type of interceptor is used for single request and single response operations?
   a. Unary interceptor
   b. Streaming interceptor
   c. Recovery interceptor
   d. Circuit breaker interceptor
4. Which of the following is a potential use case for implementing a logging interceptor in gRPC?

   a. Handling user authentication
   b. Modifying protocol buffers
   c. Monitoring and debugging requests
   d. Load balancing operations

5. What is the purpose of a recovery interceptor in gRPC?
   a. Enhancing load balancing
   b. Recovering from network failures
   c. Modifying request payloads
   d. Handling user authentication

6. How does gRPC contribute to resilient communication?
   a. By minimizing the use of interceptors
   b. By avoiding streaming operations
   c. By handling cascading failures
   d. By ignoring context and deadlines

7. What is the role of context and deadlines in gRPC?
   a. Controlling execution flow
   b. Defining protocol buffers
   c. Managing database connections
   d. Handling user authentication

8. Which pattern is employed to limit the time a gRPC operation can take?
   a. Logging pattern
   b. Timeout pattern
   c. Retry pattern
   d. Circuit breaker pattern

9. How does the retry pattern contribute to resilient gRPC communication?
   a. By ignoring failures
   b. By reducing request payload size
   c. By attempting an operation again on failure
   d. By modifying protocol buffers

10. In gRPC, what does the circuit breaker pattern aim to prevent?

a. Request modifications
b. Cascading failures
c. Streaming operations
d. Middleware conflicts

Answers

1	b
2	c
3	a
4	c
5	b
6	c
7	a
8	b
9	c
10	b

CHAPTER 6
Load balancing in gRPC

Introduction

In the previous chapter, we delved into the powerful world of gRPC interceptors, drawing parallels with traditional middlewares. We explored both unary and streaming interceptors, and implemented specific examples like logging and recovery interceptors. The focus shifted towards building resilient gRPC communication, addressing challenges such as cascading failures. Context and deadlines took the spotlight, and we implemented patterns like timeout, retry, and circuit breaker to enhance system robustness. These techniques contribute to gRPC's effectiveness in managing complex communication scenarios. The chapter concluded by highlighting the significance of these advanced concepts in optimizing gRPC applications.

This chapter delves into the pivotal role of load balancing within the realm of gRPC servers. The necessity for load balancing arises from the perpetual aim of software engineering to scale applications and products. As most applications are developed with the foresight of serving a large user base, the initial challenge lies in designing a system capable of handling both single users and scaling to accommodate millions. The architecture of modern software relies on indispensable components such as caching, Content Delivery Networks (CDNs), database replication, messaging queues, sharding, observability, and more.

Among these, load balancing emerges as a cornerstone, a non-negotiable element in ensuring a seamless and efficient user experience. It becomes particularly challenging in the context of gRPC servers due to their unique characteristics. This chapter navigates through the intricacies of load balancing in gRPC, shedding light on the complexities that make this task challenging.

To tackle these challenges, the chapter unfolds various strategies and tools. It begins by exploring client-side load balancing, a technique where the client is responsible for distributing the incoming requests across multiple servers. This approach is contrasted with look-aside load balancing, where an external entity manages the distribution of requests. We shall also look into how gRPC load balancing can be achieved with Istio, a powerful service mesh framework in Kubernetes.

As the chapter progresses, it provides practical insights and guidance on implementing these load balancing techniques, offering a comprehensive understanding of their implications on performance, reliability, and scalability. The exploration of real-world scenarios and hands-on implementations enriches the reader's knowledge, emphasizing the pivotal role of effective load balancing in the success of distributed systems.

Structure

In this chapter, we will cover the following topics:

- Usage of load balancing
- Tricky load balancing in gRPC servers
- Various ways to handle load balancing in gRPC
    - Client-side load balancing
    - Look-aside load balancing
    - gRPC load balancing with Istio

Usage of load balancing

In the realm of software engineering, the overarching perspective during the development of an application or product has consistently been scalability. This is rooted in the understanding that most applications or products are crafted with the intention of serving a substantial user base. Consequently, initiating the design of an application or product with the capacity to accommodate a single user and subsequently scaling it to support a multi-million user base poses a formidable challenge. Numerous concepts and tools, including caching, Content Delivery Networks (CDNs), database replication, messaging queues, sharding, and observability, have evolved into indispensable components of modern software architecture. Among these, load balancing stands out as a crucial necessity.

Load balancers play a crucial role in distributing network traffic efficiently across multiple servers to enhance the overall performance, reliability, and availability of applications. Various types of load balancers cater to different needs. Server-side load balancers operate on the server or application side, handling incoming requests and distributing them among server instances. In contrast, client-side load balancers are embedded in client applications, enabling them to distribute requests intelligently. Look-aside load balancers, like Istio in Kubernetes, function independently, providing flexibility in routing decisions. Furthermore, hardware load balancers are dedicated physical devices, while software load balancers are implemented in software. Each type of load balancer addresses specific requirements, offering solutions tailored to diverse network architectures and application demands.

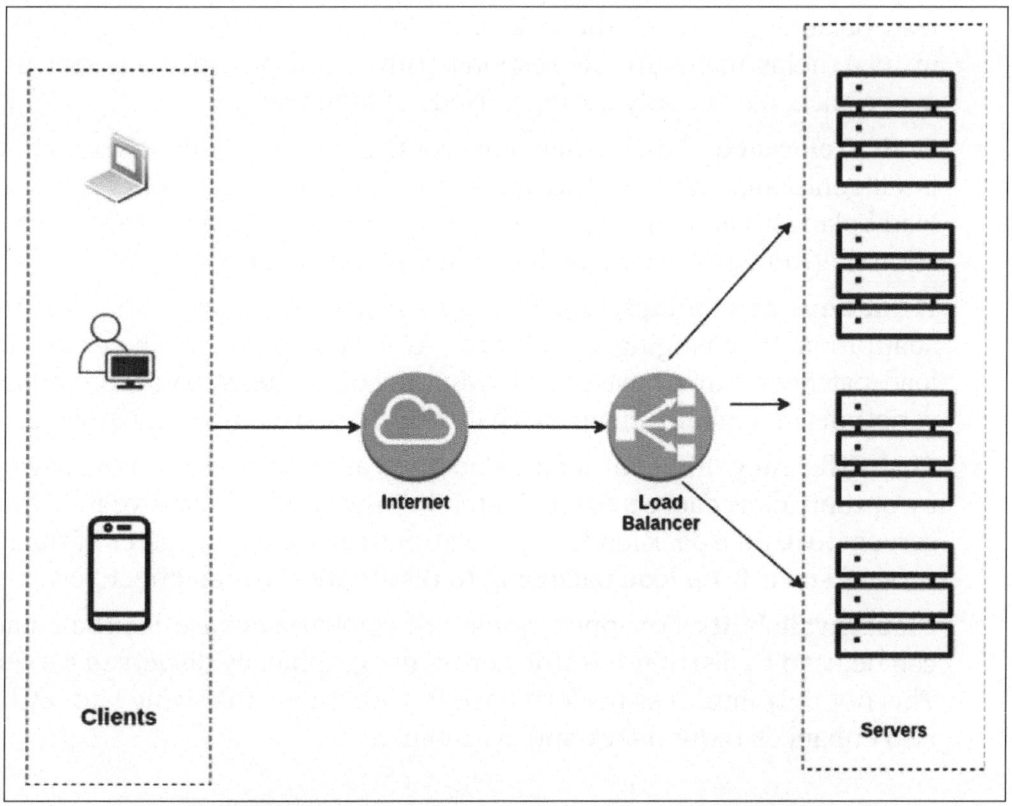

Figure 6.1: *Traffic management using load balancer*

Load balancing is a critical requirement in application and product development for several reasons, which are as follows:

- **Scalability**: Most applications and products are designed with the expectation of serving a large and potentially growing user base. Load balancing is essential for distributing incoming traffic efficiently across multiple servers or resources, ensuring that the system can scale horizontally to handle increased load.
- **High Availability**: Load balancing improves the availability and reliability of a system by distributing traffic among multiple servers. If one server becomes unavailable due to maintenance, failure, or other issues, the load balancer redirects traffic to other healthy servers, minimizing downtime and ensuring continuous service.
- **Optimal Resource Utilization**: Load balancing helps distribute incoming requests evenly across servers, preventing any single server from becoming a bottleneck. This optimal utilization of resources enhances the overall performance and responsiveness of the system.
- **Improved Performance**: By spreading the load across multiple servers, load balancing reduces the risk of overloading any single server. This, in turn, helps maintain low response times and provides a better user experience, particularly during periods of high traffic.
- **Fault Tolerance**: Load balancing contributes to fault tolerance by intelligently managing traffic. If a server fails or experiences issues, the load balancer can reroute traffic to healthy servers, ensuring that users are not adversely affected by individual server failures.
- **Flexibility and Adaptability**: Load balancing allows for dynamic adaptation to changing conditions. As traffic patterns fluctuate, the load balancer can adjust the distribution of requests to accommodate variations in demand, ensuring that resources are efficiently utilized.
- **Cost Efficiency**: Efficient load balancing can contribute to cost savings by optimizing resource usage. Instead of investing in massive individual servers to handle peak loads, organizations can deploy a cluster of smaller servers and rely on load balancing to distribute the load effectively.
- **Global Availability**: For applications with a global user base, load balancing can be used to distribute traffic across geographically dispersed servers. This not only improves performance for users by minimizing latency but also enhances redundancy and availability.

The adoptability of load balancing is a critical consideration in modern computing environments, and it is characterized by several factors, including:

- **Scalability Requirements**: Load balancing becomes crucial as applications and services need to scale to accommodate an increasing number of users or growing data loads. The adoption of load balancing is high in scenarios where scalability is a primary concern.
- **Distributed Architectures**: As organizations move towards microservices and distributed architectures, the need for load balancing becomes more pronounced. Adopting load balancing mechanisms is essential to ensure that traffic is distributed efficiently across various services and instances.
- **High Availability Needs**: Applications that demand high availability and fault tolerance are strong candidates for load balancing. The adoption of load balancing is high in situations where minimizing downtime and ensuring continuous service availability are critical requirements.
- **Cloud and Virtualized Environments**: Load balancing is particularly well-suited for cloud-based and virtualized environments due to their dynamic and scalable nature. In these settings, where resources can be provisioned on-demand and scaled up or down as needed, load balancers play a pivotal role in optimizing resource usage and ensuring consistent performance across applications and services. By distributing incoming traffic evenly across multiple servers or instances, load balancers effectively prevent any single resource from becoming overwhelmed, thus improving overall system reliability and resilience. Additionally, load balancers can intelligently route traffic based on factors such as server health, geographical location, and application-specific requirements, further enhancing performance and user experience in highly dynamic environments.
- **Complex Traffic Patterns**: Applications with complex and variable traffic patterns, such as those with seasonal fluctuations or sudden spikes in user activity, benefit significantly from load balancing. The adoption is high when dealing with unpredictable and dynamic workloads.
- **Cost Optimization**: Load balancing contributes to cost optimization by allowing organizations to distribute workloads efficiently across available resources. This is especially relevant in cloud environments, where resource usage directly influences costs. The adoption of load balancing is high in contexts where cost efficiency is a priority.
- **Global Presence**: For applications serving a global user base, load balancing is crucial for optimizing response times and minimizing

latency. The adoption of load balancing is evident in scenarios where a distributed global presence is required to provide a seamless user experience.

- **Adaptability to Change**: Load balancing solutions that can adapt to changing conditions, such as variations in traffic or the addition/removal of resources, are more likely to be adopted. The flexibility and adaptability of load balancing mechanisms contribute to their overall adoption.
- **Integration with Other Technologies**: The ease with which load balancing solutions can integrate with other technologies, such as container orchestration platforms or service meshes, impacts their adoption. Seamless integration facilitates the incorporation of load balancing into the broader technological landscape.
- **Security Considerations**: Load balancing can also contribute to security by distributing and isolating traffic. The adopt-ability of load balancing is high when it comes to implementing security measures such as SSL termination, DDoS protection, and access controls.

In summary, load balancing is a fundamental architectural component that addresses the challenges of scalability, availability, and performance in modern applications. It is a key enabler for building robust, responsive, and resilient systems that can handle the demands of a diverse and potentially vast user audience. The adoption of load balancing is driven by the specific needs and characteristics of modern applications, architectures, and operational environments. As organizations strive to build scalable, resilient, and high-performance systems, load balancing emerges as a foundational and widely adopted component of their infrastructure.

Tricky load balancing in gRPC servers

Having affirmed the critical role of load balancing as a fundamental component of software architecture, it's imperative to acknowledge that gRPC servers are no exception. The distribution of traffic across gRPC servers is equally essential to ensure optimal performance and resource utilization.

Before delving into the intricacies of load balancing challenges in gRPC servers, let's first explore the concept of **Sticky Sessions**. This exploration will provide us with a better understanding and context for the upcoming discussion. **Sticky sessions** aren't exclusive to gRPC servers; instead, they represent a design choice applicable to specific use cases.

Sticky sessions

Sticky sessions, also known as session affinity or session persistence, is a mechanism employed in load balancing scenarios where it ensures that requests from a particular client are consistently directed to the same server. This means that once a client establishes a connection to a server, subsequent requests from that client during the session will be routed to the same server.

Sticky sessions contribute to a more consistent user experience, especially in scenarios where user-specific data is stored on the server. For example, in e-commerce applications, it ensures that a user's shopping cart or session data is consistently available. Sticky sessions are commonly used in web applications, especially those that rely on server-side session management. This includes scenarios where maintaining context, such as shopping carts, user preferences, or authentication status, is crucial.

While sticky sessions provide benefits in terms of session consistency, they can introduce challenges. For instance, if a server goes down, clients associated with that server may experience disruptions until the session affinity is re-established. While sticky sessions provide one approach to session persistence, alternative strategies exist. For example, session data can be stored externally (in a database or shared cache), allowing any server to handle any request without relying on sticky sessions.

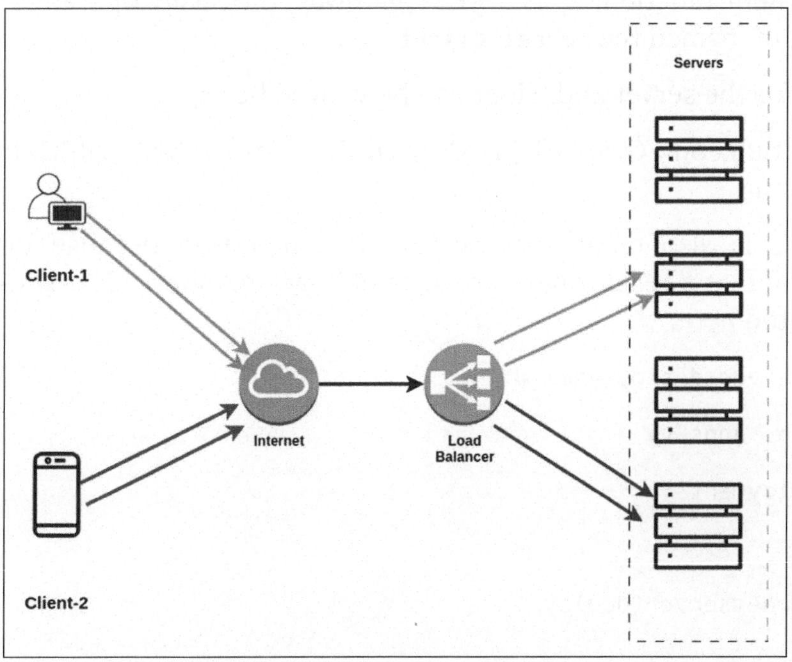

Figure 6.2: *Depiction of sticky session*

While sticky sessions can be beneficial for certain use cases, they can also impact scalability. If not managed properly, it might lead to uneven distribution of load among servers, limiting the scalability benefits of load balancing.

Chink in the armour of gRPC

gRPC boasts several advantages, such as multiplexing numerous requests through the same connection, support for both traditional client-server request-response and duplex streaming, and the utilization of a rapid, lightweight binary protocol for structured data communication between services. While these features make gRPC an enticing choice, there are considerations, particularly concerning load balancing.

Despite the resolution of latency issues through persistent connections, gRPC introduces a new challenge in the realm of load balancing. With gRPC (or HTTP2) establishing persistent connections, even in the presence of a load balancer, the client forms a lasting connection with the server situated behind the load balancer. This situation is akin to a sticky session.

To proceed, we need a specific arrangement. This arrangement encompasses the following components:

1. A gRPC server, referred to as the **'Greet Server'.**
2. A client functioning as a REST gateway, internally operating as a gRPC client, named the **'Greet Client'.**

The code for the server and client can be viewed here:

https://github.com/OrangeAVA/Modern-API-Design-with-gRPC/tree/main/loadbalancing

Kubernetes is also employed for the demonstration because of the wide adoption, and as a result, there are several YAML manifest files. These files will be elucidated here:

```
## greetserver-deploy.yaml ##

apiVersion: apps/v1

kind: Deployment

metadata:

  name: greetserver-deploy

spec:
```

```
replicas: 3
selector:
  matchLabels:
    run: greetserver
template:
  metadata:
    labels:
      run: greetserver
  spec:
    containers:
      - image: hiteshpattanayak/greet-server:1.0
        imagePullPolicy: IfNotPresent
        name: greetserver
        ports:
          - containerPort: 50051
        env:
          - name: POD_IP
            valueFrom:
              fieldRef:
                fieldPath: status.podIP
          - name: POD_NAME
            valueFrom:
              fieldRef:
                fieldPath: metadata.name
```

This Kubernetes manifest file (**`greetserver-deploy.yaml`**) specifies the deployment configuration for the **'`Greet Server.`'** Here's a breakdown:

- **`apiVersion`**: Specifies the version of the Kubernetes API to use.

- **kind**: Defines the type of resource, in this case, a Deployment.
- **metadata**: Contains information about the deployment, such as the name.
- **spec**: Describes the desired state for the deployment.
    - **replicas**: Specifies the desired number of replicas (pods) for the deployment, set to **3**.
    - **selector**: Defines how the Deployment finds which Pods to manage. It uses labels.
    - **template**: Describes the pods that will be created, including their labels.
        - **metadata**: Specifies labels for the pod.
        - **spec**: Defines the pod's specification.
- **containers**: Specifies the containers within the pod.
    - **image**: Specifies the container image (**greet-server:1.0**).
    - **imagePullPolicy**: Specifies when to pull the image (IfNotPresent means only pull if it's not already present).
    - **name**: Names the container **'greetserver'**
    - **ports**: Specifies the container's port (**50051**) for gRPC communication.
    - **env**: Specifies environment variables for the container, including the pod's IP address and name.

This manifest sets up a deployment with three replicas of the **'Greet Server'** container, each accessible through gRPC on port **50051.** The environment variables capture the pod's IP and name for internal communication.

What are the roles of individual pods in the aforementioned server setup?

Each pod serves as an rpc or service endpoint that anticipates both a **first_name** and a **last_name** as inputs. In return, it generates a response in the following format:

```
reponse from Greet rpc: Hello, <first_name> <last_name> from pod: name(<pod_
name>), ip(<pod_ip>).
```

Based on the response, we can infer the specific pod that handled our request.

```
## greet.svc.yaml ##

apiVersion: v1

kind: Service
```

```
metadata:
  labels:
    run: greetserver
  name: greetserver
  namespace: default
spec:
  ports:
    - name: grpc
      port: 50051
      protocol: TCP
      targetPort: 50051
  selector:
    run: greetserver
```

The YAML manifest **greet.svc.yaml** defines a Kubernetes Service named **greetserver** in the default namespace. This service is associated with the pods labelled as **run: greetserver**. It exposes a port named grpc with port number **50051** for TCP communication. The selector field ensures that the service directs traffic to pods labelled with **run: greetserver**. Essentially, this service enables communication with the pods of the **greetserver** deployment through the specified port.

```
## greetclient-deploy.yaml ##
apiVersion: apps/v1
kind: Deployment
metadata:
  name: greetclient-deploy
spec:
  replicas: 1
  selector:
    matchLabels:
```

```
      run: greetclient
  template:
    metadata:
      labels:
        run: greetclient
    spec:
      containers:
        - image: hiteshpattanayak/greet-client:4.0
          name: greetclient
          ports:
            - containerPort: 9091
          env:
            - name: GRPC_SERVER_HOST
              value: greetserver.default.svc.cluster.local
            - name: GRPC_SVC
              value: greetserver
            - name: POD_NAMESPACE
              valueFrom:
                fieldRef:
                  fieldPath: metadata.namespace
```

The YAML manifest **greetclient-deploy.yaml** specifies a Kubernetes Deployment named **greetclient-deploy**. This deployment is configured to run one replica of a pod labelled as **run: greetclient**. The pod, defined within the template section, uses the container image **hiteshpattanayak/greet-client:4.0**. It exposes port **9091** for communication.

The environment variables set for the container include:

1. **GRPC_SERVER_HOST**: Specifies the hostname of the gRPC server (**greetserver.default.svc.cluster.local**).

2. **GRPC_SVC**: Indicates the name of the gRPC service (greetserver).
3. **POD_NAMESPACE**: Retrieves the namespace of the pod using field reference.

Essentially, this deployment creates a pod running the **greet-client** container, which communicates with the gRPC server specified in the **GRPC_SERVER_HOST** variable and targets the **greetserver** service.

As previously stated, the pod operates an application functioning as a REST gateway, connecting to the Greet Server to handle requests. The deployment utilizes the **hiteshpattanayak/greet-client:4.0** container image, and it's important to note that the version tagged as **4.0** exhibits a load balancing issue. The GitHub repository link provided earlier refers to the main branch, where the gRPC client implementation has been incorporated into the Docker image tagged as **hiteshpattanayak/greet-client:4.0.**

```
## greetclient-svc.yaml ##

apiVersion: v1

kind: Service

metadata:

  labels:

    run: greetclient

  name: greetclient

  namespace: default

spec:

  ports:

    - name: restgateway

      port: 9091

      protocol: TCP

      targetPort: 9091

  selector:

    run: greetclient

  type: LoadBalancer
```

The preceding YAML manifest (**greetclient-svc.yaml**) describes a Kubernetes Service named **greetclient** within the default namespace. Here are the key elements explained:

- **Type**: The service type is specified as `LoadBalancer`, indicating that the Kubernetes cluster should allocate an external load balancer to manage incoming traffic to this service.
- **Ports**: The service exposes a port named **restgateway** on port **9091** within the cluster. This port is associated with the **9091** port of the pods selected by this service.
- **Selector**: The service selects pods with the label **run: greetclient**. This implies that any pods with the label **run: greetclient** will be included in the set of pods targeted by this service.

In summary, this service (**greetclient**) is configured to expose port **9091** externally, directing traffic to pods labelled **run: greetclient** within the default namespace, and utilizing a **LoadBalancer** for external access.

```
## greet-ingress.yaml ##

apiVersion: networking.k8s.io/v1

kind: Ingress

metadata:

  name: greet-ingress

  namespace: default

  annotations:

    nginx.ingress.kubernetes.io/ssl-redirect: "false"

spec:

  rules:

    - host: greet.com

      http:

        paths:

          - path: /

            pathType: Prefix
```

```
            backend:
              service:
                name: greetclient
                port:
                  name: restgateway
```

The preceding YAML manifest defines an **Ingress** resource named **"greet-ingress"** within the **"default"** namespace. This resource is annotated with **nginx.ingress.kubernetes.io/ssl-redirect: "false"** to indicate that SSL redirection should be disabled. The Ingress specifies a rule for the host **"greet.com"** and sets up routing based on HTTP paths. In particular, any requests to the root path ("/") are directed to the backend service named **"greetclient"** on the **"restgateway"** port. This Ingress configuration is crucial for routing external requests to the appropriate backend service within the Kubernetes cluster.

Important:

The cluster configuration has been established using **minikube**. By default, **minikube** does not enable the ingress feature.

- To verify whether ingress is enabled, run: **minikube addons list**.
- If it is not enabled, you can enable the ingress addon by executing: **minikube addons enable ingress.**

```
## greet-clusterrole.yaml ##
kind: ClusterRole
apiVersion: rbac.authorization.k8s.io/v1
metadata:
  namespace: default
  name: service-reader
rules:
  - apiGroups: [""]
    resources: ["services"]
    verbs: ["get", "watch", "list"]
```

```
---

## greet-clusterrolebinding.yaml ##

apiVersion: rbac.authorization.k8s.io/v1

kind: ClusterRoleBinding

metadata:

  name: service-reader-binding

roleRef:

  apiGroup: rbac.authorization.k8s.io

  kind: ClusterRole

  name: service-reader

subjects:

  - kind: ServiceAccount

    name: default

    namespace: default
```

These YAML manifests define a Kubernetes **`ClusterRole`** (**`greet-clusterrole.yaml`**) named "**`service-reader,`**" granting permissions to read services within the default namespace. The accompanying **`ClusterRoleBinding`** (**`greet-clusterrolebinding.yaml`**) binds this **`ClusterRole`** to the default **`ServiceAccount`**, allowing it the specified permissions. This setup is useful for scenarios where a pod, using the default **`ServiceAccount`**, needs to read information about services in the same namespace.

The necessity for the cluster role and cluster role binding arises from the limited permissions of the default service account, which lacks the authority to retrieve service details. As the **greet client** pod internally attempts to access service information, establishing this binding becomes imperative.

Let's establish the setup or cluster by applying the manifests in the following sequence:

1. `kubectl create -f greet-clusterrole.yaml`
2. `kubectl create -f greet-clusterrolebinding.yaml`
3. `kubectl create -f greetserver-deploy.yaml`

4. kubectl create -f greet.svc.yaml
5. kubectl create -f greetclient-deploy.yaml
6. kubectl create -f greet-client.svc.yaml
7. kubectl create -f greet-ingress.yaml

As we've exposed the **Greet Client** outside the cluster through **`greet-ingress`**, the endpoint can be accessed at: **http://greet.com/greet**.

Thus, when we issue a curl request:

Request#1

```
curl --request POST \
  --url http://greet.com/greet \
  --header 'Content-Type: application/json' \
  --data '{
 "first_name": "Hitesh",
 "last_name": "Pattanayak"
}

## Response
## reponse from Greet rpc: Hello, Hitesh Pattanayak from pod: name(greetserver-deploy-7595ccbdd5-l8kmv), ip(172.17.0.2).
```

Request#2

```
curl --request POST \
  --url http://greet.com/greet \
  --header 'Content-Type: application/json' \
  --data '{
 "first_name": "Hitesh",
 "last_name": "Pattanayak"
}

## Response
```

```
## reponse from Greet rpc: Hello, Hitesh Pattanayak from pod: name(greetserver-deploy-7595ccbdd5-l8kmv), ip(172.17.0.2).
```

Request#3

```
curl --request POST \
  --url http://greet.com/greet \
  --header 'Content-Type: application/json' \
  --data '{
 "first_name": "Hitesh",
 "last_name": "Pattanayak"
}

## Response
## reponse from Greet rpc: Hello, Hitesh Pattanayak from pod: name(greetserver-deploy-7595ccbdd5-l8kmv), ip(172.17.0.2).
```

The challenge arises because, regardless of the number of requests made, they consistently reach the same server due to the sticky nature of HTTP/2. The very advantage of gRPC becomes a pitfall in this scenario.

Various Ways to Handle Load Balancing in gRPC

Load balancing is a crucial element, and gRPC is a high-performance framework. We wouldn't want to compromise either aspect based on specific requirements. Instead, we aim to leverage the strengths of both. Therefore, let's explore different approaches to navigate this intricate situation with gRPC.

Client-side Load Balancing

Upon closer examination of the greet-client's code, it becomes evident that the client employs extra server options during the dialing process to the server.

```
a.conn, err = grpc.Dial(
      servAddr,                               grpc.
      WithDefaultServiceConfig(`{"loadBalancingPolicy":"round_robin"}`),
```

```
        grpc.WithBlock(),
        opts,
    )
```

In the past, this would have appeared somewhat like the following:

```
a.conn, err = grpc.Dial(
        servAddr,
        opts,
    )
```

The additional server options serve the following purpose:

1. **`grpc.WithDefaultServiceConfig({"loadBalancingPolicy":"round_robin"})`**: This line sets the default service configuration for the gRPC client. In this case, it specifies a load balancing policy of **"round_robin,"** indicating that requests should be distributed evenly among available servers.
2. **`grpc.WithBlock()`**: This option makes the grpc. Dial call blocking until a connection to the server is established or the connection attempt fails. This is commonly used to ensure that the application waits for a successful connection before proceeding.

The primary intent behind incorporating these extra server options is to align the behaviour of the gRPC server with the conventional request-response cycle, eliminating the extended duration connections. This adjustment ensures that connections are established and utilized more akin to traditional communication patterns. Although we forgo the advantages associated with prolonged connections, we can still harness other benefits inherent to gRPC.

Now let's use **'hiteshpattanayak/greet-client:11.0'** image of the greet client in the manifest of the deployment and redeploy it in the cluster. This image has the client-side load balancing configured.

```
apiVersion: apps/v1
kind: Deployment
metadata:
  name: greetclient-deploy
spec:
```

```
  replicas: 1
  selector:
    matchLabels:
      run: greetclient
  template:
    metadata:
      labels:
        run: greetclient
    spec:
      containers:
        - image: hiteshpattanayak/greet-client:11.0
          name: greetclient
          ports:
            - containerPort: 9091
          env:
            - name: GRPC_SVC
              value: greetserver
            - name: POD_NAMESPACE
              valueFrom:
                fieldRef:
                  fieldPath: metadata.namespace
```

The server address that is used to dial the greet server from the client is a DNS address of the server, we have used **GetServiceDnsName** to extract the kubernetes DNS server address.

```
func GetServiceDnsName(clientset *kubernetes.Clientset, serviceName, namespace string) string {
    service, err := clientset.CoreV1().Services(namespace).Get(context.
    Background(), serviceName, metav1.GetOptions{})
```

```
    if err != nil {
        panic(err.Error())
    }
    var hostname string
    if len(service.Status.LoadBalancer.Ingress) > 0 {
        hostname = service.Status.LoadBalancer.Ingress[0].Hostname
    } else {
        fmt.Printf("Service %s in namespace %s has no external IP address
        or hostname\n", serviceName, namespace)
    }

    if hostname == "" {
        hostname = service.Name + "." + service.Namespace + ".svc.
        cluster.local"
    }

    return fmt.Sprintf("dns:///%s", hostname)
}
```

`GetServiceDnsName` function, is designed to retrieve the DNS name of a Kubernetes service. Here's a breakdown of its functionality:

- **Input Parameters**:
    - o **`clientset`**: The Kubernetes clientset is used to interact with the Kubernetes API.
    - o **`serviceName`**: The name of the Kubernetes service.
    - o **`namespace`**: The namespace in which the service resides.
- **Function Execution**:
    - o The function attempts to fetch the details of the specified service using the Kubernetes clientset.
    - o If an error occurs during the retrieval process, the function panics, terminating the program with the corresponding error message.

- **DNS Name Extraction**:
  - The function checks if the service has an external IP address or hostname associated with it. If so, it extracts the hostname from the service status.
  - If the service lacks an external IP address or hostname, a message is printed to the console, indicating this absence.
- **Fallback Mechanism**: If no hostname is obtained, the function constructs a default hostname based on the service name and namespace, conforming to the typical Kubernetes DNS naming convention.
- **Output**: The function returns a formatted DNS URL, using the obtained or constructed hostname.

In summary, this function provides a convenient way to obtain the DNS name of a Kubernetes service, handling scenarios where external IP addresses or hostnames may be available or unavailable. It ensures the resilience of the process, with a fallback mechanism for cases where external details are not present.

Furthermore, during the initial replication of the issue, the service (**`greetserver`**) established for the **Greet server pods** was of the standard **`ClusterIP`** type. However, for this solution, a **headless ClusterIP** service is necessary.

```
apiVersion: v1

kind: Service

metadata:

  labels:

    run: greetserver

  name: greetserver

  namespace: default

spec:

  ports:

    - name: grpc

      port: 50051

      protocol: TCP
```

```
      targetPort: 50051
  selector:
    run: greetserver
  clusterIP: None
```

This YAML manifest defines a Kubernetes Service named **`greetserver`** in the default namespace. Here are the key components of this manifest:

- **Service Metadata**:
  - **labels**: It assigns the label **`run: greetserver`** to the service.
  - **name**: The name of the service is set to greetserver.
  - **namespace**: The service is deployed in the default namespace.
- **Service Specification (spec)**:
  - **ports**: Specifies the ports that the service should expose.
    - **`name: grpc`**: A named port called grpc.
    - **`port: 50051`**: The port on which the service will be accessible.
    - **`protocol: TCP`**: The protocol used for the port is TCP.
    - **`targetPort: 50051`**: The target port to which the traffic will be forwarded.
  - **selector**: Identifies the set of Pods to which the network traffic should be forwarded.
    - **`run: greetserver`**: It matches the Pods with the label **`run: greetserver`**.
  - **`clusterIP`**: None: This setting indicates that the service should not be assigned a cluster IP. This is typical for headless services, where the service is used to define a set of Pods but without a stable virtual IP.

This headless service (**`clusterIP: None`**) is often used when you want to discover individual Pods directly rather than routing through a stable service IP. In the context of gRPC, this could be used when each Pod exposes a gRPC service, and clients may need to directly connect to individual Pods for specific reasons.

In Kubernetes, clients can discover pod IPs through DNS lookups. Typically, when conducting a DNS lookup for a service, the DNS server provides a single IP—the service's cluster IP. However, by indicating to Kubernetes that a cluster IP is unnecessary for your service (achieved by setting the **`clusterIP`** field to **`None`** in the service specification), the DNS server will respond with the pod IPs instead of a singular service IP. In this scenario, the DNS server returns multiple

A records for the service, each indicating the IP of an individual pod supporting the service at that moment. Consequently, clients can perform a straightforward DNS A record lookup and obtain the IPs of all the pods associated with the service. Armed with this information, clients can decide how they wish to connect, whether to one, many, or all of the available pods. Essentially, the service empowers the client to make choices regarding pod connections.

Follow these steps to verify headless service DNS lookup:

1. create the headless service: **`kubectl create -f greet.svc.yaml`**
2. create aan utility pod: **`kubectl run dnsutils --image=tutum/dnsutils --command -- sleep infinity`**
3. verify by running **'`nslookup`'** command on the utility pod:

```
kubectl exec dnsutils --  nslookup greetserver


## Result

Server:         10.96.0.10

Address:        10.96.0.10#53

Name:   greetserver.default.svc.cluster.local

Address: 172.17.0.4

Name:   greetserver.default.svc.cluster.local

Address: 172.17.0.3

Name:   greetserver.default.svc.cluster.local

Address: 172.17.0.2
```

As observed, the headless service resolves to the IP addresses of all pods linked through the service. This stands in contrast to the output obtained for a non-headless service:

```
kubectl exec dnsutils --  nslookup greetclient


## Result

Server:  10.96.0.10

Address: 10.96.0.10#53
```

```
Name: greetclient.default.svc.cluster.local
Address: 10.110.255.115
```

Now let's test the changes by making curl requests to the exposed ingress.

Request#1

```
curl --request POST \
  --url http://greet.com/greet \
  --header 'Content-Type: application/json' \
  --data '{
 "first_name": "Hitesh",
 "last_name": "Pattanayak"
}

## Response
## reponse from Greet rpc: Hello, Hitesh Pattanayak from pod: name(greetserver-deploy-7595ccbdd5-k6zbl), ip(172.17.0.3).
```

Request#2

```
curl --request POST \
  --url http://greet.com/greet \
  --header 'Content-Type: application/json' \
  --data '{
 "first_name": "Hitesh",
 "last_name": "Pattanayak"
}

## Response
## reponse from Greet rpc: Hello, Hitesh Pattanayak from pod: name(greetserver-deploy-7595ccbdd5-67bmd), ip(172.17.0.4).
```

Request#3

```
curl --request POST \
  --url http://greet.com/greet \
  --header 'Content-Type: application/json' \
  --data '{
 "first_name": "Hitesh",
 "last_name": "Pattanayak"
}

## Response

## reponse from Greet rpc: Hello, Hitesh Pattanayak from pod: name(greetserver-deploy-7595ccbdd5-18kmv), ip(172.17.0.2).
```

The problem has been resolved. However, what we are sacrificing in this solution is the ability of gRPC to maintain connections for an extended duration and efficiently handle multiple requests through these connections, thereby minimizing latency.

Look-aside load balancing

Previously, we explored the challenge of load balancing in gRPC and proposed a solution through client-side load balancing. Although this resolved the load balancing issue, it came at the cost of sacrificing one of gRPC's key advantages—long-duration connections. In this discussion, we aim to achieve load balancing, specifically on the client side, without compromising the aforementioned benefit of prolonged connections in gRPC.

It's crucial to emphasize that when we refer to the "client side," we are not addressing end users directly. In the context of gRPC servers, a REST gateway is utilized by end users. GPRC services are not exposed directly due to the lack of browser support.

Lookaside load balancer

The primary function of this load balancer is to determine which gRPC server to establish a connection with. Currently, the load balancer operates in two modes: round-robin and random selection. Implemented as a gRPC-based service, the load is expected to be manageable enough to operate with a single pod.

It exposes a service named **lookaside** and an RPC named **Resolve**. The **Resolve** RPC expects information about the type of routing, as well as details about the gRPC servers, such as the Kubernetes service name and the namespace they are located in.

Utilizing the service name and namespace, the load balancer retrieves the Kubernetes endpoints object associated with it. This object contains the IP addresses of the servers, which are stored in memory. Periodically, these IPs are refreshed based on a set interval. For each request to resolve an IP, the load balancer rotates through the IPs based on the routing type specified in the request.

The code for lookaside load balancer can be found here: https://github.com/OrangeAVA/Modern-API-Design-with-gRPC/tree/loadbalancing-lookaside/loadbalancing/internal/app/lookaside

We are using the image **`'hiteshpattanayak/lookaside:9.0'`** for the lookaside pod.

```
apiVersion: v1

kind: Pod

metadata:

  labels:

    run: lookaside

  name: lookaside

  namespace: default

spec:

  containers:

    - image: hiteshpattanayak/lookaside:9.0

      name: lookaside

      ports:

        - containerPort: 50055

      env:
```

```
        - name: LB_PORT
          value: "50055"
```

This YAML configuration defines a Kubernetes Pod. The pod is labelled as **lookaside** and belongs to the **default** namespace. It is configured to run a single container based on the Docker image **hiteshpattanayak/lookaside:9.0.** This container is named **lookaside** and exposes port **50055**.

In terms of environment variables, it sets a variable named **LB_PORT** with the value **"50055".** This environment variable likely indicates the port on which the load balancer inside the container will be accessible.

In summary, this Pod configuration sets up a containerized instance named **lookaside** running an image tagged **9.0.** The container exposes port **50055** and has an environment variable **LB_PORT** set to **"50055".**

The service manifest that exposes the pod is as follows:

```
apiVersion: v1
kind: Service
metadata:
  labels:
    run: lookaside-svc
  name: lookaside-svc
  namespace: default
spec:
  ports:
    - port: 50055
      protocol: TCP
      targetPort: 50055
  selector:
    run: lookaside
  clusterIP: None
```

This YAML configuration defines a Kubernetes Service named **`lookaside-svc`.** The service is labelled as **`lookaside-svc`** and belongs to the **`default`** namespace. It exposes port **`50055`** on the cluster's internal network using the TCP protocol, and it directs traffic to pods with the label **`run: lookaside`.** The **`clusterIP`** field is set to **`None`,** indicating that this is a headless service. In Kubernetes, a headless service is one that does not allocate a cluster IP and instead allows DNS resolution to individual pod IPs.

We chose headless service here also, but a normal clusterIP service would have sufficed.

Updated the **`ClusterRole`** to include the ability to fetch **`endpoints`** and **`pod`** details.

```
kind: ClusterRole

apiVersion: rbac.authorization.k8s.io/v1

metadata:

  namespace: default

  name: service-reader

rules:

  - apiGroups: [""]

    resources: ["services", "pods", "endpoints"]

    verbs: ["get", "watch", "list"]
```

Changes with Greet Client:

1. Greet Client is now integrated with lookaside load balancer: https://github.com/OrangeAVA/Modern-API-Design-with-gRPC/blob/9856488479fc3caca31e61e032726fc789fed156/loadbalancing/internal/app/greetclient/app.go#L38.
2. The client is set to use the **`RoundRobin`** routing type but can be made configurable via configmap or environment variables: https://github.com/OrangeAVA/Modern-API-Design-with-gRPC/blob/9856488479fc3caca31e61e032726fc789fed156/loadbalancing/internal/app/greetclient/app.go#L131.
3. Removed server options **load-balancing policy** and forcefully terminated connection by setting **`WithBlock`** option while dialing.

So, how does it address the previous load balancing challenge, where we sacrificed terminating long-duration connections in favour of load balancing? The approach involved storing previous connections to the server and reusing them while rotating for each new request.

```
if c, ok := a.greetClients[host]; !ok {

    servAddr := fmt.Sprintf("%s:%s", host, serverPort)


    fmt.Println("dialing greet server", servAddr)


    conn, err := grpc.Dial(

        servAddr,

        opts,

    )

    if err != nil {

        log.Printf("could not connect greet server: %v", err)

        return err

    }


    a.conn[host] = conn


    a.currentGreetClient = proto.NewGreetServiceClient(conn)

    a.greetClients[host] = a.currentGreetClient

} else {

    a.currentGreetClient = c

}
```

The preceding code checks if a gRPC client for a specific host exists in a map (**`a.greetClients`**). If it doesn't exist, it creates a new gRPC connection (**`grpc.Dial`**) to the specified server address (**`servAddr`**). If the connection is established successfully, it creates a new gRPC client using **`proto.NewGreetServiceClient(conn)`**. Both the connection and the client are then stored in their respective maps (**`a.conn`** and **`a.greetClients`**). If the client for the given host already exists, it retrieves the existing client from the map and sets it as the current client (**`a.currentGreetClient`**). This logic ensures that existing connections are reused when available.

gRPC load balancing with Istio

Establishing a custom intelligent load balancer solely for the purpose of load balancing can be a cumbersome task. Instead, we can make use of tools that inherently provide this functionality. Istio stands out as one such tool that can be deployed in your Kubernetes cluster to perform tasks similar to a lookaside load balancer.

Let's see what changes we can make to our original greet client-server setup using Istio.

Use the following annotations for both gRPC client and server deployment manifests:

```
annotations:
        inject.istio.io/templates: grpc-agent
       proxy.istio.io/config: '{"holdApplicationUntilProxyStarts": true}'
```

These annotations are utilized to configure Istio's behaviour for a specific workload. The **`inject.istio.io/templates: grpc-agent`** annotation instructs Istio's automatic sidecar injection process to include templates specific to handling gRPC traffic.

The **`proxy.istio.io/config: '{"holdApplicationUntilProxyStarts": true}'`** annotation configures Istio to ensure that the application does not start until the Istio proxy (sidecar) is fully initialized. This is a measure to guarantee that the application is fully prepared to handle traffic with Istio's features before it starts receiving requests. This can be crucial for scenarios where the application's initialization depends on Istio's proxy being ready.

Change in server startup

Original Code::

```
s := grpc.NewServer(opts...)
```

Modified Code:

```
s := xds.NewGRPCServer(opts...)
```

Change in client code

Original Code::

```
servAddr := fmt.Sprintf("%s:%s", serverHost, serverPort)
```

Modified Code:

```
servAddr := fmt.Sprintf("xds:///%s:%s", serverHost, serverPort)
```

The change suggests that instead of creating a regular gRPC server using **`grpc.NewServer`**, the application is now using a server created by **`xds.NewGRPCServer.`** And usage of **`xds`** protocol while dialing the gRPC server from gRPC client.

- **As a result**:
  - **`xDS`** **(Discovery Service)**: The prefix **`xds`** in **`xds.NewGRPCServer`** indicates that this server creation is associated with **`xDS (Extension Discovery Service)`** in the context of service mesh or dynamic configuration. The **`xds:///`** format in client dialing is a convention indicating that the address is resolved dynamically through **`xDS.`**
  - **Dynamic Configuration**: **`xDS`** is often used in service meshes like Istio for dynamic configuration and load balancing. It allows for the dynamic update of configuration parameters for services.

In summary, the change indicates a shift from using a standard gRPC server to a server that might be tailored for dynamic configuration and service discovery, possibly leveraging the **`xDS`** protocol.

Istio uses a component known as Pilot, which includes the Extension Discovery Service (xDS), to manage dynamic configuration and service discovery for microservices within a service mesh. In the context of gRPC and load balancing, xDS plays a crucial role in providing dynamic configuration to Envoy proxies that handle traffic within the Istio service mesh.

Here's how the Extension Discovery Service helps with gRPC load balancing in Istio:

- **Dynamic Configuration**: Istio uses xDS to dynamically configure Envoy proxies. This includes configuration related to routing, load balancing, and other features.
- **Service Discovery**: xDS facilitates service discovery by providing a centralized mechanism for Envoy proxies to obtain information about available services and their endpoints.

- **Load Balancing Policies**: xDS allows Istio to apply various load balancing policies dynamically. This is crucial for gRPC services, where efficient load balancing is essential for distributing traffic among healthy instances.
- **Health Checks**: xDS enables health checks on service instances. Envoy proxies can be dynamically updated with health status, allowing Istio to route traffic only to healthy instances.
- **gRPC-Specific Features**: Istio, through xDS, can apply gRPC-specific features for load balancing. This includes handling gRPC retries, timeouts, and other aspects critical for a reliable and performant gRPC communication.
- **Circuit Breaking and Rate Limiting**: xDS allows Istio to apply circuit breaking and rate limiting policies dynamically, which is important for managing traffic effectively, especially in microservices architectures.
- **Consistent Configuration Across Envoy Proxies**: xDS ensures that configuration changes are applied consistently across all Envoy proxies in the mesh, providing a uniform and dynamic control plane.
- **Integration with Envoy**: Envoy, as the data plane proxy used by Istio, listens to xDS updates and adjusts its behaviour accordingly. This ensures that the entire service mesh is synchronized with the latest configuration.

In summary, the Extension Discovery Service (xDS) in Istio is integral for managing dynamic configurations, service discovery, and load balancing policies, especially when dealing with gRPC services. It provides a centralized and dynamic control panelplane for Istio's service mesh architecture.

Conclusion

In the realm of application and product development, the imperative of load balancing cannot be overstated. It emerges as a critical mechanism for efficiently managing incoming network traffic across multiple servers, ensuring optimal resource utilization, preventing server overload, and ultimately enhancing overall system performance and reliability. This foundational principle lays the groundwork for addressing challenges that arise in distributed and scalable architectures.

However, the adoption of gRPC, a high-performance RPC framework, introduces a unique set of challenges to the conventional understanding of load balancing. The use of long-duration persistent connections in gRPC, designed to improve latency, gives rise to the sticky session problem. Unlike traditional load balancing, where connections are terminated swiftly and each request is directed to the most suitable server, gRPC's persistent connections may cause requests to consistently land on the same server. This introduces complexities that need thoughtful consideration and innovative solutions.

To address the intricacies of load balancing in gRPC, several strategies have come to the fore. Client-side load balancing, where the onus is on the client to decide which server to connect to, offers flexibility but may result in sticky sessions. Look-aside load balancing, employing external load balancers separate from gRPC, proves effective in mitigating sticky session issues. Additionally, leveraging service mesh solutions like Istio, with features such as Extension Discovery Service (xDS), provides a holistic and dynamic approach to load balancing, aligning with the specific requirements of microservices communication.

Moreover, the use of headless ClusterIP services in Kubernetes allows clients to decide how they connect to individual pods, enhancing control and flexibility. Custom load balancing solutions or extensions tailored to gRPC's characteristics can be developed to meet specific application needs. In conclusion, the multifaceted landscape of load balancing in gRPC demands a thoughtful and strategic approach, considering the trade-offs and benefits associated with each solution. As the chapter concludes, it's evident that a nuanced understanding of load balancing intricacies is crucial for architects and developers navigating the complex terrain of modern application development.

In the upcoming chapter, we shall delve into the crucial aspect of securing gRPC communications, ensuring that the exchange of data is not only efficient but also safeguarded against potential threats. The exploration begins with a focus on TLS security, understanding how it facilitates one-way secured communication within the gRPC framework. The chapter shall explore the practical implementation of authenticating gRPC calls. Two distinct approaches are covered – the utilization of basic authentication mechanisms and the integration of JSON Web Tokens (JWT) for enhanced security. Readers will gain not only a theoretical understanding of TLS security and mTLS authentication in the context of gRPC but also practical insights into implementing robust authentication mechanisms. The exploration of basic authentication and JWT integration adds a practical layer to the theoretical foundations, providing a well-rounded understanding of securing gRPC communications in real-world scenarios.

Multiple Choice Questions

1. Why is load balancing essential in application development?
    a. It reduces the overall load on servers
    b. It ensures fair distribution of requests among multiple servers
    c. It improves the performance and scalability of applications
    d. All of the above
2. What challenges does gRPC face in terms of load balancing?
    a. Inefficient multiplexing of requests
    b. Difficulty in maintaining persistent connections
    c. Lack of support for modern load balancing algorithms
    d. None of the above
3. Which term best describes the load balancing challenge specific to gRPC's long-duration connections?
    a. Latency trade-off
    b. Cascading failures
    c. Persistent connection dilemma
    d. None of the above
4. What is a potential trade-off when resolving the load balancing issue in gRPC through client-side load balancing?
    a. Reduced latency
    b. Improved long-duration connections
    c. Sacrificing one of gRPC's advantages
    d. Seamless load balancing
5. Which approach does the chapter recommend to address the load balancing issue in gRPC?
    a. Server-side load balancing
    b. Client-side load balancing
    c. Look-aside load balancing
    d. Both a and b

6. What role does the "lookaside" load balancer play in the recommended solution?
    a. Distributing traffic among gRPC servers
    b. Resolving DNS for clients
    c. Storing previous connections for reuse
    d. None of the above
7. In the context of load balancing in gRPC, what does "sticky sessions" refer to?
    a. Sessions with persistent connections
    b. Sessions that stick to a single server
    c. Randomized session distribution
    d. None of the above
8. How can Kubernetes enhance load balancing in gRPC?
    a. By introducing round-robin algorithms
    b. By providing native support for gRPC
    c. By enabling headless ClusterIP services
    d. All of the above
9. What is a potential drawback of headless ClusterIP services in gRPC load balancing?
    a. Improved latency
    b. Loss of gRPC's long-duration connection advantage
    c. Enhanced security
    d. None of the above
10. Which tool is recommended for handling gRPC load balancing in a Kubernetes cluster in the chapter?
    a. Istio
    b. Nginx
    c. HAProxy
    d. Kubernetes native load balancer

Answers

1	d
2	b
3	a
4	c
5	b
6	c
7	b
8	c
9	b
10	a

References

https://www.infracloud.io/blogs/understanding-grpc-concepts-best-practices/

CHAPTER 7

Secured gRPC

Introduction

In the chapter on gRPC load balancing, we delved into the crucial need for load balancing in application development and explored the intricacies that gRPC servers face in achieving effective load distribution. The challenges arise due to the persistent connections created by gRPC, which, while addressing latency issues, pose difficulties for load balancing. We explored various solutions to this problem, including client-side load balancing, lookaside load balancing, and integrating gRPC load balancing with Istio. The chapter discussed implementing custom load balancing solutions, such as an intelligent lookaside load balancer, and highlighted the trade-offs involved, particularly concerning the longevity of connections. Additionally, we explored how Istio, with its Extension Discovery Service, contributes to gRPC load balancing. The chapter aimed to provide a comprehensive understanding of the complexities associated with load balancing in gRPC and the diverse strategies to address them.

In this chapter, we will delve into the realm of security considerations in gRPC, particularly focusing on the implementation of Transport Layer Security (TLS) to enhance the overall security posture. The chapter outlines the steps for enabling TLS security in gRPC, emphasizing the importance of securing both client-server communication through mutual TLS (mTLS). Furthermore, we will explore two distinct approaches to authenticate gRPC calls–utilizing basic authentication and leveraging JSON Web Tokens (JWT). The discussion will encompass the implementation details and considerations associated with each authentication method. Finally, the chapter will conclude by summarizing the key takeaways and highlighting the significance of robust security measures in gRPC-based applications.

Structure

In this chapter, we will cover the following topics:

- Enabling TLS security in gRPC
- Securing both client-server communication with mTLS
- Authenticating gRPC calls by:
  - Using basic auth
  - Using JWT

Enabling TLS Security in gRPC

Ensuring the security of communication over APIs between machines and the applications and services they interact with remains a paramount concern for both security and engineering teams. Throughout the evolution of technology, protocols such as SSL (Secure Sockets Layer) and its successor TLS (Transport Layer Security) have played a pivotal role in furnishing enterprises with robust mechanisms to encrypt data during its transfer within a network or across its boundaries. The implementation of these protocols has become a foundational element in safeguarding sensitive information, contributing significantly to the overall cybersecurity posture of organizations. As technology advances, the continuous emphasis on securing communication channels underscores the critical nature of protecting data integrity and confidentiality in the dynamic landscape of modern applications and services.

TLS (Transport Layer Security), previously recognized as SSL (Secure Sockets Layer), stands as a ubiquitous encryption protocol extensively employed across the Internet. In the context of a client-server interaction, TLS fulfills the crucial roles of authenticating the server and encrypting transactions between the client and server, thereby preventing third-party entities from deciphering the transmitted data.

To delve into the operational intricacies of TLS, it is imperative to grasp several fundamental components that constitute its functioning:

- **Public key and private key**: TLS incorporates a cryptographic method called public-key encryption, a sophisticated approach that involves the utilization of two distinctive keys within the encryption and decryption process. These keys, namely the public key and the private key, form a paired set with a unique relationship. Specifically, only the private key possesses the capability to decrypt any information that has been encrypted using the corresponding public key, and conversely, the public key can decrypt content encrypted with the private key. This asymmetric key system establishes a secure communication channel, ensuring that confidential data remains protected during transmission. The intricacies of this encryption methodology contribute significantly to the robust security measures offered by TLS in the realm of data transfer across networks.

- **TLS certificate**: A TLS certificate stands as a crucial data file within the context of secure communications, encapsulating vital information essential for server or device authentication. This file contains not only the public key but also pertinent details such as the identity of the certificate issuer and the expiration date of the certificate. Through this comprehensive set of information, the TLS certificate serves as a trusted credential, validating the authenticity of servers or devices engaged in communication. The public key within the certificate plays a pivotal role in encryption processes, ensuring that data transmitted between entities remains confidential and secure. Furthermore, the details regarding the certificate issuer and its expiration date contribute to the verification of the certificate's legitimacy and currency. This multifaceted nature of TLS certificates enhances the overall security infrastructure, reinforcing the integrity and trustworthiness of communications over the Internet.
- **TLS handshake**: The TLS handshake constitutes a critical process in establishing a secure communication channel by verifying not only the authenticity of the TLS certificate but also confirming the ownership of the server's private key. This intricate procedure serves as a foundational step in securing the exchange of information between entities engaged in a TLS interaction. During the TLS handshake, the mechanism for encryption is not only established but also precisely defined for the subsequent communication. This involves the negotiation of encryption algorithms and parameters that will be employed to safeguard the confidentiality and integrity of the data transmission. Therefore, the TLS handshake acts as a pivotal moment in the initiation of secure communication, ensuring that both parties can trust the encryption methods selected and confirming the legitimacy of the participating entities in the process.

Ordinarily, the server is equipped with a TLS certificate along with a set of public and private keys, while the client lacks these components. The standard TLS process unfolds in the following manner:

1. The client initiates communication with the server.
2. The server presents its TLS certificate.
3. The client authenticates the server's certificate.
4. Subsequently, the client and server engage in exchanging information over a secure TLS connection that ensures encryption of the transmitted data.

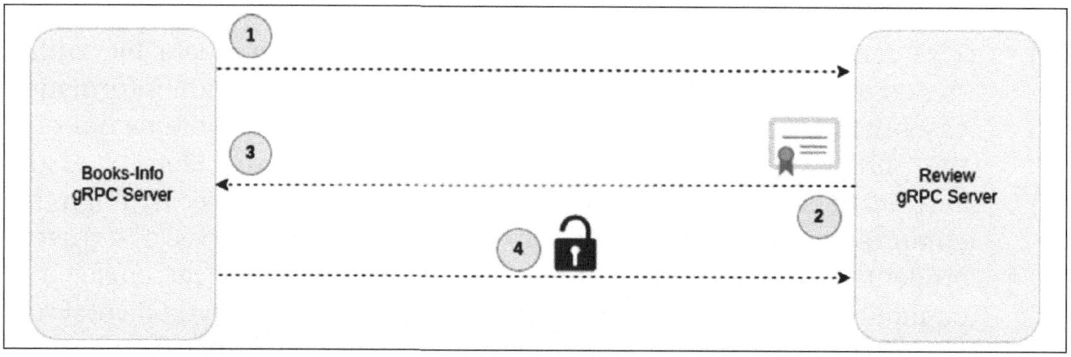

Figure 7.1: *Books-Info Server <-> Review Server Communication TLS Handshake*

While gRPC inherently utilizes HTTP/2, enabling TLS (Transport Layer Security) offers an additional layer of security to the communication. TLS ensures that the data exchanged between the client and server is encrypted, preventing unauthorized access or tampering. Even though HTTP/2 provides certain security features, such as header compression and multiplexing, it does not inherently guarantee data confidentiality. By enabling TLS, gRPC enhances its security posture by encrypting the traffic, protecting sensitive information from interception and manipulation by malicious entities. In summary, TLS complements the foundational benefits of HTTP/2 in gRPC by addressing data privacy and integrity concerns.

As TLS took over from its predecessor SSL, ushering in enhanced security features, it became apparent that both protocols were susceptible to various vulnerabilities. TLS, despite its advancements, faced challenges such as renegotiation attacks, vulnerabilities associated with RC4, and the notorious POODLE attacks. The identification of these exploitable weaknesses in TLS prompted security professionals to recognize the need for additional security measures. In response to these concerns, Mutual Transport Layer Security (mTLS) emerged as a robust solution. Unlike traditional TLS, mTLS goes beyond one-way authentication; instead, it establishes a mutual authentication mechanism where both communicating parties authenticate each other using certificates. This elevated level of authentication significantly enhances the security of cross-network communications, addressing the limitations observed in traditional TLS.

Mutual TLS (mTLS) serves as a robust mutual authentication mechanism, ensuring the identity verification of parties engaged in a network connection. This authentication process involves validating the private keys of the communicating entities, reinforced by the information encapsulated in their respective TLS certificates. In essence, mTLS acts as a stringent gatekeeper, confirming the authenticity of each party in the communication loop. Beyond mere authentication, mTLS plays a pivotal role in the implementation of a Zero-Trust security framework. This strategic security approach dispels the notion of inherent trust within an enterprise, necessitating thorough verification of individuals, connections, and servers. Leveraging mTLS in this context provides a robust defense against unauthorized access and potential security threats. Furthermore, mTLS is widely employed to fortify the security posture of an organization's APIs, extending Zero-Trust guarantees to every facet of network activity. This proactive stance contributes to the mitigation of unnecessary security risks, creating a more resilient and secure operational environment.

While mTLS shares similarities with conventional TLS, it introduces an extra layer of security by providing certificates to both the client and the server, allowing each party to leverage its public/private key pair for authentication. The mTLS handshake process involves the following steps for mutual validation:

1. **Client-Server Interaction**: The client initiates communication with the server.
2. **Server Presents TLS Certificate**: The server presents its TLS certificate to the client.
3. **Client Validates Server Certificate**: The client rigorously validates the server's certificate, ensuring its authenticity.
4. **Client Provides TLS Certificate**: The client reciprocates by presenting its TLS certificate to the server.
5. **Server Verifies Client's Certificate**: The server thoroughly verifies the client's certificate, confirming its legitimacy.
6. **Server Grants Access**: Upon successful verification, the server grants access to the client.

7. **Encrypted Data Transfer**: With mutual authentication established, both the client and server engage in information exchange over an encrypted TLS connection.

This meticulous mutual validation process ensures a heightened level of security, mitigating the risks associated with unauthorized access and bolstering the integrity of the communication channel between the client and the server.

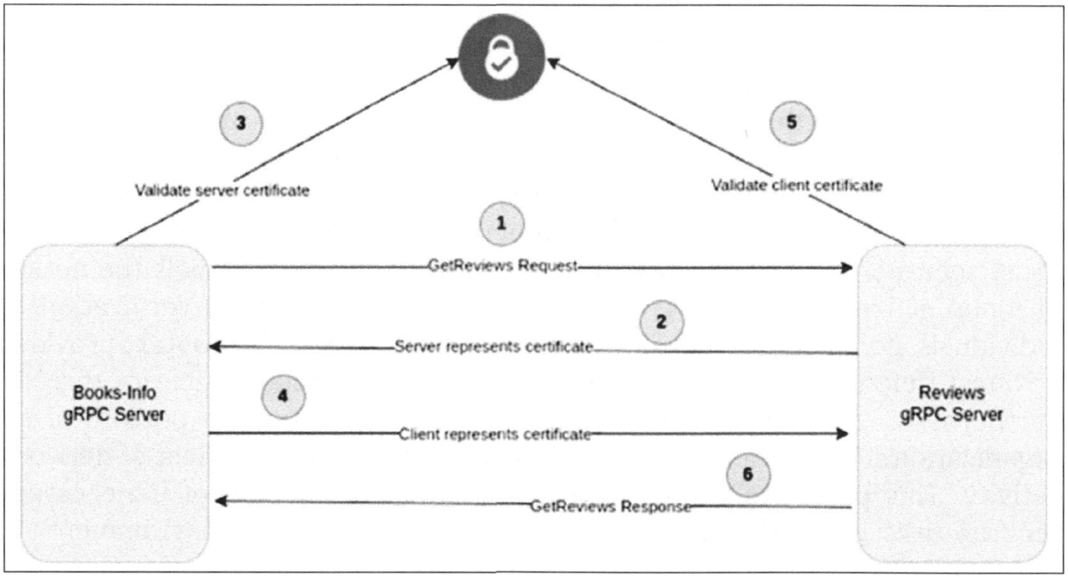

Figure 7.2: *Books-Info Server <-> Review Server gRPC mTLS Communication*

Let us now explore in detail the implementation of TLS/mTLS in our microservices environment, specifically focusing on the Reviews gRPC server, and Books-Info gRPC server. TLS has been activated in the **Reviews** server, and likewise, TLS has been implemented in the **Books-Info** server, which serves as a client when engaging with the **Reviews** server.

Certificate Generation

These commands will help us establish a secure communication infrastructure by creating a CA, generating server keys and certificates, and converting the private key to a suitable format for gRPC. This will ensure that our microservices can communicate over a secure and authenticated channel.

```
openssl genrsa -passout pass:1111 -des3 -out books-app/ssl/ca.key 4096
```

The command you provided generates an RSA private key using OpenSSL. Here is a breakdown of the options:

1. **`openssl genrsa`**: This initiates the process of generating an RSA private key.
2. **`-passout pass:1111`**: This sets the password for the private key. In this case, the password is set to **`'1111'`**.
3. **`-des3`**: This specifies the use of the triple DES encryption algorithm to encrypt the private key.
4. **`-out books-app/ssl/ca.key`**: This indicates the output file for the generated private key. In this case, it's being saved in the **`'ca.key'`** file within the **`'ssl'`** directory of the **`'books-app'`** folder.
5. **`4096`**: This specifies the number of bits in the generated key. In this case, it is a 4096-bit key.

```
openssl req -passin pass:1111 -new -x509 -days 365 -key books-app/
ssl/ca.key -out books-app/ssl/ca.crt -subj "//CN=${SERVER_CN}" -addext
"subjectAltName=DNS:${SERVER_CN}"
```

This OpenSSL command is used to generate a self-signed X.509 certificate for the Certificate Authority (CA). Here is an explanation of the options:

1. **`openssl req`**: This command is used for **X.509** certificate requests. In this case, it is used to generate a self-signed certificate.
2. **`-passin pass:1111`**: This specifies the password for the private key. The password is set to **`'1111'`**, and it is used to unlock the private key generated in the previous step.
3. **`-new`**: This option indicates that a new certificate request is being made.
4. **`-x509`**: This option tells OpenSSL that the output is a self-signed certificate rather than a certificate request.
5. **`-days 365`**: This sets the validity period of the certificate to **`365`** days.
6. **`-key books-app/ssl/ca.key`**: This specifies the private key to be used for generating the certificate.
7. **`-out books-app/ssl/ca.crt`**: This is the output file where the generated self-signed certificate will be stored.
8. **`-subj "//CN=${SERVER_CN}"`**: This sets the subject of the certificate. The Common Name (CN) is set to the value of the environment variable **`SERVER_CN`**.
9. **`-addext "subjectAltName=DNS:${SERVER_CN}"`**: This adds a Subject Alternative Name (SAN) extension to the certificate, specifying that the certificate is valid for the DNS name specified in the **`SERVER_CN`** variable.

```
openssl genrsa -passout pass:1111 -des3 -out books-app/ssl/server.key
4096
```

This command generates RSA Private Key:

1. **genrsa**: Generate an RSA private key.
2. **-passout pass:1111**: Set a password for the private key. The password is **'1111'.**
3. **-des3**: Use the Triple DES encryption algorithm to encrypt the private key.
4. **-out books-app/ssl/server.key**: Specify the output file for the private key.
5. **4096**: Specify the number of bits in the key (4096 bits in this case).

```
openssl req -passin pass:1111 -new -key books-app/ssl/server.key
-out books-app/ssl/server.csr -subj "//CN=${SERVER_CN}" -addext
"subjectAltName=DNS:${SERVER_CN}"
```

This command generates Certificate Signing Request (CSR):

1. **req**: PKCS#10 certificate request and certificate generating utility.
2. **-passin pass:1111**: Input password for the private key.
3. **-new**: Generate a new CSR.
4. **-key books-app/ssl/server.key**: Specify the private key file.
5. **-out books-app/ssl/server.csr**: Specify the output file for the CSR.
6. **-subj "//CN=${SERVER_CN}"**: Set the subject of the certificate (Common Name).
7. **-addext "subjectAltName=DNS:${SERVER_CN}"**: Add a Subject Alternative Name (SAN) extension with the DNS name.

```
openssl x509 -req -passin pass:1111 -days 365 -in books-app/ssl/server.
csr -CA books-app/ssl/ca.crt -CAkey books-app/ssl/ca.key -set_serial 01
-out books-app/ssl/server.crt
```

This command signs the CSR with the CA:

1. **x509**: Certificate display and signing utility.
2. **-req**: Indicates that a certificate signing request is being processed.
3. **-passin pass:1111**: Password for the CA key.
4. **-days 365**: Set the certificate's validity period to 365 days.
5. **-in books-app/ssl/server.csr**: Input file containing the CSR.

6. **-CA books-app/ssl/ca.crt**: CA certificate.
7. **-CAkey books-app/ssl/ca.key**: CA private key.
8. **-set_serial 01**: Set the serial number for the certificate.
9. **-out books-app/ssl/server.crt**: Output file for the signed certificate.

```
openssl pkcs8 -topk8 -nocrypt -passin pass:1111 -in books-app/ssl/server.
key -out books-app/ssl/server.pem
```

This command converts a Private Key Format to pem format:

1. **pkcs8**: PKCS#8 format private key conversion tool.
2. **-topk8**: Convert a private key to PKCS#8 format.
3. **-nocrypt**: Do not encrypt the output private key.
4. **-passin pass:1111**: Input password for the private key.
5. **-in books-app/ssl/server.key**: Input file containing the original private key.
6. **-out books-app/ssl/server.pem**: Output file for the converted private key.

Following the generation of certificates, it becomes imperative to provide their file paths to our applications through configurations, enabling their utilization. However, for the sake of simplicity in this scenario, we have opted to define them as constants within the **'configs'** package as follows:

```
package configs


const (

   TLS              = "true"

   SSL_CERT_PATH    = "ssl/server.crt"

   SSL_KEY_PATH     = "ssl/server.pem"

   SSL_CA_CERT_PATH = "ssl/ca.crt"

)
```

In order to enable TLS in **Reviews** server, we made the following changes while it's startup:

```
tlsOrNot := configs.TLS

tls, _ := strconv.ParseBool(tlsOrNot)
```

```
if tls {
  certFilePath := configs.SSL_CERT_PATH
  keyFilePath := configs.SSL_KEY_PATH
  creds, sslErr := credentials.NewServerTLSFromFile(certFilePath,
  keyFilePath)
  if sslErr != nil {
    log.Fatalf("Failed to load certificates: %v", sslErr)
    return
  }

  opts = append(opts, grpc.Creds(creds))
}
```

Where we check whether TLS (Transport Layer Security) is enabled based on the configuration. We read the configuration variable **TLS** and convert it to a boolean value. If the TLS is enabled, we proceed to load the server certificates from the specified file paths. The paths for the SSL certificate and key are retrieved from the configuration variables **`SSL_CERT_PATH`** and **`SSL_KEY_PATH`.** We then create gRPC server credentials using the loaded certificates, and these credentials are added to the gRPC server options (**opts**). If any error occurs during the SSL certificate loading process, we log the error and terminate the program. This code is part of a larger system that sets up a gRPC server with TLS if configured to do so.

When establishing a connection from the Books-info server to the Reviews server, it is imperative to utilize a CA (Certificate Authority) certificate for secure communication. This requirement is fulfilled through the following modifications in the code of the Books-info server:

```
tlsOrNot := configs.TLS
tls, _ := strconv.ParseBool(tlsOrNot)
if tls {
  certFilePath := configs.SSL_CA_CERT_PATH
  creds, sslErr := credentials.NewClientTLSFromFile(certFilePath, "")
```

```
  if sslErr != nil {
    log.Fatalf("Failed to loading ca trust certificates: %v", sslErr)
    return
  }
  opts = grpc.WithTransportCredentials(creds)
}
```

If TLS is enabled, we retrieve the **CA (Certificate Authority)** certificate file path from the configuration and use it to create **TLS** credentials for the client using **`credentials.NewClientTLSFromFile()`**. If any error occurs during the certificate loading process, we log an error message and exit the application. The resulting TLS credentials are then added to the gRPC options using **`grpc.WithTransportCredentials(creds)`**. This ensures that secure communication is established when the **`Books-info`** server connects to the **`Reviews`** server.

Authenticating gRPC Calls

Despite the majority of gRPC calls occurring within the microservice architecture, the implementation of authentication mechanisms remains necessary. Authenticating gRPC calls in microservice communication is a fundamental practice for securing the interactions between services, preventing unauthorized access, and ensuring the integrity of the entire microservices architecture. Authenticating gRPC calls in microservice communication is essential for several reasons:

- **Protect Against Unauthorized Access**: Authentication ensures that only authorized and authenticated users or services can make gRPC calls. This helps in preventing unauthorized access to sensitive information or functionalities.
- **Prevent Data Tampering**: Authentication provides a way to verify the integrity of the data exchanged between microservices. It ensures that the data has not been tampered with during transit.
- **Verify Service Identities**: For service-to-service communication, authentication ensures that the calling service is who it claims to be. This is crucial for maintaining the trustworthiness of the entire microservices ecosystem.
- **Enforce Access Control**: Authentication is often coupled with authorization. Once a service is authenticated, authorization mechanisms

can be employed to control what actions or resources the authenticated service is allowed to access.

- **Logging and Auditing**: Authentication events can be logged for auditing purposes. This creates an audit trail, helping in tracking who accessed which service and when.
- **Meet Regulatory Requirements**: Many industries and applications have specific regulatory requirements regarding data security. Authentication helps in meeting these requirements.
- **Build Trust in the System**: Authenticating gRPC calls helps build trust between microservices. Each service can rely on the identity of the calling service, making the system more robust.
- **Avoid Impersonation Attacks**: Without authentication, there is risk of impersonation attacks where an unauthorized entity pretends to be a legitimate service.
- **Ensure Confidentiality**: Authentication often goes hand-in-hand with encryption. Together, they ensure that communication channels are secure and that sensitive information remains confidential.
- **Prevent Malicious Behavior**: Authenticating calls helps in preventing malicious entities from injecting harmful or unauthorized requests into the system.

Using Basic Auth

Authentication of gRPC requests using basic auth involves intercepting the requests, extracting credentials from the request context, and validating them using a specific logic. Depending on the validation result, the request is either allowed to proceed or rejected.

The following code snippets illustrate the process:

1. Define a basic auth interceptor:

```
// Basic authentication interceptor

func authInterceptor(ctx context.Context, req interface{}, info
*grpc.UnaryServerInfo, handler grpc.UnaryHandler) (interface{},
error) {

    // Extract credentials from the context

    username, password, ok := extractBasicAuth(ctx)

    if !ok {
```

```
        return nil, fmt.Errorf("Failed to extract basic auth
        credentials.")
    }

    // Validate credentials (example: check against hardcoded
    credentials)
    if !isValidUser(username, password) {
        return nil, grpc.Errorf(codes.Unauthenticated, "Invalid
        credentials")
    }

    // Proceed to the actual service method
    return handler(ctx, req)
}
```

2. Define extract credentials:

```
// extractBasicAuth extracts basic authentication credentials from
the context.
func extractBasicAuth(ctx context.Context) (username, password
string, ok bool) {
    md, ok := metadata.FromIncomingContext(ctx)
    if !ok {
        return "", "", false
    }

    // Check if the "authorization" metadata header exists.
    authHeaders, ok := md["authorization"]
    if !ok || len(authHeaders) == 0 {
        return "", "", false
    }

    // Parse the "Authorization" header for basic authentication.
    authHeader := authHeaders[0]
    authParts := strings.Fields(authHeader)
```

```
    if len(authParts) != 2 || strings.ToLower(authParts[0]) !=
    "basic" {
        return "", "", false
    }

    // Decode the base64-encoded credentials.
    decoded, err := decodeBase64(authParts[1])
    if err != nil {
        return "", "", false
    }

    // Split the credentials into username and password.
    creds := strings.Split(decoded, ":")
    if len(creds) != 2 {
        return "", "", false
    }

    return creds[0], creds[1], true
}

// decodeBase64 decodes a base64-encoded string.
func decodeBase64(encoded string) (string, error) {
    decoded, err := grpc.DecodeBase64(encoded)
    if err != nil {
        return "", err
    }
    return string(decoded), nil
}
```

3. Define validate credentials:

```
// isValidUser checks if the provided credentials match a known
user.
func isValidUser(username, password string) bool {
```

```
    // this logic to validate needs to be replaced to validate
    against a user database or known set of users.
    // For simplicity, we have a hard-coded user here.
    validUser := User{Username: "uname", Password: "safePass"}
    return username == validUser.Username && password == validUser.
    Password
}
```

4. Integrate the interceptor with server as a server option:

```
// Register the gRPC server and attach the interceptor for basic
authentication
grpcServer := grpc.NewServer(
    grpc.UnaryInterceptor(authInterceptor),
     // ... other server options
)
```

5. Client dials with 'Bearer <token/credentials>' request header.

```
ctx := metadata.NewIncomingContext(context.Background(), metadata.
Pairs("authorization", "Basic dW5hbWU6c2FmZVBhc3M="))

 // Set up a connection to the server
 conn, err := grpc.Dial("localhost:50051", grpc.WithInsecure())
if err != nil {
    log.Fatalf("did not connect: %v", err)
}
defer conn.Close()

// Create a gRPC client
client := proto.NewBookServiceClient(conn)

// Assume you have a request to send
req := &proto.BookRequest{ /*...*/ }

// Make an authenticated gRPC call
resp, err := client.GetBook(ctx, req)
if err != nil {
```

```
        log.Fatalf("Error calling GetBook: %v", err)
    }

    // Handle the response...
```

Using JWT

Now, let us explore the implementation of authentication in gRPC using JWT.

To achieve this, we will develop a comprehensive gRPC auth server and establish an interceptor to ensure the authentication of all incoming requests.

We will start with **auth.proto**

```
syntax = "proto3";

package prot;

option go_package="./proto";

message LoginRequest {
    string username = 1;
    string password = 2;
}

message LoginResponse {
    string access_token = 1;
}

service AuthService {
    rpc Login(LoginRequest) returns (LoginResponse);
}
```

This is a Protocol Buffers (proto3) file defining a simple gRPC service for authentication. Let us break down the components:

1. **Package Declaration**: package prot; specifies the package name as `"prot".` This helps organize related protobuf files.
2. **Go Package Option**: option `go_package="./proto";` indicates the Go package path generated from this proto file. In this case, it suggests that the Go files should be placed in a `"proto"` directory.
3. **Message Definitions**:
   a. **LoginRequest**: A message that represents the request for user login. It contains fields for the username and password.
   b. **LoginResponse**: A message representing the response after a login attempt. It contains an access token.
4. **Service Definition**:
   a. **AuthService**: This declares a gRPC service named `"AuthService"` with one RPC method:
   b. **Login**: Takes a `LoginRequest` and returns a `LoginResponse`. This RPC is responsible for handling user login.

In summary, this proto file defines a basic authentication service with a single method for user login, and it utilizes Protocol Buffers for data serialization. The **LoginResponse** includes an access token, which is a common practice in token-based authentication systems. The Go implementation generated from this proto file will be placed in the "./proto" directory.

The corresponding golang code can be generated by the following command:

```
protoc --go_out=books-app/internal/pkg --go-grpc_out=books-app/internal/
pkg books-app/internal/pkg/proto/auth.proto
```

Before moving ahead, certain foundational components need implementation:

1. **User model**: This will encapsulate user attributes.
2. **User repository**: To store and retrieve user information.
3. **JWT manager**: Essential for generating verifiable tokens.

We can represent an user with some basic attributes for simplicity:

```
package model


import "golang.org/x/crypto/bcrypt"


type User struct {
```

```
    Username       string
    HashedPassword string
    Role           string
}

func (user *User) IsCorrectPassword(password string) bool {
    err := bcrypt.CompareHashAndPassword([]byte(user.HashedPassword), []
    byte(password))
    return err == nil
}

func (user *User) Clone() *User {
    return &User{
        Username:       user.Username,
        HashedPassword: user.HashedPassword,
        Role:           user.Role,
    }
}
```

We will utilize an in-memory repository for storing and retrieving user details.

```
package repo

import (
    "fmt"
    "log"
    "sync"

    "github.com/OrangeAVA/Modern-API-Design-with-gRPC/books-app/
    internal/pkg/configs"
    "github.com/OrangeAVA/Modern-API-Design-with-gRPC/books-app/
```

```
    internal/pkg/model"
)

var (
    userStore UserStore
    onceInit  sync.Once
)

type UserStore interface {
    Save(user *model.User) error
    Find(username string) (*model.User, error)
}

func init() {
    onceInit.Do(func() {
        userStore = NewInMemoryUserStore()
        err := configs.SeedUsers(userStore)
        if err != nil {
            log.Fatal("could not create seed users")
        }
    })
}

type inMemoryUserStore struct {
    mutex sync.RWMutex
    users map[string]*model.User
}
```

```
func NewInMemoryUserStore() UserStore {
    return userStore
}

func (store *inMemoryUserStore) Save(user *model.User) error {
    store.mutex.Lock()
    defer store.mutex.Unlock()

    if store.users[user.Username] != nil {
        return fmt.Errorf("user(%s) already exists", user.Username)
    }

    store.users[user.Username] = user.Clone()
    return nil
}

func (store *inMemoryUserStore) Find(username string) (*model.User,
error) {
    store.mutex.RLock()
    defer store.mutex.RUnlock()

    user := store.users[username]
    if user == nil {
        return nil, nil
    }

    return user.Clone(), nil
}
```

We will introduce a user service layer specifically designed to confine the functionality of the user repository to storage and retrieval tasks only.

```
package service

import (
    "fmt"

    "github.com/OrangeAVA/Modern-API-Design-with-gRPC/books-app/
    internal/pkg/model"
    "golang.org/x/crypto/bcrypt"
)

func NewUser(username, password, role string) (*model.User, error) {
    hashedPassword, err := bcrypt.GenerateFromPassword([]byte(password),
    bcrypt.DefaultCost)
    if err != nil {
        return nil, fmt.Errorf("cannot hash password: %v", err)
    }

    user := &model.User{
        Username:       username,
        HashedPassword: string(hashedPassword),
        Role:           role,
    }

    return user, nil
}
```

Now let us define some roles to restrict access to services based on it.

```
package configs
```

```
import (
   “time”

   “github.com/OrangeAVA/Modern-API-Design-with-gRPC/books-app/
   internal/pkg/repo”
   “github.com/OrangeAVA/Modern-API-Design-with-gRPC/books-app/
   internal/pkg/service”
)

const (
   SecretKey     = “secret”
   TokenDuration = 15 * time.Minute

   bookServicePath       = “/prot.BookService/”
   bookReviewServicePath = “/prot.ReviewService/”
   bookInfoServicePath   = “/prot.BookInfoService/”
)

func SeedUsers(userStore repo.UserStore) error {
   err := createUser(userStore, “admin1”, “12345”, “admin”)
   if err != nil {
      return err
   }

   return createUser(userStore, “user1”, “54321”, “user”)

}

func AccessibleRoles() map[string][]string {
```

```
    return map[string][]string{
        bookServicePath + "AddBook":     {"admin"},
        bookServicePath + "UpdateBook": {"admin"},
        bookServicePath + "RemoveBook": {"admin"},

        bookServicePath + "GetBook":                          {"admin", "user"},
        bookReviewServicePath + "GetBookReviews":             {"admin", "user"},
        bookReviewServicePath + "SubmitReviews":              {"admin", "user"},
        bookInfoServicePath + "GetBookInfoWithReviews": {"admin", "user"},
    }
}

func createUser(userStore repo.UserStore, username, password, role string)
error {
    user, err := service.NewUser(username, password, role)
    if err != nil {
        return err
    }

    return userStore.Save(user)
}
```

This preceding code defines a package named configs that contains constants, functions for seeding users, and defining accessible roles. Let us break down the code:

1. **Constants**:
    a. **`SecretKey`**: A constant representing a secret key.
    b. **`TokenDuration`**: A constant representing the duration for which a token is valid (15 minutes).
    c. **`bookServicePath`, `bookReviewServicePath`, `bookInfoServicePath`**: Constants representing paths for different gRPC services.

2. **Function SeedUsers**:
    a. Takes a **`userStore`** of type **`repo.UserStore`** as a parameter.
    b. Calls the createUser function twice to seed users: an admin with username "**`admin1`**" and a user with username "**`user1`**".
    c. Returns any error encountered during user creation.
3. **Function AccessibleRoles:**
    a. Returns a map where keys are gRPC service paths and values are slices of roles that have access to the corresponding service.
    b. Specifies roles that have access to various methods of gRPC services (**`AddBook`**, **`UpdateBook`**, and so on).
4. **Function createUser:**
    a. Takes a **`userStore`** and user details (username, password, role) as parameters.
    b. Uses the **`service.NewUser`** function to create a new user.
    c. Saves the user to the provided **`userStore`**.
    d. Returns any error encountered during user creation.

In summary, this code provides constants for secret keys, token duration, and service paths. It includes functions to seed users with specific roles and to define accessible roles for different gRPC services. The code structure suggests that it is a part of a larger system that involves user authentication and authorization for gRPC services.

The preceding code defines a package named **`jwt`** that manages JSON Web Tokens (JWT) for user authentication and authorization. Let's break down the code:

1. Singleton Pattern:
    a. The package uses the singleton pattern to create a single instance (**`jwtMgr`**) of the **`JWTManager`** type.
    b. This ensures that there is only one instance of the JWT manager throughout the application.
2. JWTManager Struct:
    a. Represents the JWT manager with fields for **`secretKey`** and **`tokenDuration`** (the duration for which a token is valid).

3. UserClaims Struct:
   a. Extends the standard JWT claims **(`jwt.StandardClaims`)** to include additional user-specific claims like **`Username`** and **`Role`**.
4. init Function:
   a. Uses the **`sync.Once`** package to ensure that the JWT manager is initialized only once.
   b. Sets up the **`jwtMgr`** with the **`SecretKey`** and **`TokenDuration`** from the **configs** package.
5. NewJWTManager Function:
   a. Returns the singleton instance of the JWT manager.
6. Generate Method:
   a. Generates a JWT token for a given user.
   b. Creates a **`UserClaims`** structure with expiration time, username, and role.
   c. Uses the HMAC SHA-256 signing method and signs the token with the secret key.
   d. Returns the signed token as a string.
7. Verify Method:
   a. Verifies the authenticity of a given JWT token.
   b. Parses the token using the provided secret key.
   c. Checks the token signing method and verifies it's using HMAC SHA-256.
   d. Returns the decoded claims (including username and role) if verification is successful.

In summary, this code provides a thread-safe JWT manager that can generate and verify JWT tokens for user authentication. It follows best practices by using HMAC SHA-256 for signing tokens and includes user-specific claims in the token payload. The singleton pattern ensures that there is a single instance of the JWT manager across the application.

Now that we have the foundational components in place, let us create the auth server.

```
package authserver


import (
```

```
    "context"
    "fmt"
    "log"
    "net"

    "github.com/OrangeAVA/Modern-API-Design-with-gRPC/books-app/
    internal/pkg/configs"
    "github.com/OrangeAVA/Modern-API-Design-with-gRPC/books-app/
    internal/pkg/jwt"
    "github.com/OrangeAVA/Modern-API-Design-with-gRPC/books-app/
    internal/pkg/middleware"
    "github.com/OrangeAVA/Modern-API-Design-with-gRPC/books-app/
    internal/pkg/proto"
    "github.com/OrangeAVA/Modern-API-Design-with-gRPC/books-app/
    internal/pkg/repo"
    "google.golang.org/grpc"
    "google.golang.org/grpc/codes"
    "google.golang.org/grpc/reflection"
    "google.golang.org/grpc/status"
)

type App struct {
    proto.UnimplementedAuthServiceServer

    userStore  repo.UserStore
    jwtManager *jwt.JWTManager
}

func NewApp(userStore repo.UserStore, jwtManager *jwt.JWTManager) *App {
    return &App{userStore: userStore, jwtManager: jwtManager}
```

```
}

func (a *App) Start() {

    appConfig, err := configs.ProvideAppConfig()
    if err != nil {
        log.Fatal(err)
    }

    servAddr := fmt.Sprintf("0.0.0.0:%d", appConfig.ServerConfig.Port)

    fmt.Println("starting auth gRPC server at", servAddr)

    lis, err := net.Listen("tcp", servAddr)
    if err != nil {
        log.Fatalf("Failed to listen: %v", err)
    }

    opts := []grpc.ServerOption{}
    middlewareOpts := middleware.ProvideGrpcMiddlewareServerOpts()
    opts = append(opts, middlewareOpts...)

    s := grpc.NewServer(opts...)

    proto.RegisterAuthServiceServer(s, a)

    reflection.Register(s)

    if err := s.Serve(lis); err != nil {
        log.Fatalf("Failed to serve: %v", err)
```

```
    }
}

func (a *App) Shutdown() {}

func (a *App) Login(ctx context.Context, req *proto.LoginRequest) (*proto.
LoginResponse, error) {
    user, err := a.userStore.Find(req.GetUsername())
    if err != nil {
        return nil, status.Errorf(codes.Internal, "cannot find user: %v",
        err)
    }

    if user == nil || !user.IsCorrectPassword(req.GetPassword()) {
        return nil, status.Errorf(codes.InvalidArgument, "invlid username
        or password")
    }

    token, err := a.jwtManager.Generate(user)
    if err != nil {
        return nil, status.Errorf(codes.Internal, "cannot generate access
        token: %v", err)
    }

    res := &proto.LoginResponse{
        AccessToken: token,
    }

    return res, nil
}
```

The preceding code defines a gRPC server for an authentication service (AuthService). Let us break down the code:

1. **App Struct**:
    a. Implements the **`AuthServiceServer`** interface from the generated gRPC code.
    b. Holds instances of the user repository (**`userStore`**) and JWT manager (**`jwtManager`**).
2. **`NewApp` Function**: Creates a new instance of the **App** struct with the provided **user store** and **JWT manager.**
3. **Start Method**:
    a. Reads the server configuration using **`configs.ProvideAppConfig()`**
    b. Constructs the server address based on the configuration.
    c. Sets up gRPC server options and middleware using the **`middleware.ProvideGrpcMiddlewareServerOpts()`** function.
    d. Creates a new gRPC server (s) with the specified options.
    e. Registers the authentication service on the server.
    f. Registers reflection service for debugging purposes.
    g. Starts serving on the specified network address.
4. **`Shutdown` Method**: Placeholder for any cleanup or shutdown procedures (currently empty).
5. **`Login` Method**:
    a. Implements the gRPC service method for user login.
    b. Retrieves user information from the user store based on the provided username.
    c. Validates the user's credentials, returning an error if the user is not found or the password is incorrect.
    d. Generates a JWT token using the JWT manager.
    e. Creates and returns a **`LoginResponse`** with the generated access token.

In summary, this code defines a gRPC authentication service with a **`Login`** method that authenticates users, generates JWT tokens, and provides them as part of the response. The server is configured to listen on a specified address, and middleware can be added to the gRPC server for additional functionalities.

Now let us define an interceptor with the aforementioned **`Auth Server`** and **`jwtManager`** to intercept requests and authenticate them.

```
package middleware

import (
   “context”
   “log”

   “google.golang.org/grpc”
   “google.golang.org/grpc/codes”
   “google.golang.org/grpc/metadata”
   status “google.golang.org/grpc/status”

   “github.com/OrangeAVA/Modern-API-Design-with-gRPC/books-app/
   internal/pkg/jwt”
)

type AuthInterceptor struct {
   jwtManager      *jwt.JWTManager
   accessibleRoles map[string][]string
}

func NewAuthInterceptor(jwtManager *jwt.JWTManager, accessibleRoles
map[string][]string) *AuthInterceptor {
   return &AuthInterceptor{jwtManager, accessibleRoles}
}

func (interceptor *AuthInterceptor) Unary() grpc.UnaryServerInterceptor {
   return func(ctx context.Context, req interface{}, info *grpc.
   UnaryServerInfo, handler grpc.UnaryHandler) (interface{}, error) {
      log.Println(“--> unary interceptor: “, info.FullMethod)
```

```
        err := interceptor.Authorize(ctx, info.FullMethod)
        if err != nil {
            return nil, err
        }

        return handler(ctx, req)
    }
}

func (interceptor *AuthInterceptor) Stream() grpc.StreamServerInterceptor
{
    return func(srv interface{}, ss grpc.ServerStream, info *grpc.
    StreamServerInfo, handler grpc.StreamHandler) error {
        log.Println("--> stream interceptor: ", info.FullMethod)

        err := interceptor.Authorize(ss.Context(), info.FullMethod)
        if err != nil {
            return err
        }

        return handler(srv, ss)
    }
}

func (interceptor *AuthInterceptor) Authorize(ctx context.Context, method
string) error {
    accessibleRoles, ok := interceptor.accessibleRoles[method]
    if !ok {
        return nil
```

```
    }

    md, ok := metadata.FromIncomingContext(ctx)
    if !ok {
        return status.Errorf(codes.Unauthenticated, "metadata is not
        provided")
    }

    values := md["authorization"]
    if len(values) == 0 {
        return status.Errorf(codes.Unauthenticated, "auth token is not
        provided")
    }

    accessToken := values[0]
    claims, err := interceptor.jwtManager.Verify(accessToken)
    if err != nil {
        return status.Errorf(codes.Unauthenticated, "auth token is
        invalid: %v", err)
    }

    for _, role := range accessibleRoles {
        if role == claims.Role {
            return nil
        }
    }

    return status.Errorf(codes.PermissionDenied, "user has no permission
    to access this RPC")
}
```

The preceding code defines a gRPC middleware for authentication (**`AuthInterceptor`**). Let us go through its key components:

1. AuthInterceptor Struct:
    a. Holds instances of **`JWTManager`** and a map of accessible roles for each gRPC method.
2. NewAuthInterceptor Function:
    a. Creates a new instance of **`AuthInterceptor`** with the provided **`JWTManager`** and a map of accessible roles.
3. Unary and Stream Methods:
    a. Define the gRPC unary and stream interceptors.
    b. These interceptors are functions that can be used to pre-process gRPC unary and streaming RPCs, respectively.
    c. The interceptors log the intercepted method and then call the **`Authorize`** method to check for authorization.
4. Authorize Method:
    a. Validates the authorization of a user based on the provided JWT token and accessible roles for a specific gRPC method.
    b. Retrieves metadata (including the authorization token) from the incoming context.
    c. Verifies the JWT token using the **`Verify`** method of the **`JWTManager`**.
    d. Checks if the user's role matches one of the accessible roles for the given method.
    e. Returns an error if authorization fails, including cases where metadata is not provided, the auth token is missing, or it is invalid.

In summary, this middleware ensures that gRPC requests are authorized based on JWT tokens and accessible roles. It logs the intercepted gRPC methods and performs the necessary authorization checks before allowing the request to proceed to the actual gRPC handler. If the authorization fails, appropriate error statuses are returned.

Now integrate the **`AuthInterceptor`** with the **`books`** server.

```
jwtMgr := jwt.NewJWTManager()

authInterceptor := middleware.NewAuthInterceptor(jwtMgr, configs.
AccessibleRoles())
```

```
opts := []grpc.ServerOption{}

middlewareOpts := middleware.ProvideGrpcMiddlewareServerOpts()

opts = append(opts, middlewareOpts...)

opts = append(opts, grpc.UnaryInterceptor(authInterceptor.Unary()), grpc.
StreamInterceptor(authInterceptor.Stream()))
```

The complete code for the TLS and authentication via JWT mechanism can be viewed here: https://github.com/OrangeAVA/Modern-API-Design-with-gRPC/tree/chapter-7

Conclusion

In this chapter, we delved into the critical aspects of securing gRPC communication within a microservices architecture. We initiated the discussion by recognizing the inherent need for load balancing in such distributed systems, highlighting the challenges faced by gRPC in load balancing and exploring strategies to address these challenges while retaining the advantages of long-duration connections. Subsequently, the focus shifted to the implementation of security measures, primarily through the adoption of Transport Layer Security (TLS). The significance of enabling TLS was underscored, and the process of securing gRPC servers and clients using certificates, private keys, and CA certificates was elucidated through practical code examples. The chapter further extended its exploration into Mutual TLS (mTLS), a powerful security mechanism where both the client and server authenticate each other using certificates. The inherent vulnerabilities of TLS were acknowledged, prompting the adoption of mTLS to fortify the security posture, especially within a Zero-Trust framework. Authentication mechanisms for gRPC calls were rigorously examined, covering basic authentication and the implementation of JSON Web Tokens (JWT) for more robust authentication. The chapter culminated in the creation of a comprehensive authentication server, incorporating JWT-based user authentication and authorization through role-based access control. By integrating these elements, this chapter laid the foundation for a secure, authenticated, and well-structured microservices communication architecture using gRPC. The implementation details, code snippets, and practical considerations provided throughout equip the reader with actionable insights to fortify their microservices infrastructure, fostering a resilient and secure environment for gRPC-based communication.

In the upcoming chapter, we will delve into crucial aspects of gRPC-based microservices, starting with unit testing to ensure the integrity of servers and clients. We will then cover integration testing, logging strategies, observability with Prometheus metrics and Datadog tracing, and conclude with practical deployment guidance using Docker and Kubernetes, alongside tools like Postman for comprehensive testing.

Multiple Choice Questions

1. What does TLS stand for in the context of gRPC security?
   a. Transport Layer Service
   b. Tokenized Linking System
   c. Transparent Layer Security
   d. Transport Layer Security
2. Which encryption protocol does gRPC predominantly use for secure communication?
   a. SSL
   b. HTTPS
   c. TLS
   d. SSH
3. Why is Mutual TLS (mTLS) considered a robust security mechanism for gRPC?
   a. It encrypts data in transit.
   b. It ensures only one party is authenticated.
   c. It authenticates both client and server.
   d. It uses symmetric key encryption.
4. What is the role of a TLS certificate in gRPC security?
   a. Authenticate the client.
   b. Encrypt communication.
   c. Authenticate the server.
   d. Both a and b.
5. Which gRPC service is essential for handling user authentication and token generation?
   a. JWTManager
   b. SecurityService

   c. TokenService
   d. AuthService

6. What does JWT stand for in the context of gRPC authentication?
   a. Java Web Tokens
   b. JSON Web Tokens
   c. JavaScript Web Tokens
   d. Java Web Security
7. In the context of gRPC, what is the purpose of the SeedUsers function in the provided code?
   a. Seed data for testing.
   b. Create initial user roles.
   c. Initialize user data in the repository.
   d. Generate random user credentials.
8. What role does the AuthInterceptor play in the middleware package?
   a. Encrypts communication.
   b. Handles JWT token verification.
   c. Implements Mutual TLS.
   d. Provides logging functionalities.
9. Which gRPC interceptor is responsible for handling authentication during unary operations?
   a. StreamInterceptor
   b. AuthInterceptor
   c. UnaryInterceptor
   d. LoggingInterceptor
10. In the AuthService server, what does the Login function primarily handle?
    a. Initiates a gRPC connection.
    b. Handles user authentication and token generation.
    c. Manages server shutdown.
    d. Verifies JWT tokens in the stream.

Answers

1	d
2	c
3	c
4	c
5	d
6	b
7	c
8	b
9	b
10	b

CHAPTER 8

Production Grade gRPC Applications

Introduction

In the preceding chapter, we delved into fortifying gRPC communication with robust security measures. The implementation of Transport Layer Security (TLS) emerged as a pivotal aspect, elevating the security of client-server interactions. We not only explored the fundamental utilization of TLS for encrypting data but also ventured into the realm of mutual TLS (mTLS), where both, the client and the server, authenticate each other through certificates, adding an extra layer of verification. Furthermore, we scrutinized the authentication of gRPC calls using two distinct methods: basic authentication and the sophisticated JWT (JSON Web Token) approach. Basic authentication, relying on simple credentials, and JWT, employing digitally signed tokens, provided diverse options to suit security requirements. This comprehensive security discussion sets the stage for the upcoming chapters, where we will delve into topics like testing, logging, observability, and deployment strategies, ensuring a holistic understanding of securing and optimizing gRPC applications.

In this chapter, we delve into the crucial aspects of ensuring production readiness for gRPC-based applications. We start by exploring the importance of meeting production requirements and the key considerations for achieving this milestone. The focus then shifts to testing strategies, beginning with detailed insights into unit testing and integration testing tailored specifically for gRPC services. Additionally, we address the significance of observability in maintaining and monitoring these services, with a spotlight on seamless integrations with Prometheus and Datadog. The chapter further navigates through the intricacies of deploying gRPC applications, including revisiting Dockerfiles and Kubernetes manifests for optimal performance. To complete our comprehensive approach, we conclude with an exploration of API testing using Postman, offering a well-rounded guide for developers and operators seeking to ensure the robustness and reliability of their gRPC-based systems.

Structure

In this chapter, we will cover the following topics:

- Requirement of production readiness
- Tests for gRPC:
  - Unit testing
  - Integration testing
- Observability:
  - Integration with Prometheus
  - Integration with Datadog
- Deployments:
  - Revisit dockerfiles
  - K8s manifests
- API testing with Postman

Requirement of Production Readiness

Ensuring production readiness during the development of an application or product is paramount for several reasons. First and foremost, it is a critical step to guarantee that the software is capable of handling real-world operational conditions and user loads. Production readiness assessments help identify and mitigate potential issues, ensuring the application's stability, performance, and reliability in a live environment.

Furthermore, addressing production readiness early in the development lifecycle helps minimize the risk of encountering unexpected problems or failures when the application is deployed to production. This proactive approach contributes to a smoother and more efficient transition from development to production, reducing the likelihood of downtime, customer dissatisfaction, and business disruptions.

Production readiness also involves considerations beyond the application's core functionality, such as security, scalability, and monitoring. By incorporating these aspects into the development process, teams can build applications that are not only feature-rich but also resilient and secure, meeting the expectations and requirements of end-users.

In summary, looking into production readiness while building an application is essential for delivering a robust and reliable product that performs well in real-world scenarios, provides a positive user experience, and minimizes the risk of post-deployment issues.

The production readiness considerations for gRPC applications share similarities with those for other types of applications, but there are also specific aspects that differentiate them. Here are some key factors to consider when evaluating the production readiness of gRPC applications:

- **Protocol and Communication Style:** gRPC uses a binary protocol, which can have performance benefits compared to text-based protocols like HTTP/JSON. Ensuring that the network infrastructure and proxies can efficiently handle this binary format is crucial.
- **Testing Strategies:** gRPC often utilizes Protocol Buffers (Protobufs) for message serialization. Testing strategies need to account for the specific challenges and requirements of working with Protobufs, ensuring robust unit and integration tests.
- **Service Contracts and Versioning:** As gRPC relies on Protocol Buffers for service contracts, any changes to proto files impact service contracts. Production readiness involves establishing a solid strategy for versioning and handling backward compatibility to minimize disruptions during updates.
- **Observability:** Monitoring and observability solutions must be tailored to capture gRPC-specific metrics, such as request/response times, streaming metrics, and error rates. Integration with tools like Prometheus or Datadog should be fine-tuned for gRPC characteristics.
- **Deployment:** Gaining production readiness for gRPC applications involves optimizing containerization, revisiting Dockerfiles, and ensuring compatibility with container orchestration platforms like Kubernetes. Managing the lifecycle of gRPC services in a containerized environment requires specific considerations.
- **Security:** gRPC provides support for mutual TLS (mTLS) by default, ensuring secure communication between services. Production readiness

involves configuring and managing mTLS effectively, addressing security considerations unique to gRPC.

- **Error Handling:** gRPC uses a rich set of status codes for communication. Production-ready gRPC applications should handle these status codes appropriately and provide meaningful error messages to facilitate debugging and troubleshooting.
- **Circuit Breaking and Retry Policies**: In a production setting, circuit breaking and retry policies are vital components for gRPC applications, safeguarding against service failures and transient issues. They contribute significantly to the resilience of the system, preventing widespread outages and maintaining consistent service availability.
- **Timeouts and Deadlines**: In a production environment, precise timeouts and deadlines in gRPC are crucial for managing resources efficiently, preventing potential bottlenecks, and enhancing system responsiveness, ensuring a reliable and stable user experience.
- **Load Balancing:** For distributed systems, load balancing is crucial. Production readiness requires setting up and configuring load-balancing mechanisms that are aware of gRPC's characteristics, such as the ability to balance based on methods and headers.
- **Client Considerations:** Ensuring that client libraries across various programming languages are up-to-date and well-maintained is essential for production readiness. Compatibility and performance of gRPC clients impact the overall user experience.

In summary, while the fundamental principles of production readiness apply to gRPC applications, addressing the unique features and challenges of gRPC, such as binary protocols, Protocol Buffers, and specialized metrics, is crucial for ensuring a smooth and reliable production deployment.

Tests for gRPC

Testing strategies for gRPC applications and RESTful applications share some common principles, but they also differ in certain aspects due to the distinct nature of communication protocols and data formats. Here is a comparison of unit and integration testing for gRPC apps and REST apps:

Unit Testing

	gRPC	REST
Message format	**Protobuf Considerations:** Unit testing in gRPC involves testing individual components, such as gRPC service methods, in isolation. Special attention is given to handling Protobuf messages, ensuring correct serialization and deserialization. Mocking is often utilized to isolate the units under test.	**JSON Handling:** In REST applications, where JSON is a common data format, unit testing focuses on ensuring proper handling of JSON payloads. Unit tests validate the correctness of request parsing, response generation, and JSON serialization/deserialization.
Service Contracts	Requires strict adherence to Protobuf-based service contracts, and changes to these contracts may impact multiple services.	Relies on well-defined API endpoints, and changes to the API contract may affect clients consuming the RESTful API.
Error Handling	Has a well-defined status code and metadata for error handling, making it clear when an error occurs.	Relies on HTTP status codes and may include error details in the response body.

Table 8.1: *gRPC versus REST: Considerations for unit testing*

Integration Testing

	gRPC	REST
Communication Mechanism	**Streaming and RPC Calls:** Integration testing for gRPC apps includes scenarios involving streaming and Remote Procedure Call (RPC) interactions. It ensures that services communicate seamlessly and handle streaming data appropriately. Tests may involve deploying services in a controlled environment to simulate real-world interactions.	**HTTP Endpoint Testing:** Integration testing for RESTful apps typically revolves around testing HTTP endpoints. It involves making requests to RESTful APIs and validating the responses. This testing ensures that the API adheres to the expected behavior, handles various HTTP methods, and interacts correctly with external services.
Communication Protocol	Uses a binary protocol and relies on Protocol Buffers for message serialization.	Typically uses text-based protocols like HTTP and data formats such as JSON or XML.

	gRPC	REST
Statelessness	Supports both synchronous (unary) and asynchronous (streaming) communication. Testing asynchronous behavior may involve using frameworks or concurrency in Golang.	Primarily follows synchronous communication patterns. Asynchronous operations may be handled using technologies like WebSockets or additional asynchronous endpoints.

Table 8.2: *gRPC versus REST: Considerations for integration testing*

Unit Testing

Unit testing for gRPC applications involves testing individual components, such as service methods and business logic, in isolation. Developers create unit tests to verify that specific functions within the application, especially those defined in gRPC service implementations, behave as expected. Mocking is often employed to isolate the unit under test, and special attention is given to testing the handling of gRPC-specific constructs like Protobuf messages. This ensures that each unit of the codebase performs its designated function accurately and reliably.

Let us view these in action.

We established a simplified version of our book application in the previous chapter.

We also developed a books server that provides a predefined list of books when its RPC `ListBooks` is called. The implementation of the books server can be viewed here: https://github.com/OrangeAVA/Modern-API-Design-with-gRPC/blob/chapter-8/chapter-8/book-server/server.go

We designed a books client with the capability to call the book server's RPC **ListBooks**. The implementation of books client can be viewed here: https://github.com/OrangeAVA/Modern-API-Design-with-gRPC/blob/chapter-8/chapter-8/book-server/server.go

For effective unit testing of the given gRPC server code, consider the following points:

- **Isolation of Logic:** Ensure that each function in the App struct is tested in isolation. For example, the unit test of the `ListBooks` method should be separated from the other unit tests.

- **Mock Dependencies:** Utilize mocking to isolate the `ListBooks` method from external dependencies, such as the `GetAllBooks` method. This ensures that the test focuses solely on the logic within the method.
- **Input Variations:** Test the `ListBooks` method with various input scenarios, including cases where the context is canceled or different values of the `proto.Empty` parameter are provided.
- **Error Handling:** Test error scenarios to ensure that error paths are handled appropriately. For instance, simulate errors during the server's startup or when attempting to listen on the network.
- **Server Initialization:** Verify that the gRPC server is initialized correctly by checking that it is bound to the expected address and port.
- **Listen and Serve:** Test the `Serve` method to ensure that the server starts and serves requests as expected. Check for errors during the serving process.
- **Return Values:** Validate the return values of the `ListBooks` method, ensuring that the response contains the expected list of books or handles errors appropriately.

By addressing these points in your unit tests, you can comprehensively evaluate the functionality and reliability of the gRPC server code.

The code for how we have achieved unit testing of the books server can be viewed here: https://github.com/OrangeAVA/Modern-API-Design-with-gRPC/blob/chapter-8/chapter-8/book-server/server_test.go

Here is an explanation of key elements and how the testing is achieved:

- **Test Suite Setup:**
  - o The `BookServerTestSuite` struct embeds the `suite.Suite` from the `github.com/stretchr/testify/suite` package, providing convenient assertion methods and suite management.
  - o `SetupSuite` is called before any tests are run and initializes the in-memory listener, gRPC server, and the application under test.
- **Teardown Suite:**
  - o `TeardownSuite` is called after all tests have been run and is responsible for closing resources like the in-memory listener and stopping the gRPC server.

- **Test Case Setup:**
  - The `TestBookService_ListBooks` method sets up a goroutine to serve the gRPC server. This allows the test to call the server's methods via a client.
- **gRPC Client Setup:**
  - The `setupGRPCClient` method creates a gRPC client connection to the in-memory listener (`bufconn`). It uses a custom dialer to connect to the in-memory listener and returns a cleanup function to close the client connection after the test.
- **gRPC Call:**
  - The `callListBooksRPC` method makes a gRPC call to the `ListBooks` method on the server. It uses the client connection created in `setupGRPCClient` and returns the response.
- **Assertion:**
  - The actual testing is done in the `TestBookService_ListBooks` method. It makes a gRPC call to `ListBooks`, gets the response, and asserts that the returned list of books matches the expected list obtained from the application's `GetAllBooks` method.
- **Goroutine for Server Serving:**
  - The gRPC server is started in a goroutine to allow the test to proceed without blocking. This ensures that the test can make gRPC calls to the server while it is serving.
- **Context Handling:**
  - The gRPC client is created with an insecure connection, and the custom dialer is used to connect to the in-memory listener. The `callListBooksRPC` method utilizes the context to make the gRPC call.
- **Error Handling:**
  - The test uses `require.NoError` to assert that there are no errors during the gRPC call or any other critical steps. This ensures that the test fails if unexpected errors occur.
- **Cleanup:**
  - The test cleans up resources using the `defer` statement, ensuring that the client connection is closed after the test completes.

To effectively unit test the given gRPC client code, consider the following points:

- **Dependency Injection**: Utilize dependency injection to provide mock implementations for the gRPC client and the server connection. This allows you to control the behavior of the client during testing.
- **Error Handling**: Test error scenarios by simulating connection failures or unexpected errors during the gRPC calls. Ensure that the client handles errors appropriately and returns the expected error types.
- **Context Handling**: Test the client's behavior with different contexts, including canceled contexts or contexts with deadlines. Verify that the client correctly respects context cancellation and deadlines.
- **Server Connection**: In unit tests, use a mocked server connection or a testing-specific server to ensure that the client behaves as expected in the absence of a real server. This helps isolate client behavior from server issues during testing.
- **ListBooks Method**: Test the `ListBooks` method by providing various scenarios, such as an empty response, responses with different numbers of books, and different book attributes. Ensure that the client processes the response correctly.
- **Mocks and Stubs**: Use mocking frameworks or handcrafted mocks and stubs to simulate the gRPC server's behavior and responses. This allows you to focus on testing the client's logic independently of the server.

We created a mock server to independently test this without relying on the book server.

Command to create mock for the preceding book server:

```
mockgen -source=chapter-8/proto/book_grpc.pb.go -destination=chapter-8/
proto/mock/book_grpc.pb.go
```

Note: **`mockgen`** (https://github.com/golang/mock) is deprecated.

The command **`mockgen`** is part of the **`mockgen`** tool, which is used to generate mock implementations of Go interfaces for testing purposes. In your provided command:

1. **`-source=chapter-8/proto/book_grpc.pb.go`**: specifies the source file from which the interface declarations are extracted. In this case, it is the **`book_grpc.pb.go`** file located in the **`chapter-8/proto`** directory.
2. **`-destination=chapter-8/proto/mock/book_grpc.pb.go`**: specifies the destination file where the generated mock implementations will be saved.

The generated file will be named **book_grpc.pb.go** and will be placed in the **chapter-8/proto/mock** directory.

Essentially, this command is instructing **mockgen** to analyze the specified source file (**book_grpc.pb.go**) containing gRPC service interfaces and generate corresponding mock implementations. These mock implementations can be useful for testing components that depend on gRPC services without having to interact with the actual services during testing. The generated mocks can be customized to simulate various scenarios, making it easier to write comprehensive tests for components that use gRPC interfaces.

Following is how we have achieved unit testing of the books client:

```
package bookclient


import (

   "context"

   "testing"


   "github.com/OrangeAVA/Modern-API-Design-with-gRPC/chapter-8/proto"

   mock_proto "github.com/OrangeAVA/Modern-API-Design-with-gRPC/
   chapter-8/proto/mock"

   "github.com/golang/mock/gomock"

   "github.com/stretchr/testify/assert"

   "github.com/stretchr/testify/suite"

)


type BookClientTestSuite struct {

   *suite.Suite


   controller        *gomock.Controller

   bookServiceClient *mock_proto.MockBookServiceClient

}
```

```
func TestBookServerTestSuite(t *testing.T) {
    suite.Run(t, &BookClientTestSuite{
        Suite: new(suite.Suite),
    })
}

func (suite *BookClientTestSuite) SetupSuite() {
    suite.controller = gomock.NewController(suite.T())
    suite.bookServiceClient = mock_proto.NewMockBookServiceClient(suite.
    controller)
}

func (suite *BookClientTestSuite) TeardownSuite() {
    if suite.controller != nil {
        suite.controller.Finish()
    }
}

func (suite *BookClientTestSuite) TestBookClient_ListBooks() {
    t := suite.T()

    client := App{
        client: suite.bookServiceClient,
    }

    // Expected data
    expectedBooks := []*proto.Book{
        {
            Isbn:      1234,
```

```
            Name:      "book-1",
            Publisher: "publisher-1",
        },
        {
            Isbn:      1235,
            Name:      "book-2",
            Publisher: "publisher-2",
        },
    }

    // Set up the mock
    suite.bookServiceClient.EXPECT().
        ListBooks(gomock.Any(), gomock.Any()).
        Return(&proto.ListBooksRespose{Books: expectedBooks}, nil)

    // Call the ListBooks method on the client
    resp, err := client.ListBooks(context.Background(), &proto.Empty{})

    // Assert that the response and error match the expected values
    assert.NoError(t, err)
    assert.Equal(t, expectedBooks, resp.Books)
}
```

Let us break down the key components and the flow of the test:

1. **Test Suite Setup and Teardown:** **BookClientTestSuite** is a test suite struct that embeds the **suite.Suite** from the **github.com/stretchr/testify/suite** package. It has methods for setting up (**SetupSuite**), tearing down (**TeardownSuite**), and running (**TestBookServerTestSuite**) the suite.
2. **Mock Controller and Client Initialization:** In **SetupSuite**, a new instance of **gomock.Controller** is created to manage the lifecycle of the mocks. The mock **BookServiceClient** is created using **mock_proto.**

`NewMockBookServiceClient` with the controller. This mock client will replace the actual gRPC client during testing.

3. **Test for `ListBooks` Method**:
   a. `TestBookClient_ListBooks` is the actual unit test for the `ListBooks` method of the **App** struct.
   b. An instance of the **App** struct is created with the mock `BookServiceClient`.
   c. `expectedBooks` is a slice of `proto.Book` objects representing the expected response from the mock service.
   d. The mock client's behavior is set up using `EXPECT()` to specify the expected parameters for the `ListBooks` method and the return values. It expects any context and any `proto.Empty` parameter and returns a response with the `expectedBooks` slice and a `nil` error.
   e. The `ListBooks` method of the **App** struct is then called, and the response and error are captured.
   f. `assert.NoError(t, err)` checks that there is no error returned from the ListBooks method.
   g. `assert.Equal(t, expectedBooks, resp.Books)` asserts that the returned books match the expected books.
4. **Mock Controller Cleanup**: In `TeardownSuite`, the mock controller's `Finish` method is called to ensure that resources associated with the controller are released.
5. **Test Execution**: The test suite is executed using `suite.Run(t, &BookClientTestSuite{Suite: new(suite.Suite)})`.

Overall, this unit test uses the `gomock` library to create a controlled environment for testing the `ListBooks` method of the **App** struct. The mock client allows the test to specify and verify the behavior of the client under specific conditions, ensuring that it interacts correctly with the gRPC service.

Integration Testing

Integration testing for gRPC applications focuses on validating the interaction and collaboration between different components, services, and external dependencies. In the context of gRPC, integration testing ensures that communication between gRPC services occurs seamlessly, including scenarios involving streaming and error handling. This testing phase often includes testing against a real gRPC server and may involve deploying services in a controlled environment to simulate real-world interactions. By assessing the integration points, developers ensure that the entire system functions cohesively, adhering to the specified gRPC contracts and handling various use cases effectively.

Following is how we have achieved integration testing of the books client and server combined:

```
package integration_test

import (
    "context"
    "fmt"
    "path/filepath"
    "testing"
    "time"

    bookclient "github.com/OrangeAVA/Modern-API-Design-with-gRPC/
    chapter-8/book-client"
    "github.com/OrangeAVA/Modern-API-Design-with-gRPC/chapter-8/proto"
    "github.com/stretchr/testify/assert"
    "github.com/testcontainers/testcontainers-go"
    "github.com/testcontainers/testcontainers-go/wait"
)

func TestIntegration(t *testing.T) {
    ctx := context.Background()

    // Start a gRPC server container
    serverContainer := startGRPCServerContainer(ctx, t)

    // Cleanup the container after the test
    defer func() {
```

```
        assert.NoError(t, serverContainer.Terminate(ctx))
    }()

    // Create a gRPC client connected to the server container
    client := createGRPCClient(ctx, t, serverContainer)

    // Test your gRPC client against the server
    resp, err := client.ListBooks(ctx, &proto.Empty{})
    assert.NoError(t, err)
    assert.NotNil(t, resp)
}

// startGRPCServerContainer starts a gRPC server container using testcontainers
func startGRPCServerContainer(ctx context.Context, t *testing.T) testcontainers.Container {
    req := testcontainers.ContainerRequest{
        FromDockerfile: testcontainers.FromDockerfile{
            Context:    filepath.Join("."),
            Dockerfile: "args.Dockerfile",
        },
        ExposedPorts: []string{"50091"},
        WaitingFor:   wait.ForListeningPort("50091").
        WithStartupTimeout(30 * time.Second),
    }

    container, err := testcontainers.GenericContainer(ctx,
    testcontainers.GenericContainerRequest{
        ContainerRequest: req,
```

```
        Started:         true,
    })
    assert.NoError(t, err)

    return container
}

// createGRPCClient creates a gRPC client connected to the specified server
container
func createGRPCClient(ctx context.Context, t *testing.T, serverContainer
testcontainers.Container) proto.BookServiceClient {
    port, err := serverContainer.MappedPort(ctx, "50091")
    assert.NoError(t, err)

    // Use the mapped port to create a gRPC client
    client := bookclient.NewApp(fmt.Sprintf("localhost:%s", port.Port()))
    return client
}
```

Let us break down the key components and the flow of the integration test:

1. **Test Function**:
    a. `TestIntegration` is the main test function that initiates the integration test.
    b. It starts by creating a context `(ctx)` for the test.
    c. The test consists of three main steps: starting the gRPC server container, creating a gRPC client connected to the server container, and testing the gRPC client against the server.
2. **Starting the gRPC Server Container**:
    a. The `startGRPCServerContainer` function is responsible for starting a gRPC server container using the `testcontainers` library.
    b. It defines a `ContainerRequest` with details such as the Dockerfile, exposed ports, and waiting conditions for the container to be ready.

   c. The **GenericContainer** function creates and starts the container based on the specified request.
   d. The function returns the reference to the started container.
3. **Creating the gRPC Client**:
   a. The **createGRPCClient** function creates a gRPC client connected to the specified server container.
   b. It extracts the mapped port from the running server container and uses it to create the gRPC client.
   c. The client is an instance of the **bookclient.App** struct with the server address configured based on the mapped port.
4. **Testing the gRPC Client Against the Server**:
   a. With the gRPC client created, the test calls the **ListBooks** method on the client.
   b. Assertions using **assert** from the **testify** library validate that there are no errors (**assert.NoError**) and that the response is not nil (**assert.NotNil**).
5. **Dockerfile and Docker Compose:**
   a. The Dockerfile (**args.Dockerfile**) is referenced to build the Docker image for the gRPC server container. This file is expected to contain instructions for setting up the server environment.
6. **Cleanup**:
   a. A deferred cleanup step ensures that the server container is terminated after the test finishes. This is done to clean up resources and avoid lingering containers.
7. **Integration with gRPC Client Library**:
   a. The integration test demonstrates the integration of the gRPC client (**bookclient.App**) with the gRPC server running in a Docker container.

Overall, this integration test verifies the end-to-end interaction between the gRPC client and the gRPC server, providing a comprehensive validation of the client's ability to communicate with the server in a real-world scenario. The use of the **testcontainers** library facilitates the setup and teardown of Docker containers for integration testing purposes.

Observability

Observability is crucial in any software application, including gRPC-based applications, as it provides insights into the system's behavior, performance, and overall health. Here are some key reasons highlighting the importance of observability in gRPC apps:

- **Understanding System Behavior**: Observability allows you to gain insights into how your gRPC services are behaving in real-time. It provides visibility into the internal workings of your application, helping you understand how components interact and identifying potential issues.
- **Performance Monitoring**: Monitoring metrics like response times, latency, and throughput help in assessing the performance of gRPC services. Observability tools enable you to track these metrics and identify performance bottlenecks, ensuring that the application meets performance expectations.
- **Error Detection and Troubleshooting**: Observability tools provide detailed information about errors and exceptions occurring within your gRPC services. This information is invaluable for debugging and troubleshooting issues quickly. You can identify the root cause of errors and address them proactively.
- **Logging and Tracing**: Logging and tracing are essential components of observability. They allow you to trace the flow of requests across different services, helping you understand the complete journey of a request. This is especially important in microservices architectures where gRPC is often used.
- **Resource Utilization**: Observability tools enable you to monitor the utilization of system resources such as CPU, memory, and network bandwidth. Understanding resource consumption helps in optimizing the performance and scalability of gRPC services.
- **Service Level Objectives (SLOs) and Service Level Indicators (SLIs)**: Observability is critical for establishing and monitoring SLOs and SLIs. These metrics define the level of service performance and reliability that your gRPC services are expected to meet. Observability tools help track these metrics and ensure that your services align with the defined objectives.

- **Capacity Planning**: By analyzing historical data and trends gathered through observability, you can make informed decisions about capacity planning. This involves scaling resources based on anticipated load and usage patterns, ensuring that the system can handle increased demand.
- **Security Monitoring**: Observability tools can also contribute to security monitoring by tracking and analyzing access patterns, authentication events, and potential security threats. Monitoring and alerting on unusual behavior can help detect security incidents promptly.
- **Continuous Improvement**: Observability facilitates continuous improvement by providing data-driven insights. Regularly analyzing observability data allows you to identify areas for optimization, make informed decisions for architectural enhancements, and implement changes to improve overall system reliability.

In summary, observability in gRPC applications is essential for maintaining a high level of reliability, performance, and responsiveness. It enables developers and operators to gain deep insights into the system's behavior, diagnose issues efficiently, and continuously enhance the overall quality of the application.

Integration with Prometheus

Integrating with Prometheus offers significant benefits in enhancing the observability of gRPC applications. Prometheus serves as a robust monitoring and alerting solution, collecting detailed metrics and exposing them in a standardized format. By instrumenting gRPC services with Prometheus-compatible metrics, teams can gain valuable insights into the performance, latency, and error rates of their services. Prometheus enables the establishment of SLIs and facilitates the creation of meaningful dashboards for real-time visibility. Moreover, its alerting capabilities empower teams to proactively address potential issues before they impact the user experience. The integration with Prometheus enhances the overall observability of gRPC applications, providing a comprehensive view of their health and performance, which is essential for troubleshooting, capacity planning, and continuous improvement.

Let us explore the integration of Prometheus as middleware to expose key metrics, offering valuable insights into the system's performance.

To achieve this, we utilized the books app introduced in the previous chapters. You can review the entire set of code modifications built upon the existing solution here: https://github.com/OrangeAVA/Modern-API-Design-with-gRPC/commit/bf87b87e52b4a38dc16bebad6d7d5e530fb53e34

We have first created a prometheus middleware. The code for the same can be viewed here: https://github.com/OrangeAVA/Modern-API-Design-with-gRPC/blob/chapter-8/books-app/internal/pkg/middleware/prometheus.go

Let us break down its key components:

- **Custom Prometheus Metrics**: The middleware defines several custom Prometheus counters to track specific metrics related to the gRPC application's functionality, such as counting incoming API requests, successful and failed attempts to fetch, create, update, and delete books.
- **Register Function**: The `Register` function initializes and registers the custom Prometheus metrics. It logs the start and end of the registration process.
- **RunPrometheusServer Function**: The `RunPrometheusServer` function sets up an HTTP server for serving Prometheus metrics on the specified port (`promPort`). It registers the custom metrics using the `Register` function. The server runs in a goroutine, and its status is logged.
- **AddPrometheus Function**: The `AddPrometheus` function is responsible for adding Prometheus interceptors to gRPC unary and stream interceptors. It appends the `grpc_prometheus` library's unary and stream server interceptors to the provided slices.
- **Middleware Initialization**:
  - The code initializes and registers the custom Prometheus metrics during application startup using the `Register` function.
  - It runs the Prometheus HTTP server in the background, exposing metrics at the `/metrics` endpoint.
- **Integration with gRPC Server**: The `AddPrometheus` function is intended to be used to integrate Prometheus interceptors with gRPC servers. It adds the necessary interceptors to track metrics related to unary and stream gRPC calls.
- **Logging**: The code includes logging statements using a custom logger (`logger.Log`) to provide information about the registration of custom metrics and the status of the Prometheus server.

While starting the application, we need to start the Prometheus server:

```
grpc_prometheus.Register(s)

middleware.RunPrometheusServer(appConfig.ServerConfig.PrometheusPort)
```

Also similar to how logging and recovery middlewares were integrated with the books server in **`ProvideGrpcMiddlewareServerOpts`** function, we need to perform the same here as well:

```
AddPrometheus(&uInterceptors, &sInterceptors)
```

Then we need to increment/adjust the counter metrics in their respective locations:

- **`Incoming_api_req_counter`**: This counter is incremented at every request handler **`AddBook`, `UpdateBook`, `ListBooks`, `GetBook`, `RemoveBook`**.

  ```
  middleware.Incoming_api_req_counter.Add(1)
  ```

- **`Book_create_pass_counter`**: This counter is incremented in the **`AddBook`** handler.

  ```
  middleware.Book_create_pass_counter.Add(1)
  ```

- **`Book_update_pass_counter`**: This counter is incremented in the **`UpdateBook`** handler.

  ```
  middleware.Book_update_pass_counter.Add(1)
  ```

- **`Book_get_pass_counter`**: This counter is incremented in the **`ListBooks`, `GetBook`** handler.

  ```
  middleware.Book_get_pass_counter.Add(1)
  ```

- **`Book_get_fail_counter`**: This counter is incremented in the **`ListBooks`** handler while there is an error in retrieving books from repository, serializing the books and deserializing into proto format.

  ```
  middleware.Book_get_fail_counter.Add(1)
  ```

- **`Book_delete_pass_counter`**: This counter is incremented in the **`RemoveBook`** handler.

  ```
  middleware.Book_delete_pass_counter.Add(1)
  ```

This is the process of defining, modifying, and making metrics available in the **`OpenTelemetry`** format. These metrics can then be polled by Prometheus agents deployed within the cluster where our books servers and clients are deployed.

Integration with Datadog

Integrating with Datadog offers several benefits for monitoring and managing gRPC applications. One of them is tracing. Integrating with Datadog Tracing offers several benefits for gaining insights into the behavior and performance of gRPC applications:

- **Distributed Tracing**: Datadog Tracing provides distributed tracing capabilities, allowing you to trace the flow of requests across various services in a gRPC microservices architecture. This enables a holistic view of request journeys and helps in identifying dependencies and potential performance bottlenecks.
- **End-to-End Visibility**: With distributed tracing, you can achieve end-to-end visibility into the entire lifecycle of a gRPC request. This includes details about each service the request traverses, the time taken at each step, and any potential errors encountered during the process.
- **Root Cause Analysis**: Datadog Tracing facilitates root cause analysis by providing detailed information about the interactions between services. When an issue occurs, such as increased latency or errors, the trace data helps pinpoint the root cause and identify the specific service or component responsible.
- **Performance Optimization**: By analyzing traces, you can identify areas for performance optimization in your gRPC services. This includes understanding where delays occur, optimizing service dependencies, and improving overall request response times.
- **Service Dependencies Mapping**: Datadog Tracing automatically maps service dependencies, creating a visual representation of how different services interact with each other. This mapping aids in understanding the overall architecture and relationships between services.
- **Latency Analysis**: Tracing data includes information about latency at each hop in the request journey. This allows you to analyze and optimize latency, ensuring that your gRPC services meet performance expectations.
- **Error Analysis**: Trace data includes information about errors encountered during the execution of a request. By analyzing traces, you can gain insights into the types and frequency of errors, facilitating proactive issue resolution.
- **Service-Level Agreement (SLA) Monitoring**: Datadog Tracing enables you to monitor and enforce SLAs by tracking the performance of individual services. This ensures that your gRPC services consistently meet the defined performance criteria.
- **Custom Instrumentation**: Datadog Tracing supports custom instrumentation, allowing you to add trace points and context information to your gRPC code. This flexibility is valuable for capturing application-specific details and enhancing trace data.

- **Integration with Other Observability Tools**: Datadog Tracing seamlessly integrates with other Datadog observability tools, including metrics, logs, and dashboards. This integration provides a unified platform for monitoring and troubleshooting gRPC applications.

Let us take a look at how we have achieved the same.

To achieve this, modifications have been implemented in the **`book info server`** compared to the previous chapters. To revise, the **`book info server`** initiates distinct calls to both the **`book server`** and **`review server`**, consolidates the respective responses, and subsequently delivers a unified and comprehensive response.

We opted for this service with the intention of determining the duration a request spends in each server throughout its lifecycle.

We need to start the tracer while starting the book info server:

```
tracer.Start(tracer.WithAgentAddr(appConfig.ServerConfig.DataDogServerAd-
dress))
```

Library used is: "`gopkg.in/DataDog/dd-trace-go.v1/ddtrace/tracer`"

This is how existing implementation of **`GetBookInfoWithReviews`** handler looks like:

```
func (a *App) GetBookInfoWithReviews(ctx context.Context, req *proto.
GetBookInfoRequest) (*proto.GetBookInfoResponse, error) {

   log.Println("fetching book and reviews")


   book, err := a.bookServerClient.GetBook(ctx, &proto.
   GetBookRequest{Isbn: req.GetIsbn()})

   if err != nil {

      return nil, err

   }


   resp, err := a.reviewServerClient.GetBookReviews(ctx, &proto.
   GetBookReviewsRequest{Isbn: req.GetIsbn()})

   if err != nil {

      return nil, err
```

```
    }

    return &proto.GetBookInfoResponse{
        Isbn:      req.GetIsbn(),
        Name:      book.Name,
        Publisher: book.Publisher,
        Reviews:   resp.GetReviews(),
    }, nil
}
```

When data dog spans are added, this looks as follows:

```
func (a *App) GetBookInfoWithReviews(ctx context.Context, req *proto.
GetBookInfoRequest) (*proto.GetBookInfoResponse, error) {
    // Start a root span.
    rootSpan := tracer.StartSpan("get.bookInfo.withReviews")
    defer rootSpan.Finish()

    log.Println("fetching book and reviews")

    bookSpan := spawnChildSpan(rootSpan, "get.bookInfo", fmt.
    Sprintf("%d", req.GetIsbn()))

    book, err := a.bookServerClient.GetBook(ctx, &proto.
    GetBookRequest{Isbn: req.GetIsbn()})
    bookSpan.Finish(tracer.WithError(err))
    if err != nil {
        return nil, err
    }
```

```
    reviewSpan := spawnChildSpan(rootSpan, "get.bookReview", fmt.
    Sprintf("%d", req.GetIsbn()))

    resp, err := a.reviewServerClient.GetBookReviews(ctx, &proto.
    GetBookReviewsRequest{Isbn: req.GetIsbn()})
    reviewSpan.Finish(tracer.WithError(err))
    if err != nil {
        return nil, err
    }

    return &proto.GetBookInfoResponse{
        Isbn:      req.GetIsbn(),
        Name:      book.Name,
        Publisher: book.Publisher,
        Reviews:   resp.GetReviews(),
    }, nil
}

func spawnChildSpan(parentSpan ddtrace.Span, spanName, resourceName
string) ddtrace.Span {
    child := tracer.StartSpan(spanName, tracer.ChildOf(parentSpan.
    Context()))
    child.SetTag(ext.ResourceName, resourceName)

    // If you are using 128 bit trace ids and want to generate the high
    // order bits, cast the span's context to ddtrace.SpanContextW3C.
    if w3Cctx, ok := child.Context().(ddtrace.SpanContextW3C); ok {
        fmt.Printf("128 bit trace id = %s\n", w3Cctx.TraceID128())
    }
```

```
    return child
}
```

Here are the key changes from the previous implementation:

1. **Distributed Tracing Initialization**: The code begins by initializing a root span named **`get.bookInfo.withReviews`** using Datadog's tracer.
2. **Child Spans for Book and Review Operations**:
   a. Two child spans are created within the root span, each representing a distinct operation: **`get.bookInfo`** for fetching book details and **`get.bookReview`** for obtaining book reviews.
   b. The **`spawnChildSpan`** function is introduced to streamline the creation of child spans, taking the parent span, span name, and resource name as parameters.
3. **Tagging and Resource Naming**: Each child span is tagged with a resource name corresponding to the ISBN of the requested book. This helps in associating spans with specific resources and facilitates detailed tracing.
4. **Span Completion with Error Handling**: Each child span is finished with additional information, including potential errors. This ensures that the spans accurately reflect the duration and outcomes of the respective operations.
5. **Returning Traced Response**:
   a. The response is constructed as usual, encapsulating book and review details.
   b. The root span, which encapsulates the entire process, is automatically finished upon returning the response.

This can be further dissected to examine the duration a request spends on a specific action as well.

Deployments

To expedite the deployment of gRPC servers and clients within the cluster, it is imperative to meticulously craft Dockerfiles and Kubernetes (K8s) manifests. These artifacts play a crucial role in defining the configuration, dependencies, and runtime environment of the gRPC applications. Dockerfiles serve as blueprints for container images, encapsulating the necessary dependencies and configurations, while K8s manifests provide a declarative specification for orchestrating the deployment, scaling, and management of these containers within a Kubernetes environment. By thoughtfully preparing these artifacts, the process of deploying gRPC services becomes streamlined, ensuring efficient and consistent deployment practices across the cluster.

Revisiting Dockerfiles

We have previously covered the process of creating Dockerfiles for both a gRPC client and a gRPC server. Let us revisit and delve into these steps once more.

Dockerfile of the gRPC book server:

```
FROM golang:1.16 AS builder


WORKDIR /app

COPY go.mod .

COPY go.sum .

RUN go mod download

COPY . .

RUN CGO_ENABLED=0 GOOS=linux go build -a -installsuffix cgo -o grpc-server
cmd/book-server/main.go



FROM alpine:latest

WORKDIR /app

COPY --from=builder /app/grpc-server .

EXPOSE 50091

CMD [“./grpc-server”]
```

This Dockerfile consists of two stages to efficiently build and deploy a gRPC server written in Go:

1. Builder Stage (**`FROM golang:1.16 AS builder`**):
    a. The build process begins with the official Golang 1.16 image, designated as the builder stage.
    b. The working directory is set to **`/app`**, and the **`go.mod`** and **`go.sum`** files are copied to facilitate dependency management.

   c. The **`go mod download`** command is executed to download the necessary dependencies.
   d. The entire application code is then copied into the working directory.
   e. Finally, the **`go build`** command is used to compile the Go application. The resulting binary is named **`grpc-server`**, and CGO is disabled to ensure compatibility with a minimal Alpine-based image.
2. Final Stage (**`FROM alpine:latest`**):
   a. The second stage utilizes a lightweight Alpine Linux image as its base, minimizing the overall image size.
   b. The working directory is set to **`/app`** within this stage.
   c. The binary **`grpc-server`** is copied from the builder stage to the current working directory of the final image using **`COPY --from=builder.`**
   d. Port 50091 is exposed to allow external communication with the gRPC server.
   e. The CMD instruction specifies the command to run when the container starts, launching the **`grpc-server`** binary.

Commands to build and run the gRPC server:

```
docker build -t grpc-server:v1 .

docker run -p 50091:50091 grpc-server:v1
```

Dockerfile of the gRPC book client:

```
FROM golang:1.16 AS builder

WORKDIR /app

COPY go.mod .

COPY go.sum .

RUN go mod download

COPY . .

RUN CGO_ENABLED=0 GOOS=linux go build -a -installsuffix cgo -o grpc-client
cmd/book-client/main.go


FROM alpine:latest

WORKDIR /app
```

```
COPY --from=builder /app/grpc-client .

CMD [“./grpc-client”]
```

Here is a breakdown of each stage:

1. Builder Stage (**`FROM golang:1.16 AS builder`**):
    a. The build process begins with the official Golang 1.16 image, serving as the builder stage.
    b. The working directory is set to **`/app`**.
    c. Dependencies are managed by copying the go.mod and go.sum files into the working directory and executing **`go mod download`** to download them.
    d. The entire application code is copied into the working directory.
    e. The **`go build`** command is then used to compile the Go application. The resulting binary, named **`grpc-client`**, is created with CGO disabled to ensure compatibility with a minimal Alpine-based image.
2. Final Stage (**`FROM alpine:latest`**):
    a. The second stage utilizes a lightweight Alpine Linux image as its base, reducing the overall image size.
    b. The working directory is set to **`/app`** within this stage.
    c. The binary **`grpc-client`** is copied from the builder stage to the current working directory of the final image using **`COPY --from=builder`**.
    d. The CMD instruction specifies the command to run when the container starts, launching the **`grpc-client`** binary.

Commands to build and run the gRPC client:

```
docker build -t grpc-client:v1 .

docker run grpc-client:v1
```

This multi-stage Dockerfile optimizes the resulting image size by using a separate builder stage with a larger base image that includes the Go toolchain. The final image, based on Alpine, only contains the compiled binary and necessary runtime dependencies, resulting in a smaller and more efficient container for deploying the gRPC server and client.

K8s Deployments

Kubernetes manifest for a gRPC server:

```
apiVersion: apps/v1
```

```yaml
kind: Deployment
metadata:
  name: grpc-server
spec:
  replicas: 3 # Adjust the number of replicas as needed
  selector:
    matchLabels:
      app: grpc-server
  template:
    metadata:
      labels:
        app: grpc-server
    spec:
      containers:
        - name: grpc-server
          image: grpc-server:1.0
          ports:
            - containerPort: 50051
---
apiVersion: v1
kind: Service
metadata:
  name: grpc-server-service
spec:
  selector:
    app: grpc-server
  ports:
```

```
    - protocol: TCP
      port: 80
      targetPort: 50051
  type: LoadBalancer # Adjust the service type as needed
```

This YAML configuration defines a Kubernetes Deployment and Service for a gRPC server. Let us break down each section:

Deployment:

- `apiVersion`: Specifies the Kubernetes API version being used (apps/v1 for Deployments).
- `kind`: Defines the type of Kubernetes resource (Deployment in this case).
- `metadata`: Provides metadata for the Deployment, including the name.
- `spec`: Describes the desired state of the Deployment.
    - `replicas`: Specifies the number of desired replicas (in this case, 3 instances of the gRPC server).
    - `selector`: Defines how the Deployment selects which Pods to manage. It uses labels, and Pods with the label `app: grpc-server` will be managed.
    - `template`: Specifies the template for creating new Pods.
        - `metadata`: Labels assigned to Pods created from this template.
        - `spec`: Defines the Pod specification.
- `containers`: Describes the containers within the Pod.
    - `name`: Name of the container.
    - `image`: Docker image for the gRPC server.
    - `ports`: Specifies the container port (50051) the gRPC server is running on.

Service:

- The --- indicates the separation between different YAML documents.
- `apiVersion`: Specifies the Kubernetes API version (v1 for Services).
- `kind`: Defines the type of Kubernetes resource (Service in this case).
- `metadata`: Provides metadata for the Service, including the name.
- `spec`: Describes the desired state of the Service.

- **selector**: Defines the Pods that this Service will select. It matches Pods with the label **app: grpc-server.**
- **ports**: Specifies the ports to expose on the Service.
  - **protocol**: Specifies the protocol (TCP in this case).
  - **port**: Exposes port 80 on the Service.
  - **targetPort**: Forwards traffic to port 50051 on the selected Pods.
- **type**: Specifies the type of Service (LoadBalancer in this case, indicating that an external load balancer should be created to route external traffic to the Service). Adjust the service type as needed.

This configuration creates a scalable Deployment for the gRPC server with three replicas and a Service exposing port 80 externally, which forwards traffic to the gRPC server's port 50051.

Kubernetes manifest for a gRPC client:

```
apiVersion: apps/v1

kind: Deployment

metadata:

  name: grpc-client

spec:

  replicas: 1

  selector:

    matchLabels:

      app: grpc-client

  template:

    metadata:

      labels:

        app: grpc-client

    spec:

      containers:

        - name: grpc-client
```

```
        image: grpc-client:1.0
---
apiVersion: v1
kind: Service
metadata:
  name: grpc-client-service
spec:
  selector:
    app: grpc-client
  ports:
    - protocol: TCP
      port: 80
      targetPort: 50052
  type: LoadBalancer # Adjust the service type as needed
```

This YAML configuration defines a Kubernetes Deployment and Service for a gRPC client. Let us break down each section:

Deployment:

- **`apiVersion`**: Specifies the Kubernetes API version being used (apps/v1 for Deployments).
- **`kind`**: Defines the type of Kubernetes resource (Deployment in this case).
- **`metadata`**: Provides metadata for the Deployment, including the name.
- **`spec`**: Describes the desired state of the Deployment.
  - o **`replicas`**: Specifies the number of desired replicas (in this case, 1 instance of the gRPC client).
  - o **`selector`**: Defines how the Deployment selects which Pods to manage. It uses labels, and Pods with the label **`app: grpc-client`** will be managed.
  - o **`template`**: Specifies the template for creating new Pods.
    - **`metadata`**: Labels assigned to Pods created from this template.
    - **`spec`**: Defines the Pod specification.

- `containers`: Describes the containers within the Pod.
  - `name`: Name of the container.
  - `image`: Docker image for the gRPC client.

Service:

- The --- indicates the separation between different YAML documents.
- `apiVersion`: Specifies the Kubernetes API version (v1 for Services).
- `kind`: Defines the type of Kubernetes resource (Service in this case).
- `metadata`: Provides metadata for the Service, including the name.
- `spec`: Describes the desired state of the Service.
  - `selector`: Defines the Pods that this Service will select. It matches Pods with the label `app: grpc-client`.
  - `ports`: Specifies the ports to expose on the Service.
    - `protocol`: Specifies the protocol (TCP in this case).
    - `port`: Exposes port 80 on the Service.
    - `targetPort`: Forwards traffic to port 50052 on the selected Pods.
  - `type`: Specifies the type of Service (LoadBalancer in this case, indicating that an external load balancer should be created to route external traffic to the Service). Adjust the service type as needed.

This configuration creates a Deployment for the gRPC client with one replica and a Service exposing port 80 externally, which forwards traffic to the gRPC client's port 50052. Adjustments can be made to the number of replicas and service type based on specific requirements.

API testing with Postman

Unlike testing REST APIs with Postman or any equivalent tools like Insomnia, it is not quite comfortable to test gRPC services.

Postman has a beta version of testing gRPC services.

Here are the steps of how you can do it:

1. Open Postman, goto **'APIs'** in the left sidebar and click **'+'** sign to create a new api. In the popup window, enter **'Name'**, **'Version'**, and **'Schema Details'** and click **Create** [unless you need to import from some sources like GitHub, Bitbucket].

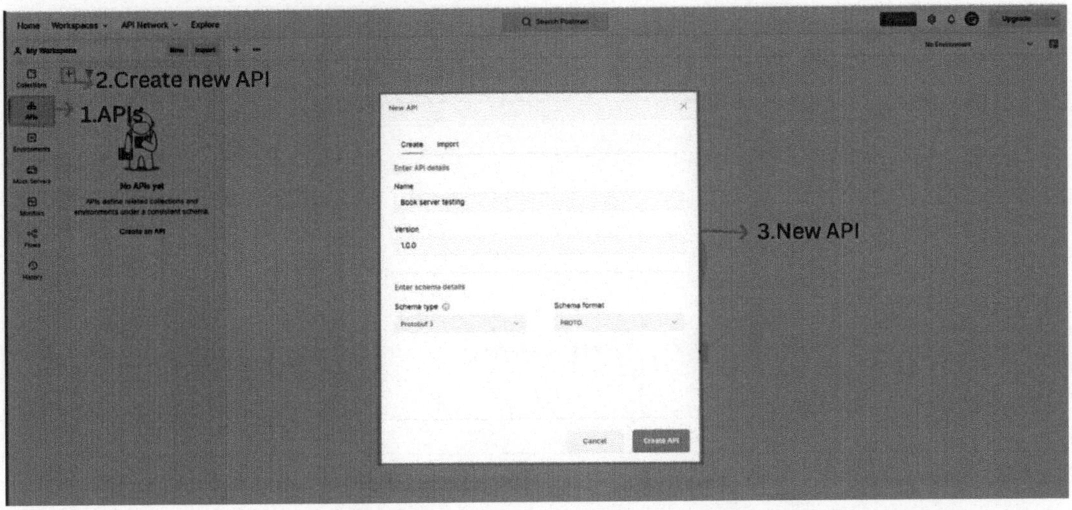

Figure 8.1: *Create New API in Postman*

2. Once Your API gets created then go to definition and enter your proto contract.

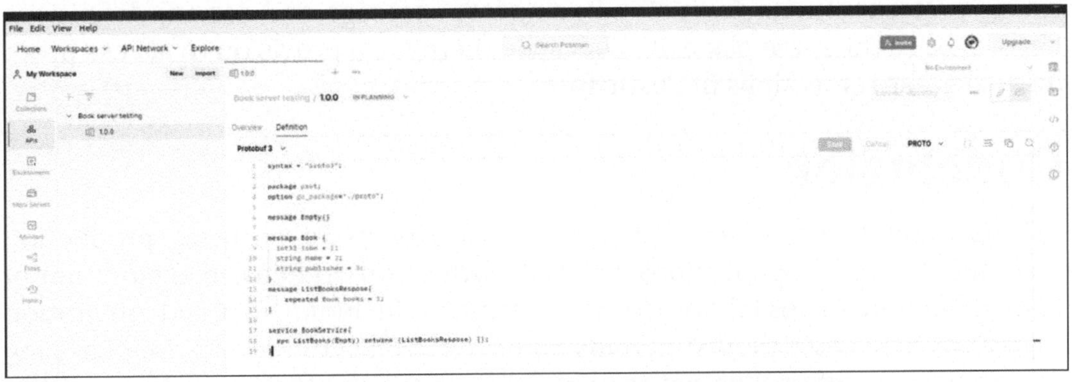

Figure 8.2: *Add Proto Definition for RPCs in Postman*

3. Remember importing does not work here, so it would be better to keep all dependent protos at one place.
4. The preceding steps will help to retain contracts for future use.
5. Then click **`'New'`** and select **`'gRPC request'`**, enter the URI and choose the proto from the list of saved **`'APIs'`** and finally enter your request message and hit **`'Invoke'`**.

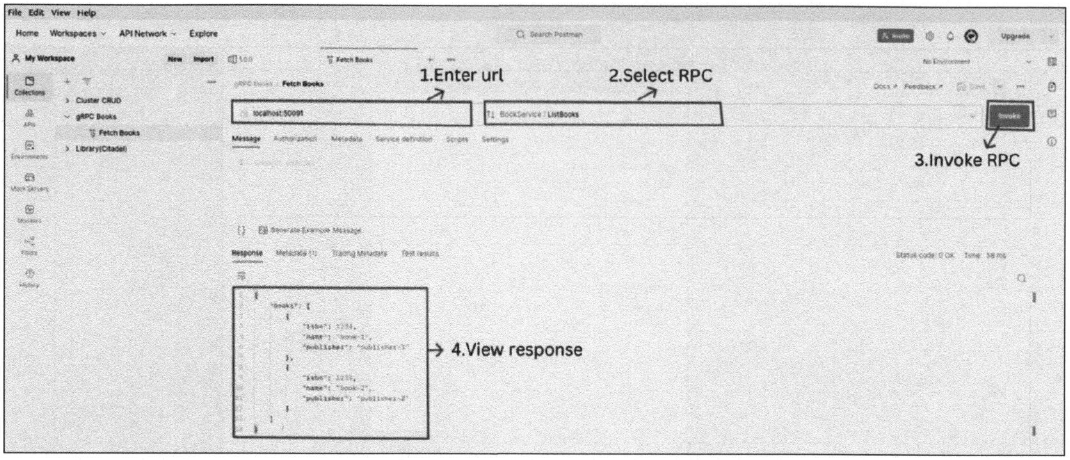

Figure 8.3: *Invoke RPCs in postman*

In the preceding steps, we figured out the process to test our gRPC APIs via Postman. The process to test gRPC endpoints is different from that of REST endpoints using Postman. One thing to remember is that while creating and saving proto contracts as in step 2, all proto message and service definitions need to be in the same place. It is because there is no provision to access proto messages across versions in Postman.

Conclusion

In this chapter, we delved into the crucial aspects of ensuring production readiness for gRPC applications. Starting with a comprehensive exploration of testing methodologies tailored for gRPC services, including unit and integration testing, we elucidated the distinctions from their REST counterparts. Emphasizing the significance of production readiness, we examined the intricacies of gRPC applications' unique requirements, shedding light on the nuanced aspects of observability. The integration of observability tools, such as Prometheus and Datadog, was elucidated to provide a comprehensive understanding of monitoring and tracing capabilities. Additionally, we navigated through the essentials of Dockerfiles and Kubernetes manifests for efficient deployment, ensuring scalability and fault tolerance. The chapter concluded with a practical guide on incorporating middleware for Prometheus metrics and the pivotal role it plays in gathering insights into the application's performance. In essence, this chapter serves as a holistic guide for gRPC application developers, covering testing strategies, deployment considerations, and observability measures indispensable for achieving robust and production-ready solutions.

In the next and final chapter, we will explore real-world applications and the widespread adoption of gRPC, discussing its practical benefits and reasons behind its success in diverse industries. This examination aims to provide concise insights into how gRPC addresses specific challenges, making it a versatile and robust communication protocol.

Multiple Choice Questions

1. What type of testing methodology did the chapter emphasize for gRPC services?
   a. Manual testing.
   b. Unit and Integration testing.
   c. Performance testing.
   d. User acceptance testing.
2. In the context of gRPC applications, what is the primary focus of observability?
   a. Security monitoring.
   b. Performance tracking.
   c. Code coverage analysis.
   d. Load testing.
3. How does production readiness for gRPC applications differ from other types of applications?
   a. It does not require testing.
   b. It involves integration with observability tools.
   c. Only unit testing is necessary.
   d. Deployment is not a consideration.
4. What is the purpose of the provided gRPC server code snippets in the chapter?
   a. To demonstrate Dockerfile creation.
   b. To illustrate unit testing principles.
   c. To showcase API testing with Postman.
   d. To discuss Kubernetes manifests.

5. In the context of gRPC applications, what is a consideration for unit testing that differs from REST apps?
   a. No need for unit testing.
   b. Focus on integration testing only.
   c. Protobuf message validation.
   d. Exclusively use Postman for testing.
6. What does the provided BookServerTestSuite in the chapter primarily focus on testing?
   a. gRPC server deployment.
   b. Dockerfile creation.
   c. Unit testing of gRPC server methods.
   d. Integration testing with Postman.
7. In the context of gRPC, what is the purpose of the **`bufconn`** package used in the testing code?
   a. Docker image creation.
   b. gRPC client creation.
   c. Buffering connections for testing.
   d. Prometheus integration.
8. What is the primary function of the provided gRPC client code in the chapter?
   a. Docker image creation.
   b. Unit testing.
   c. Interaction with the gRPC server.
   d. Prometheus integration.
9. In the integration test code, what does TestIntegration primarily aim to test?
   a. Unit testing of gRPC server.
   b. Docker image creation.
   c. Interaction between gRPC client and server.
   d. Prometheus integration.

10. Why is observability important in gRPC applications?
    a. It enhances security.
    b. It improves code readability.
    c. It provides insights into performance and behavior.
    d. It simplifies Dockerfile creation.

Answers

1	b
2	b
3	b
4	b
5	c
6	c
7	c
8	c
9	c
10	c

CHAPTER 9

Case Studies of Projects Using gRPC

Introduction

This chapter delves into the dynamic landscape of technology, exploring a few compelling case studies that showcase the transformative power of innovative solutions in the realms of cloud computing, communication protocols, and business platforms. First, we unravel LinkedIn's strategic shift from traditional data centers to the public cloud, dissecting the challenges, motivations, and outcomes of this ambitious migration. Following that, we navigate through Vendasta's success story, shedding light on how their white-label platform has revolutionized digital marketing for businesses. We follow this up with a discussion on how Uber and Netflix have used gRPC in some of their components. These case studies offer insights into technological advancements, addressing challenges, and leveraging solutions that have reshaped the way organizations operate in the contemporary digital era. Join us on this journey to unravel the intricacies of these fascinating real-world scenarios, where technology becomes a catalyst for business evolution.

Structure

In this chapter, we will cover the following topics:

- LinkedIn shifted from JSON+REST to gRPC+Protobuf
- Vendasta decided to move their APIs to gRPC

- Uber's implementation of gRPC for RealTime push platform
- Netflix optimizes Backend-to-Backend Communication with gRPC and Protobuf FieldMask

LinkedIn Shifted from JSON+REST to gRPC+Protobuf

Background

LinkedIn, serving billions of member requests daily, emphasizes quick and efficient fulfillment of member requests to enhance user experience. The platform relies on `Rest.li`, an open-source REST framework for microservices, to handle diverse member interactions.

Challenges with JSON

While JSON provided broad language support and human-readability, it posed challenges for LinkedIn, including increased network bandwidth usage and suboptimal serialization/deserialization latency. The company sought a replacement with a compact payload size, high efficiency, wide language support, and seamless integration with **Rest.li**'s existing mechanisms.

Protobuf as a solution

After evaluating various formats, LinkedIn chose Google Protocol Buffers (Protobuf) for its effectiveness across criteria like payload size, serialization efficiency, language support, and integration capabilities.

Integration process

To integrate Protobuf into Rest.li, LinkedIn introduced symbol tables, facilitating the conversion of Rest.li's schema-agnostic serialization into Protobuf's schema-dependent serialization. The symbol tables were dynamically generated at service startup and exchanged between clients and servers.

Rollout strategy

LinkedIn gradually rolled out the Protobuf integration by first incorporating it into the Rest.li library, then applying it to all services. Client configurations enabled a controlled transition, allowing the encoding of payloads using Protobuf. This approach minimized disruption, allowing gradual validation and bug fixing.

Benefits and Improvement

The adoption of Protobuf resulted in notable efficiency gains. Average throughput per-host increased, and for services with large payloads, latency improved by up to 60%. The rollout, utilizing techniques like symbol tables and configuration-based ramps, ensured a seamless transition with minimal disruption to developers and the business.

We discussed the aforementioned benefit in detail in *Chapter 2, Fundamentals of gRPC* under the heading **Serialization of Data**.

The successful integration of Protobuf at LinkedIn led to tangible efficiency gains and cost savings, showcasing the importance of strategic technology choices in large-scale platforms. The careful rollout strategy, transparent to developers, exemplifies how impactful changes can be achieved with minimal disruption.

Vendasta's Decision to Move their APIs to gRPC

Background

Vendasta is an all-in-one platform that empowers agencies and enterprises to acquire, retain, and grow their local business clientele through a suite of software solutions and services.

Problem

Vendasta faced scalability challenges as it evolved into a comprehensive platform. Initially using Python on Google App Engine (GAE) and Datastore, the introduction of the Vendasta Marketplace in 2016 necessitated a shift towards more efficient APIs to accommodate third-party vendors.

Optimizations and Challenges

To address performance concerns, Vendasta first utilized the Go programming language for higher throughput. Additionally, the replication of Datastore data into ElasticSearch allowed the transition from batch-processing to real-time APIs. The final optimization involved moving APIs to gRPC, a significant shift affecting clients but proving to be a true superset.

Benefits of gRPC Implementation

GRPC implementation delivered the following capabilities:

- **SDK Integration Simplification**:
    - gRPC facilitated the transition from publishing APIs to providing SDKs, easing integration for developers in various languages.
    - Light wrappers over generated gRPC SDKs maintained package-manager compatibility.
- **Streaming Capabilities**:
    - Built on HTTP/2, gRPC enabled client-side and server-side streaming.
    - Server-side streaming reduced the time to the first display, allowing for results to be streamed as they became available.
- **Protocol Buffers and Serialization**:
    - The switch from JSON to protocol buffers optimized serialization and deserialization times.
    - Explicit format specifications of proto provided typed objects, enabling auto-completion, type-safety, and compatibility enforcement between clients and servers.
- **Efficient Endpoint Specification**:
    - The proto format simplified defining new endpoints, enabling clear communication between development teams.
    - Simultaneous development of client and server-side APIs was achieved for the first time, significantly reducing the latency in producing new APIs and accompanying SDKs.

We discussed the above-stated benefits in detail in *Chapter 2, Fundamentals of gRPC* under the heading **Serialization of Data and Features that make gRPC Standout**.

While gRPC did not eliminate all challenges, its implementation at Vendasta demonstrated marked improvements in endpoint performance, integration processes, and efficient SDK delivery. The positive experience highlighted gRPC's role in addressing scalability concerns and enhancing overall system performance.

Uber's Implementation of gRPC for RealTime Push Platform

Background

Uber, a global multi-sided marketplace, manages real-time experiences for millions of users worldwide. The dynamic nature of real-time marketplaces necessitated constant synchronization of multiple participants, leading to challenges in the traditional polling-based approach for app updates.

Challenges with Polling

Client-side polling has several challenges, including:

- Aggressive polling results in significant backend load and degradation, causing issues such as faster battery drain, app sluggishness, and network congestion.
- Overloading existing polling APIs and creating new ones for various features lead to a complex and inconsistent API landscape.
- Cold startup of the app poses challenges due to concurrent API calls, increasing load time in poor network conditions.

Introducing RAMEN Push Platform

- To eliminate polling issues, Uber developed the RAMEN (Realtime Asynchronous Messaging Network) push platform.
- Key considerations in designing RAMEN included easier migration from polling, developer-friendly processes, reliability, and wire efficiency.

Key Components of RAMEN

1. **Fireball**
   a. Microservice determines when to generate a message payload.
   b. Listens to events and triggers push messages based on configurations.
2. **Push Message Delivery System**
   a. Responsible for delivering push messages to mobile devices.
   b. Utilizes RAMEN Server to determine payload content and priorities.
3. **Message Metadata**
   a. Configurations include priority, time to live, and deduplication.

   b. Prioritization helps manage payload delivery, especially in resource-constrained environments.

4. **RAMEN Delivery Protocol**
   a. Utilizes Server-Sent Events (SSE) for reliable delivery with acknowledgments and retries.
   b. Simple yet effective protocol scheme allowing resumability of streaming connections.

Scaling and Evolution

In addition to the adoption of gRPC, several strategic actions played a pivotal role in scaling and evaluating the RAMEN system.

- Initial implementation used Node.js and Ringpop for distributed sharding.
- As the system grew, technologies like Netty, Apache ZooKeeper, Apache Helix, Redis, and Apache Cassandra were adopted for better scalability and reliability.

Moving with gRPC

Switching to gRPC with the RAMEN enhances the following capabilities:

- The gRPC-based RAMEN protocol was introduced to address shortcomings of the SSE-based protocol.
- Improvements include instant acknowledgments, real-time measurements of network conditions, support for stream multiplexing, and flexibility in message payload serialization.
- This transition to gRPC ensures enhanced reliability, efficient data usage, and standardized implementations across languages.

We discussed the above-stated benefits in detail in *Chapter 4, Communication patterns of gRPC* while comparing REST's polling with gRPC's streaming.

Uber's adoption of gRPC in the RAMEN push platform marked a significant improvement in reliability, efficiency, and scalability. The transition showcased the benefits of standardized implementations, real-time acknowledgments, and simplified design, making it a crucial component in delivering a seamless real-time experience for Uber's diverse user base.

Netflix Optimizes Backend-to-Backend Communication with gRPC and Protobuf FieldMask

Background

Netflix relies heavily on gRPC for backend-to-backend communication, and efficient data exchange is crucial for their operations. When processing requests, it is essential to minimize latency, reduce errors, and conserve network bandwidth by understanding which fields callers are interested in.

Challenge

Netflix faced the challenge of avoiding unnecessary computations and remote calls for fields that callers ignored. This issue arose when dealing with large response payloads and the need for selective data retrieval.

Solution: gRPC and Protobuf FieldMask

To address these challenges, Netflix adopted gRPC as its communication protocol and utilized Protobuf FieldMask, a feature of Protocol Buffers, for fine-grained control over data retrieval.

Benefits

- **Selective Field Retrieval**
  - FieldMask allows callers to specify the fields they need, enabling selective retrieval of data.
  - Reduces unnecessary computations and avoids remote calls for unrequested fields.
- **Efficient Payloads**
  - Consumers can request only the necessary fields, preventing the unnecessary burden of large response payloads.
  - Particularly beneficial for applications with limited network bandwidth, such as mobile devices.
- **Improved Performance**
  - Eliminates the need for custom "include" parameters, providing a cleaner and more efficient solution.
  - Enhances backend performance by avoiding unnecessary resource-heavy computations.

- **Flexibility for Consumers**
  - Consumers have the flexibility to request specific fields without complex custom parameters.
  - Simplifies the request process while maintaining a clean API design.
- **Reusable and Scalable**
  - Protobuf FieldMask is reusable across different messages and fields, enhancing scalability.
  - Developers can create utility methods for common operations, ensuring a consistent and maintainable approach.
- **Pre-built FieldMasks**
  - API producers can ship client libraries with pre-built FieldMasks for common field combinations.
  - Simplifies API usage for frequent scenarios, providing a smoother experience for consumers.

Limitations

- Renaming message fields can be challenging due to the integration of field names in the API contract.
- Repeated fields have limitations on selecting individual subfields within a message inside a list.

Netflix successfully optimized backend-to-backend communication by leveraging gRPC and Protobuf FieldMask. This solution provided a flexible, efficient, and scalable approach to data retrieval, aligning with Netflix's commitment to delivering high-quality streaming experiences. The adoption of these technologies reflects a strategic move towards industry-standard tools, ensuring long-term stability and minimal maintenance overhead.

Conclusion

The case studies presented showcase the transformative impact of gRPC (general-purpose or generic Remote Procedure Calls) across various industries and applications. From Uber's real-time marketplace synchronization to Netflix's optimization of backend operations, gRPC emerges as a pivotal technology fostering streamlined and high-performance communication protocols. The benefits are clear: reduced latency, minimized network congestion, and improved scalability. The adoption of gRPC has not only addressed the challenges posed by traditional communication methods but has also introduced innovative solutions such as bi-directional streaming protocols, eliminating the need for resource-intensive polling. Its standardization, support for multiple languages, and compatibility with modern infrastructure make gRPC a preferred choice for organizations seeking to enhance their communication frameworks. As evident from these case studies, gRPC proves to be a key enabler for delivering real-time, efficient, and reliable services in today's dynamic technological landscape.

In wrapping up our exploration of the case studies, these stories serve as foundational chapters in a larger narrative of technological evolution. The strategic decisions and technological adoptions discussed herein offer insightful lessons that transcend temporal boundaries. Furthermore, these case studies are but the beginning of a comprehensive journey through the tech landscape. With preceding chapters already delving into the intricate realms of gRPC, the narrative unfolds to encompass broader horizons. The adoption of gRPC, as witnessed in the Uber and Netflix ecosystems, becomes a recurrent theme, highlighting its pivotal role in shaping the future of communication protocols. As we move forward, this chapter paves the way for subsequent discussions, urging businesses to glean insights, embrace innovation, and anticipate the transformative potential of emerging technologies.

Multiple Choice Questions

1. What was one of the major challenges Uber faced with its initial approach of polling for app updates?
    a. Server overloading
    b. Battery drain
    c. Network congestion
    d. All of the above

2. What protocol did Uber adopt to replace the polling strategy for real-time updates in their app?
    a. HTTP/1.1
    b. WebSockets
    c. Server-Sent Events (SSE)
    d. gRPC

3. What benefits did Uber experience after implementing the RAMEN push messaging platform?
    a. Reduced battery drain
    b. Improved app responsiveness
    c. Minimized network congestion
    d. All of the above
4. What was the main challenge addressed by LinkedIn in their migration from traditional data centers to the public cloud?
    a. Insufficient server capacity
    b. Limited data security
    c. High operational costs
    d. Inadequate network speed
5. In the context of Vendasta's white-label platform, what is the primary benefit offered to its partners?
    a. Access to exclusive discounts
    b. Customized branding and user interface
    c. Advanced analytics tools
    d. Priority customer support
6. What role does FieldMask play in optimizing backend operations in Netflix's gRPC implementation?
    a. It reduces network bandwidth consumption
    b. It avoids unnecessary computations
    c. It allows clients to specify fields of interest
    d. All of the above
7. Which Netflix service was used as an example to demonstrate the use of FieldMask in gRPC?
    a. Script service
    b. Schedule service
    c. Production service
    d. API gateway

8. What does the FieldMask message in gRPC contain to specify fields of interest?
   a. Paths
   b. Parameters
   c. Routes
   d. Destinations
9. What is a limitation associated with using FieldMask in gRPC when renaming message fields?
   a. It requires additional request parameters
   b. It limits the ability to rename fields
   c. It only works for top-level fields
   d. All of the above
10. What benefit does gRPC offer in terms of communication compared to traditional methods in the case studies?
    a. Reduced latency
    b. Improved scalability
    c. Enhanced performance
    d. All of the above

Answers

1	d
2	c
3	d
4	c
5	b
6	d
7	c
8	a
9	b
10	d

References

- https://www.linkedin.com/blog/engineering/infrastructure/linkedin-integrates-protocol-buffers-with-rest-li-for-improved-m
- https://grpc.io/blog/vendasta/
- https://www.uber.com/en-IN/blog/real-time-push-platform/?u-click_id=40a56183-5cf0-4b53-beed-893cf127c7dd
- https://www.uber.com/en-IN/blog/ubers-next-gen-push-platform-on-grpc/
- https://netflixtechblog.com/practical-api-design-at-netflix-part-1-using-protobuf-fieldmask-35cfdc606518

Index

H

I

K

L

M

O

P

R